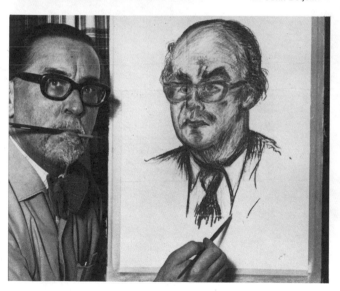

£2.60

D1621375

*This portrait of
William Shakespeare*

*Pictured below is
the Compiler,
C. John Taylor,
working upon
his portrait of
the Poet Laureate,
Sir John Betjeman.*

The Compiler acknowledges and offers his grateful thanks to Sir John Betjeman and to his Publishers, John Murray Ltd., London for permission to include "The Cottage Hospital" in this edition of "Prize Winning Poetry".

PRIZE WINNING POETRY

* More than 300 Exhibition Poems
  by New Poets.
* Selected Poems from the works of
  William Shakespeare
  John Milton
  Ben Jonson
  Robert Burns
  Thomas Grey
  Lord Byron
  Robert Browning
  Oliver Goldsmith
  William Collins
  John Keats
  Charles Lamb
  William Wordsworth
  Sir John Betjeman

Highland Arts Studios
Seil Isle, Oban, Argyll, Scotland

Highland Arts Showrooms,
Stafford Street, Oban, Argyll, Scotland

Highland Arts Exhibition Showrooms
Main Street West, Inveraray, Argyll, Scotland

Highland Arts Cottage Exhibition
The Pier, Luss Village, Luss, Loch Lomond,
Dunbarton, Scotland

Highland Arts Showroom,
The Duck Bay Marina, Loch Lomond,
Dunbarton, Scotland

"Good poetry is as a ladder, upon which our thoughts can unhindered ascend, to atmospheres uplifting, inspiring, regenerating: far, very far removed, from the ordinary, often monotonous, frequently demanding, routine of daily experience."

The Compiler
New Year's Eve, 1977

Compiler   C. John Taylor

Prize Winning
Poetry

HIGHLAND ARTS STUDIOS
Seil Isle, Oban, Scotland

821·008

TAY

I.S.B.N. 0 9504599 2 5 (Paperback) 0 9504599 3 3 (Cased)

Colour separation by Typesetting Services Ltd. Glasgow.

Published by Highland Arts Studios, Seil Isle, Oban, Scotland.

Printed in Great Britain by Wm. Collins & Co. Ltd., Bishopbriggs, Glasgow, Scotland.

CONTENTS

"Write all the words I have spoken in a book."

Habakkuk Ch. 2, v 2.

ILLUSTRATION DETAILS

1. The portrait of H.R.H. The Prince of Wales reproduced in colour upon the frontispiece is from the original portrait in oils, by the Compiler, C. John Taylor, created during the Silver Jubilee Television Appeal broadcast in April, 1977.

2. William Shakespeare portrait on the inside cover page is by an unknown artist and is reproduced by kind permission of the owners of the copyright, the National Portrait Gallery, London.

3. Sir John Betjeman's portrait, photographed with the Poet/Artist, reproduced on the inside cover, is by permission of The Highland Arts Studios.

4. The Poet/Artist with his oil portrait of H.R.H. The Prince of Wales. Inside Back Cover.

5. The photograph reproduced upon the Back Cover shows the Compiler speaking during a coloured television programme.

"The crude creations of mortal thought must finally give place to the glorious forms which we sometimes behold in the camera of divine Mind, when the mental picture is spiritual and eternal."

> *"Science and Health with Key to the Scriptures"*
> *by Mary Baker Eddy,*
> *Discoverer of Christian Science.*

PREFACE

The POEMS in this ANTHOLOGY, come from three sources.

1. PRIZE WINNING contributions, and other exhibited works, selected from the SILVER JUBILEE EXHIBITION, organised by The Highland Arts Studios.

2. "GEMS FROM OLD-MASTERS", comprising a single, short poem by each of twenty-five of the greatest Writers in our language from William Shakespeare to The Poet Laureate, Sir John Betjeman.

3. By the Compiler, new works, including "THIS ROYAL PRINCE", composed, following his Painting in Oils, of the Portrait of, "HIS ROYAL HIGHNESS, THE PRINCE OF WALES". The Portrait is reproduced as the Frontispiece of this Publication.

C. John Taylor.

Seil Isle, Oban,
Scotland. January, 1978.

"We are Labourers together with God".
St. Paul, First Corinthians, ch. 3, v. 9.

9

OTHER WORKS BY THE COMPILER

During 1977 the Compiler, C. John Taylor, has produced a series of new poems with intriguing titles and anyone wishing further information regarding these should write to The Secretary, Highland Arts Studios, Easdale, Seil Isle, Oban, Argyll, Scotland.

NEW POEMS: 1st Edition 1975
2nd Edition 1975
3rd Edition 1975
4th Edition 1975
5th Edition 1975.

One-man Exhibition, proceeds for Kilbrandon Parish Church Restoration Fund, Seil Isle, Argyll. 1963.

One-man Exhibition. Bainbridge Hall, Newcastle Upon Tyne (proceeds for Children's Charities). November, 1968.

One-man Exhibition (proceeds for Seamen's Charities), S. S. Akaroa, Shaw Saville Line. London. March, 1969.

Exhibition, New Zealand Personalities and Landscapes, New Zealand House, Haymarket, London. April, 1970.

One-man Exhibition (proceeds to Seamen's Charities), S. A. Vaal, Union Castle Line, South Africa. April, 1971.

Sir Winston Churchill Centenary Plate. November, 1974.

One-man Exhibition (proceeds for Seamen's Charities), S.S. Canberra, P & O Line, London. March, 1976.

1776/1976 U.S.A. Bicentennial Plate and Poem. Issued 4th July, 1976.

Sponsored Children's Art Exhibition (proceeds to Charity), Seil Isle. 1976.

The Silver Jubilee Queen Elizabeth Poem/Plate. November, 1976.

SILVER JUBILEE SELECTION OF POEMS: 1st Edition Published 1977
2nd Edition Published 1977
3rd Edition Published 1977
4th Edition Published 1977
5th Edition Published 1977
6th Edition Published 1977.

Poetry Competition and Silver Jubilee Exhibition (proceeds to Charity),
Seil Isle, 1977.

In preparation – "These Living Apostles". An illustrated book.
"Highland Treasures". A book and poem with
illustrations.
"Holy Bible Poems & Paintings". An illustrated
book.
"H.R.H. The Prince of Wales", Commemorative
Plate and Poem.

Published by Highland Arts Studios, Easdale, Seil Isle, Oban, Argyll,
Scotland.

INTRODUCTION

Ideas beget ideas!

This Poetry Anthology owes its existence to a Poetry/Short Story Competition sponsored with the commendable object of raising funds to be donated to H.M. The Queen's Silver Jubilee Appeal Fund.

May I explain further.

From the magnificent response, the competitors' efforts were most carefully sorted out, selected entries being numbered, arranged geographically and alphabetically in the New Exhibition Gallery.

Responding to a National advertising campaign, thousands of visitors came to see the Exhibition; accepting the invitation to vote for the poem or short story of their choice, they used the conveniently placed printed Ballot Forms which, when signed and completed, were duly deposited in the Exhibition Poetry Ballot Box. Quite properly, the principal prizes were awarded to entries obtaining the highest number of votes. A substantial sum was raised for the Silver Jubilee Appeal Fund and thus the main object of the exercise was met.

A new idea, during the Exhibition, began to take shape, formed from visitors' comments. Many said they would have liked longer, much longer, to browse, study, enjoy and sort out the many displayed poetry works. Others asked for copies of some of the poems and short stories for relatives and for friends. One visitor pointed out that any poet whose work had been submitted, studied and accepted for entry into the Exhibition might well unduly influence the result by the device of bringing several hundred friends to the Exhibition on remote Seil Isle, who presumably upon arrival would be sure to vote for the pre-arranged poem. This appeared to be a remarkable amount of trouble and expense to undertake in order to win a competition prize. In the event, nobody undertook this task. On the contrary visitors, almost without exception, expressed delight with the Exhibition and with Seil Isle, with its lovely surrounding Highland countryside and sea-scapes. Many were delighted with the Highland hospitality extended on every side.

Lots of visitors, prior to journeying to Argyll, wrote and obtained from the Exhibition Organisers a specially selected list of recommended hotel, boarding house, chalet and caravan accommodation. A large proportion of visitors expressed their pleasure and satisfaction with the accommodation arrangement that they selected from the list that they had received.

Constantly recurring, especially from visiting competitors, was the expressed wish for a more permanent form of record of some of the works exhibited.

Hence this Anthology of Prize Winning Poetry.

Readers will, I trust, forgive my indulgence in allocating a little space to include one poem each, from 25 of my favourite poets, albeit almost all ancient; also a few of my own recent poems and an old one requested in writing from many parts of the world, entitled "Upon Being Sixty".

Hope is entertained that this "over-all" offering will provide varied interest and give a number of hitherto unrecognised, unpublished poets a wider public which may happily lead them to a much wider acceptance and acclaim.

Grateful thanks are expressed to the staff of the Highland Arts Studios, to the News Media, to the Photo Separation Artists and to Wm. Collins & Sons, the book producers and printers. Acknowledgment is due to The National Gallery for permission to publish the William Shakespeare portrait; to Sir John Betjeman and his publishers, Messrs. Murray Ltd. of London, for permission to publish his poem "The Cottage Hospital"; and to the Christian Science Board of Directors, The First Church of Christ, Scientist, in Boston Massachusetts, for permission to quote from "Science and Health with Key to the Scriptures" by Mary Baker Eddy, Discoverer of Christian Science.

Before concluding, it is perhaps of interest to mention how closely the composition of poetry relates to daily living: entries listed come from almost all parts of the U.K. and since this Poetry Anthology has been in preparation a number of entrants have changed their abodes, some going overseas . . . to the U.S.A., to Canada, to the Middle East and to far away Australia and New Zealand. Alas, some have passed away, bereaved relatives accepting the sad duty of informing me of their loss. Most poignant of all, perhaps, one aspiring young poet was unfortunately involved in a road accident in which he lost beloved parents and grandmother and he himself sustained such severe head injuries that it is feared that he will never recover consciousness. His relatives have written to say they hope he will and in this way be able to read his poem which appears in this book.

Perhaps we all can benefit from renewing our acquaintance with the inspirational works committed to writing by poets ancient and modern and published through the centuries by many famous publishing houses.

Foremost amongst the ancient writers for me is the Apostle, St. Paul, whose Holy Bible philosophy, if only partially comprehended and occasionally practised, cannot fail to bring upliftment and benefit to every thinker.

C. John Taylor.
January 1978
Seil Isle.

14

"GEMS FROM OLD MASTERS"

REQUIESCAT

Strew on her roses, roses,
And never a spray of yew.
In quiet she reposes:
Ah! would that I did too.

Her mirth the world required;
She bathed it in smiles of glee.
But her heart was tired, tired,
And now they let her be.

Her life was turning, turning,
In mazes of heat and sound.
But for peace her soul was yearning,
And now peace laps her round.

Her cabined, ample Spirit,
It fluttered and failed for breath.
To-night it doth inherit
The vasty Hall of Death.

Matthew Arnold
1822–1888

NEW JERUSALEM

And did those feet in ancient time
Walk upon England's mountains green?
And was the holy Lamb of God
On England's pleasant pastures seen?

And did the Countenance Divine
Shine forth upon our clouded hills?
And was Jerusalem builded here
Among these dark Satanic mills?

Bring me my bow of burning gold!
Bring me my arrows of desire!
Bring me my spear! O clouds, unfold!
Bring me my chariot of fire!

I will not cease from mental fight,
Nor shall my sword sleep in my hand,
Till we have built Jerusalem
In England's green and pleasant land.

William Blake
1757–1827

IF THOU MUST LOVE ME

If thou must love me, let it be for nought
Except for love's sake only. Do not say
"I love her for her smile, her look, her way
Of speaking gently, for a trick of thought
That falls in well with mine, and certes brought
A sense of pleasant ease on such a day."
For these things in themselves, Beloved, may
Be changed, or change for thee, – and love, so wrought,
May be unwrought so. Neither love me for
Thine own dear pity's wiping my cheeks dry:
A creature might forget to weep, who bore
Thy comfort long, and lose thy love thereby!
But love me for love's sake, that evermore
Thou mayst love on, through love's eternity.

Elizabeth Browning
1806–1861

HOME-THOUGHTS, FROM ABROAD

Oh, to be in England
Now that April's there,
And whoever wakes in England
Sees, some morning, unaware,
That the lowest boughs and the brushwood sheaf
Round the elm-tree bole are in tiny leaf,
While the chaffinch sings on the orchard bough
In England – now!

And after April, when May follows,
And the whitethroat builds, and all the swallows –
Hark! where my blossomed pear-tree in the hedge
Leans to the field and scatters on the clover
Blossoms and dewdrops – at the bent spray's edge –
That's the wise thrush; he sings each song twice over,
Lest you should think he never could recapture
The first fine careless rapture!
And though the fields look rough with hoary dew,
All will be gay when noontide wakes anew
The buttercups, the little children's dower
– Far brighter than this gaudy melon-flower!

Robert Browning
1812–1889

O my Luve's like a red, red rose
That's newly sprung in June:
O my Luve's like the melodie
That's sweetly play'd in tune.

As fair art thou, my bonnie lass,
So deep in luve am I:
And I will luve thee still, my dear,
Till a' the seas gang dry:

Till a' the seas gang dry, my dear,
And the rocks melt wi' the sun;
I will luve thee still, my dear,
While the sands o' life shall run.

And fare thee weel, my only Luve
And fare thee weel awhile!
And I will come again my Luve,
Tho' it were ten thousand mile.

Robert Burns
1759–1796

WHEN WE TWO PARTED

When we two parted
In silence and tears,
Half broken-hearted,
To sever for years,
Pale grew thy cheek and cold,
Colder thy kiss;
Truly that hour foretold
Sorrow to this!

The dew of the morning
Sunk chill on my brow;
It felt like the warning
Of what I feel now.
Thy vows are all broken,
And light is thy fame:
I hear thy name spoken
And share in its shame.

They name thee before me,
A knell to mine ear;
A shudder comes o'er me –
Why wert thou so dear?
They know not I knew thee
Who knew thee too well:
Long, long shall I rue thee
Too deeply to tell.

In secret we met:
In silence I grieve
That thy heart could forget,
Thy spirit deceive.
If I should meet thee
After long years,
How should I greet thee? –
With silence and tears.

Lord George Gordon Noel Byron
1788–1824

YOUTH AND AGE

Flowers are lovely; Love is flower-like;
Friendship is a sheltering tree;
O! the joys, that came down shower-like,
Of Friendship, Love, and Liberty,
Ere I was old!
Ere I was old? Ah woeful Ere,
Which tells me, Youth's no longer here!
O Youth! for years so many and sweet
'Tis known that Thou and I were one,
I'll think it but a fond conceit –
It cannot be, that Thou art gone!
Thy vesper-bell hath not yet toll'd: –
And thou wert ay a masker bold!
What strange disguise hast now put on
To make believe that thou art gone?
I see these locks in silvery slips,
This drooping gait, this alter'd size:
But Springtide blossoms on thy lips,
And tears take sunshine from thine eyes
Life is but Thought: so think I will
That Youth and I are housemates still.

Samuel Coleridge Taylor
1772–1834

HOW SLEEP THE BRAVE

How sleep the Brave who sink to rest
By all their Country's wishes blest!
When Spring, with dewy fingers cold,
Returns to deck their hallow'd mould,
She there shall dress a sweeter sod
Than Fancy's feet have ever trod.

By fairy hands their knell is rung,
By forms unseen their dirge is sung:
There Honour comes, a pilgrim grey,
To bless the turf that wraps their clay;
And Freedom shall awhile repair
To dwell, a weeping hermit, there!

William Collins
1721–1759

LOSS OF THE ROYAL GEORGE

Toll for the Brave!
The brave that are no more!
All sunk beneath the wave
Fast by their native shore!
Eight hundred of the brave
Whose courage well was tried,
Had made the vessel heel
And laid her on her side,
A land-breeze shook the shrouds
And she was overset;
Down went the Royal George,
With all her crew complete.

Toll for the brave!
Brave Kempenfelt is gone;
His last sea-fight is fought,
His work of glory done.
It was not in the battle;
No tempest gave the shock;
She sprang no fatal leak,
She ran upon no rock.
His sword was in its sheath,
His fingers held the pen,
When Kempenfelt went down
With twice four hundred men.

20

Weigh the vessel up
Once dreaded by our foes!
And mingle with our cup
The tears that England owes.
Her timbers yet are sound,
And she may float again
Full charged with England's thunder,
And plough the distant main:
But Kempenfelt is gone,
His victories are o'er;
And he and his eight hundred
Shall plough the wave no more.

William Cowper
1731–1800

PAST AND PRESENT

I remember, I remember
The house where I was born,
The little window where the sun
Came peeping in at morn;
He never came a wink too soon
Nor brought too long a day;
But now, I often wish the night
Had borne my breath away.

I remember, I remember
The roses, red and white,
The violets, and the lily-cups –
Those flowers made of light!
The lilacs where the robin built,
And where my brother set
The laburnum on his birthday, –
The tree is living yet!

I remember, I remember
The fir trees dark and high;
I used to think their slender tops
Were close against the sky:
It was a childish ignorance,
But now 'tis little joy
To know I'm farther off from Heaven
Than when I was a boy.

Thomas Hood
1799–1845

THE PERFECT LIFE

It is not growing like a tree
In bulk, doth make Men better be;
Or standing long an oak, three hundred year,
To fall a log at last, dry, bald, and sere;
A lily of a day
Is fairer far in May,
Although it fall and die that night –
It was the plant and flower of Light.
In small proportions we just beauties see;
And in short measures life may perfect be.

Ben Jonson
1578–1637

WHEN

When lovely woman stoops to folly
And finds too late that men betray, –
What charm can soothe her melancholy,
What art can wash her guilt away?

The only art her guilt to cover,
To hide her shame from every eye
To give repentance to her lover
And wring his bosom, is – to die.

Oliver Goldsmith
1728–1774

ELEGY

The curfew tolls the knell of parting day,
The lowing herd wind slowly o'er the lea,
The ploughman homeward plods his weary way,
And leaves the world to darkness and to me.

Now fades the glimmering landscape on the sight,
And all the air a solemn stillness holds,
Save where the beetle wheels his droning flight,
And drowsy tinklings lull the distant folds:

Save that from yonder ivy-mantled tower
The moping owl does to the moon complain
Of such as, wandering near her secret bower
Molest her ancient solitary reign.

Beneath those rugged elms, that yew-tree's shade
Where heaves the turf in many a mouldering heap,
Each in his narrow cell for ever laid,
The rude Forefathers of the hamlet sleep.

The breezy call of incense-breathing morn,
The swallow twittering from the straw-built shed,
The cock's shrill clarion, or the echoing horn,
No more shall rouse them from their lowly bed.

For them no more the blazing hearth shall burn
Or busy housewife ply her evening care:
No children run to lisp their sire's return,
Or climb his knees the envied kiss to share.

Oft did the harvest to their sickle yield,
Their furrow oft the stubborn glebe has broke;
How jocund did they drive their team afield!
How bow'd the woods beneath their sturdy stroke!

Let not Ambition mock their useful toil,
Their homely joys, and destiny obscure;
Nor Grandeur hear with a disdainful smile
The short and simple annals of the Poor.

The boast of heraldry, the pomp of power,
And all that beauty, all that wealth e'er gave,
Awaits alike th' inevitable hour: –
The paths of glory lead but to the grave.

Thomas Grey
1716–1771

A JOY FOR EVER

A thing of beauty is a joy for ever:
Its loveliness increases; it will never
Pass into nothingness; but still will keep
A bower quiet for us, and a sleep
Full of sweet dreams, and health, and quiet breathing.
Therefore, on every morrow, are we wreathing
A flowery band to bind us to the earth,
Spite of despondence, of the inhuman dearth
Of noble natures, of the gloomy days,
Of all the unhealthy and o'er-darkened ways
Made for our searching: yes, in spite of all,
Some shape of beauty moves away the pall
From our dark spirits. Such the sun, the moon,
Trees old, and young, sprouting a shady boon
For simple sheep; and such are daffodils
With the green world they live in; and clear rills
That for themselves a cooling covert make
Gainst the hot season; the mid-forest brake,
Rich with a sprinkling of fair musk-rose blooms:
And such too is the grandeur of the dooms
We have imagined for the mighty dead;
All lovely tales that we have heard or read:
An endless fountain of immortal drink,
Pouring unto us from the heaven's brink.

John Keats
1759–1821

24

OLD FAMILIAR FACES

I have had playmates, I have had companions
In my days of childhood, in my joyful school-days;
All, all are gone, the old familiar faces.

I have been laughing, I have been carousing,
Drinking late, sitting late, with my bosom cronies;
All, all are gone, the old familiar faces.

I loved a Love once, fairest among women:
Closed are her doors on me, I must not see her –
All, all are gone, the old familiar faces.

I have a friend, a kinder friend has no man:
Like an ingrate, I left my friend abruptly;
Left him, to muse on the old familiar faces,

Ghost-like I paced round the haunts of my childhood,
Earth seem'd a desert I was bound to traverse,
Seeking to find the old familiar faces.

Friend of my bosom, thou more than a brother,
Why wert not thou born in my father's dwelling?
So might we talk of the old familiar faces.

How some they have died, and some they have left me,
And some are taken from me; all are departed;
All, all are gone, the old familiar faces.

Charles Lamb
1775–1837

PRO PATRIA MORI

When he who adores thee has left but the name
Of his fault and his sorrows behind,
O! say wilt thou weep, when they darken the fame
Of a life that for thee was resign'd!
Yes, weep, and however my foes may condemn,
Thy tears shall efface their decree;
For, Heaven can witness, though guilty to them,
I have been but too faithful to thee.

With thee were the dreams of my earliest love;
Every thought of my reason was thine:
In my last humble prayer to the Spirit above
Thy name shall be mingled with mine!
O! blest are the lovers and friends who shall live
The days of thy glory to see;
But the next dearest blessing that Heaven can give
Is thy pride of thus dying for thee.

Thomas Moore
1779–1852

THEY ALSO SERVE WHO ONLY STAND AND WAIT

When I consider how my light is spent
Ere half my days, in this dark world and wide,
And that one talent which is death to hide
Lodged with me useless, though my soul more bent

To serve therewith my Maker, and present
My true account, lest He returning chide, –
Doth God exact day-labour, light denied?
I fondly ask: – But Patience, to prevent

That murmur, soon replies; God doth not need
Either man's work, or His own gifts: Who best
Bear His mild yoke, they serve Him best: His state

Is kingly; thousands at His bidding speed
And post o'er land and ocean without rest: –
They also serve who only stand and wait.

John Milton
1608–1674

COME LIVE WITH ME

Come live with me and be my Love,
And we will all the pleasures prove
That hills and valleys, dale and field,
And all the craggy mountains yield.

There will we sit upon the rocks
And see the shepherds feed their flocks,
By shallow rivers, to whose falls
Melodious birds sing madrigals.

There will I make thee beds of roses
And a thousand fragrant posies,
A cap of flowers, and a kirtle
Embroider'd all with leaves of myrtle.

A gown made of the finest wool,
Which from our pretty lambs we pull,
Fair lined slippers for the cold,
With buckles of the purest gold.

A belt of straw and ivy buds
With coral clasps and amber studs:
And if these pleasures may thee move,
Come live with me and be my Love.

Thy silver dishes for thy meat
As precious as the gods do eat,
Shall on an ivory table be
Prepared each day for thee and me.

The shepherd swains shall dance and sing
For thy delight each May-morning:
If these delights thy mind may move,
Then live with me and be my Love.

Christopher Marlowe
1564–1593

QUIET LIFE

Happy the man, whose wish and care
A few paternal acres bound,
Content to breathe his native air
In his own ground.

Whose herds with milk, whose fields with bread,
Whose flocks supply him with attire;
Whose trees in summer yield him shade,
In winter, fire.

Blest, who can unconcern'dly find
Hours, days and years, slide soft away
In health of body, peace of mind,
Quiet by day,

Sound sleep by night; study and ease
Together mix'd; sweet recreation,
And innocence, which most does please
With meditation.

Thus let me live, unseen, unknown;
Thus unlamented let me die;
Steal from the world, and not a stone
Tell where I lie.

Alexander Pope
1688–1744

TO HIS LOVE

Shall I compare thee to a summer's day?
Thou art more lovely and more temperate:
Rough winds do shake the darling buds of May,
And summer's lease hath all too short a date:

Sometime too hot the eye of heaven shines,
And often is his gold complexion dimm'd:
And every fair from Fair sometime declines,
By chance, or nature's changing course, untrimm'd.

But thy eternal summer shall not fade
Nor lose possession of that fair thou owest;
Nor shall death brag thou wanderest in his shade,
When in eternal lines to time thou growest;

So long as men can breathe, or eyes can see,
So long lives this, and this gives life to thee.

William Shakespeare
1564–1616

PIBROCH OF DONUIL DHU

Pibroch of Donuil Dhu
Pibroch of Donuil
Wake thy wild voice anew,
Summon Clan Conuil.
Come away, come away,
Hark to the summons!
Come in your war-array,
Gentles and commons.

Come from deep glen, and
From mountain so rocky;
The war-pipe and pennon
Are at Inverlocky.
Come every hill-plaid, and
True heart that wears one,
Come every steel blade, and
Strong hand that bears one.

Leave untended the herd,
The flock without shelter;
Leave the corpse uninterr'd,
The bride at the altar;
Leave the deer, leave the steer,
Leave nets and barges;
Come with your fighting gear,
Broadswords and targes.

Come as the winds come, when
Forests are rended,
Come as the waves come, when
Navies are stranded:
Faster come, faster come,
Faster and faster,
Chief, vassal, page and groom,
Tenant and master.

Fast they come, fast they come;
See how they gather!
Wide waves the eagle plume
Blended with heather.
Cast your plaids, draw your blades,
Forward each man set!
Pibroch of Donuil Dhu
Knell for the onset!

Sir Walter Scott
1771–1832

REQUIEM

Under the wide and starry sky,
Dig the grave and let me lie,
Glad did I live and gladly die,
And I laid me down with a will.

This be the verse you grave for me:
Here he lies where he longed to be;
Home is the sailor, home from sea,
And the hunter home from the hill.

Robert Louis Stevenson
1850–1894

PEACE

My soul, there is a country
Far beyond the stars,
Where stands a winged sentry
All skilful in the wars,
There, above noise and danger,
Sweet Peace sits crown'd with smiles,
And one born in a Manger
Commands the beauteous files,

He is thy gracious Friend,
And (O my soul awake!)
Did in pure love descend
To die here for thy sake.
If thou canst get but thither,
There grows the flower of Peace,
The rose that cannot wither,
Thy fortress, and thy ease.

Leave then thy foolish ranges;
For none can thee secure,
But one, who never changes,
Thy God, thy life, thy cure.

Henry Vaughan
1622–1695

30

THE DAFFODILS

I wandered lonely as a cloud
That floats on high o'er vales and hills,
When all at once I saw a crowd,
A host, of golden daffodils;
Beside the lake, beneath the trees,
Fluttering and dancing in the breeze.

Continuous as the stars that shine
And twinkle on the Milky Way,
They stretched in never-ending line
Along the margin of a bay:
Ten thousand saw I at a glance,
Tossing their heads in sprightly dance.

The waves beside them danced; but they
Out-did the sparkling waves in glee:
A poet could not but be gay,
In such a jocund company:
I gazed – and gazed – but little thought
What wealth the show to me had brought:

For oft, when on my couch I lie
In vacant or in pensive mood,
They flash upon that inward eye
Which is the bliss of solitude;
And then my heart with pleasure fills,
And dances with the daffodils.

William Wordsworth
1770–1850

THE COTTAGE HOSPITAL

At the end of a long-walled garden
in a red provincial town,
A brick path led to a mulberry –
scanty grass at its feet.
I lay under blackening branches
where the mulberry leaves hung down
Sheltering ruby fruit globes
from a Sunday-tea-time heat.
Apple and plum espaliers
basked upon bricks of brown;
The air was swimming with insects
and children played in the street.

Out of this bright intentness
into the mulberry shade
Musca domestica (housefly)
swung from the August light
Slap into slithery rigging
by the waiting spider made
Which spun the lithe elastic
till the fly was shrouded tight,
Down came the hairy talons
and horrible poison blade
And none of the garden noticed
that fizzing, hopeless fight.

Say in what Cottage Hospital
whose pale green walls resound
With the tap upon polished parquet
on inflexible nurses' feet
Shall I myself be lying
when they range the screen around?
And say shall I groan in dying,
as I twist the sweaty sheet?
Or gasp for breath uncrying,
as I feel my senses drown'd
While the air is swimming with insects
and children play in the street?

Sir John Betjeman
Born 1906

POETRY TODAY

What is the function of Poetry today?

To provide enjoyment . . . with possibly a glimpse of existence, alas, almost extinct, of an earlier pre-television, mass educational and mechanical sound copying age. Poetry develops a deeper appreciation of the magical meaning, the sheer beauty, in the Sound of Words. Poetry flourishing in earlier generations has in modern times undergone transformations, inevitably, the consequence of twentieth century noise, and life. A life for many in leisure time consisting of an unending stream of time-consuming T.V. attractions. Combinations calculated to render quiet meditation difficult, a situation when material living almost over-powers the near spiritual self.

Originating within, poetry feeds an essential, often almost unrealised need. Discovering the Heart of a new poem to one's experience could be likened to the meeting for the first time with a new personality, one seemingly instantaneously in harmony with our thoughts, our ideas. Possibly more so. Although newly met there exists already an inner bond: inexplicably the first meeting seems as a renewal with a long lost well remembered acquaintance. Occasionally it is almost as twin souls meeting who have loved one another in some other consciousness; as space in the eternal, the experience reveals itself rarely during the present Life Span.

Poetry, like music, is capable of moving us deeply. They are arts which require quietude and are at once almost unrestricted in scope and in range: truly they are the Food of Love.

C. John Taylor.
The Poet/Artist.
Born 1915

PRIZE WINNING POETRY

Introduction to New Poetry/Short Story and Postal Competition

New poems and short stories in the following section of this Edition, each won an Exhibitor's Prize, having been selected for exhibition in the 1977 Silver Jubilee Exhibition.

Arranged by Composer's surnames, alphabetically, coming from a wide geographical section of the United Kingdom, they represent Poets and Authors of different age groups, environments and occupations. The extensive "Title" or "First-lines" range, in the index, indicates how vast is the inspirational area available to the poetical imagination! Techniques, as well as methods, understandably, are almost as varied, as are the "Titles" or "First-lines", themselves!

POSTAL COMPETITION: £1,000 in Valuable Prizes.

Available until November 1st, 1978!

Readers are invited to select one poem or short story only, from the index, which possesses for them an especial appeal!

Write (upon a postcard only, please) the "Title" or "First-line", the index page number, the name and town of the Poet or Author chosen, sign the postcard, making certain that the sender's own full name and postal reply address is also written upon the postcard.

The completed postcard should be addressed and mailed to:

Highland Arts Studios ('78 Poetry Competition),
Seil Isle,
Oban,
Scotland.

Only one vote, i.e. one postcard, per person, will be accepted.

Postcard votes will be meticulously computed.

The Poet or Author whose work receives the highest number of votes will be judged the winner.

A first prize of One Hundred Pounds (£100) will be awarded to the winning Poet or Author. Three "runners up" prizes of Fifty Pounds (£50) each will be awarded to the Poets or Authors receiving the nearest totals of votes to the winner.

Employees of Highland Studios, or employees of their advertising agents, will not be eligible to enter this competition.

One hundred and fifty (150) prizes will be available to be won by postcard voters in this Competition, comprising of signed First Edition C. John Taylor "Highland Village" fine art full natural colour, lithographic wall pictures, value, as advertised in "The Sunday Post", Five Pounds each.

These prizes will be available to be won by the first (by postmark) voters who correctly select the winning poem . . . The ultimate first winner of the first prize of One Hundred Pounds. Results will be published in December in The National Sunday Newspapers.

The decision of the Compiler of "Prize Winning Poetry" is final and binding in this Competition. Closing Date for receipt of postcard votes is November 1st, 1978.

No correspondence whatsoever can be entered into regarding this, the 1978 Poetry Competition.

Vote for the poem or short story of your choice (one only). The winner receives One Hundred Pounds cash First Prize.

Make sure your own full name and postal address is clearly written upon your postcard, otherwise your vote is invalid.

Write to:

> Highland Arts Studios,
> '78 Poetry Competition,
> Seil Isle,
> Oban,
> Scotland.

Choose your poem or short story from the following indexes.

Visitors will also be able to record their votes in this Competition, using the forms and special ballot boxes provided for the purpose, at the Studios.

PRIZE WINNING POETRY

Poet's Name Alphabetically With Poetry Title

43

DAWN

I saw the joy of morning light
Erupting from the black of night,
I saw the dawn, the morning dew,
I saw the sun the world renew,
I saw in each red glorious ray
The miracle of a new-born day.
It stirred the waters of the deep
Where silent rocks their vigil keep
It warmed the mountains slumbering there,
And woke the birds who filled the air
With joyous song which seemed to say,
Arise! Arise! and greet the day.

Dorothy Braidwood Aiken,
Stafford, Staffs.

AUTUMN

Autumn – season that I love
In richest browns and reds
You clothe yourself, while up above
A yellow paper sun her pale light sheds.

Fragrance of a misty wood
It's leaf strewn pathways lead me on
To elven glades where squirrels hoard their food
Against the barren days of Winter long.

Hedgerows jewelled with silver webs
Nature opens up her treasure chest
Yet even now that vibrant life begins to ebb
Preparing for its Winter's rest.

Mary Crawford Alexander,
Edinburgh.

OCTOBER

Unwelcome herald thrown in at the deep end,
Unwilling, yet ungallant. When winds begin to push and pull
The young trees that visibly protest against conditions.
The rain enjoins and adds it's "hear, hear" against the
Window pane and low flying birds declare about further
Deprivation and tits become aware of Humanity.
The farmer reflects on lean rewards and contemplates
The scene. The plough brings desolation and destruction
To life below while circling gulls above await the
unturned spit. We gaze through streaked and misty glass
And wistful eyes follow the ever dwindling traffic
A portent of the coming cocoon.
Huge oaks across the fields still beautifully adorned,
Swaying and casting out their wardrobes as a woman,
Apologetically, wistfully, yet unremittingly.
Children begin to feel a sense of loss
As fading light contracts their play and turns them home.
But you approach us full of compromise as
Soon we shall inwards turn to family
Soon will appear once more the books,
The sewing machine, the playing cards, the games,
And with them the early evening noise, the ready wit, the
Warmth, the mixed feeling at drawing the curtains.
Oh, October, we'd not rather seen your face for it had beauty,
But concealed disorder. Alas you are here. We cannot but accept
You for you in truth are Nature's shock absorber.

James R. Alison,
Dumfries.

A SMILE

Life, love and grace
Brought forth from that familiar face,
Her eyes so soft and kind,
Her touch so human as she kept behind.
Always there to help or to advise,
Yes, a face that through my memory of years,
I guarded, her youth, her beauty, and her pride,
And from them sprang, perch nce my melancholy mind.
For why should youth be stolen from my side?
A youth that gave me life?
And why should beauty go and age creep in?
An age that makes my feelings strive, for –
Should I cry for youth gone by,
Or rejoice in wisdom?

46

Oh life, life, life so cruel,
So cruel for we have but no choice,
But just to live and follow rules,
Rules made by us, from all our own mistakes, and cries.
Cries from our wildness,
Cries from our hearts,
Cries of fear and ignorance,
Till death does silence all.

Oh peace, oh peace break out upon our human race,
To give who live a chance of joy and grace,
Only pride can save us,
Pride that, keeps us from an animalistic state,
Pride, sent through to me,
From that familiar face,
That face that saves my melancholy mind,
Radiating life, love and grace.
Yes –
That warm true smile,
Upon a mother's gentle face.

Laura Alzapiedi,
Banchory, Kincardineshire.

TRAVELLING CIRCUS

Travelling along the road,
Dust and dirt an extra load,
Seeing sights and gaining heights,
Of knowledge, in this vast abode.
Carrying on despite the heat,
Despite the cold, must not retreat,
Creating an aura of magic, their code,
Travelling along this dusty road.
To pull the ropes, to lift the tent,
The big top stands, time to relent.
The acts they practice, work hard to please,
The public applaud – then their on their knees.
To clear up, to carry on,
When all folk to their homes have gone,
Then their off again like sifting sand,
Move with the wind, all of one brand.
They travel thus creating for us,
A magic scene, a magic of time,
The Circus comes with trumpets blowing,
Not golden bugles, but people glowing.

Mrs. Elizabeth Armstrong,
Oban, Argyll.

Sweet daughter of the Atlantic swell,
Is Loch Cuin's gentle inlet,
Fed by that ocean on its tidal travels,
Yet somehow warm, unlike her parent's cruel coldness,
Beautiful, even when emptied of her watery flow.
When Autumn golds and russets, greens and red,
Carpet the ground and clothe the trees,
Of Cuin's fair banks and tiny islets.
Yet when her empty basin starts to fill,
With the rough ocean's lively overflow,
Then is her loveliness increased;
And birds who lately walked upon dry land,
Must fly away when sensing waves approach,
To find a safer resting place until,
Loch Cuin again is made bereft of water,
By the demanding ocean.
The almost silent lilt of birdsong,
Mingles in the quiet evening how,
With the caressing sound of gently lapping water,
Stroking the greying slopes of Cuin.
And then, as if to saturate the heart,
Already full of nature's bounty,
The sun and sky, in mystic harmony,
Conspire to paint so eloquent a sunset,
Which thrusts its silver ribbons o'er the loch,
And gilds the ever darkening sky,
Till I believe that here is heaven, here perfection,
Where Cuin's serenity speaks silently of peace.

Miss Pamela Jean Artley,
Bridlington, N. Humberside.

A SUMMER BREEZE

One gorgeous day in mid July,
I heard the sea's eternal cry,
And took to dreaming.
I dreamt I felt the splashing spray,
The sun's exquisite golden ray,
And seagulls screaming.
So out I went and fixed the yacht,
Pulled up the anchor, loosed the knot,
And took to steering!
The "Lucy" skimmed the sparkling sea,
With graceful curves of ecstasy,
She slid the clearing.
And then there came like echoes soft,
A cooling, calming freshing waft,
To soothe and ease.
It sent the yacht a header on,
And filled the sail, but now 'tis gone,
A summer breeze.

Mrs. L. Ash,
Edinburgh.

NOVEMBER 1974

Still two thousand miles apart
I remember you with tenderness
Maybe you felt nothing but to me you were everything.
I loved to see and I longed to hold you,
At night I lay alone in my bed
Thinking over and over the things that you said
I dreamed of you in my sleep
And hoped to find you there on my awakening.
You saw only my young love,
You saw my face but you didn't see me.
You were not cruel yet you hurt
I forgave because love is that way.
You were hard but insecure
Behind the veil that masked your face
You felt and cared but showed no trace.
Your name was what you were . . .
      and rocks don't move.

Miss Shiela Backhouse,
Romford, Essex.

49

BUYING A CAR

"REAL LEATHER SEATS," the salesman said,
"Reversing light as well –
New tyres – twin spots – wood panelling –
THIS car will always sell.
What's more, it's done no mileage,
Look – the seats are hardly sat on."
(We'd heard it all before, of course,
He hadn't changed the pattern.)

"This make of car, you're bound to know
Is one that can't be beaten."
And so, convinced, we drove away
Our gem with leather seatin' –
All gleaming white, and spotless,
Crikey! This should stun the neighbour –
With radio for forty pounds
(And ten more for the labour!)

A year passed by – we went to sell,
He sadly dropped his head
"There's not much *call* for these, sir,
How's your sub-chassis?" he said.
"Oh fine – just fine – and what is more
Our seats are pretty slick,
We've walnut panelling – twin spots . . ."
He gave our tyres a kick.
"Twin spots don't make much difference, sir –
You might as well just lose 'em
Be honest now – it isn't very often that you use 'em,
But while you're here, you look around."
We like a grey saloon;
"Twelve-eighty pounds – one owner –
Just came in this afternoon.
Now *yours*," he said, "is getting on,
But still, I'll do a deal.
Go home and think it over, sir
Then tell me how you feel."

It seems we thought a bit too long
For next time that we met
His offer dropped by sixty pounds
(We fear it's dropping yet!)
"Your price was higher earlier," we said,
He rubbed his cheek,
"Aye – *time's* the ruddy problem, mate,
Cars lose ten quid a week."

We glanced around the showroom
And we didn't feel so "matey",
The price tag on the grey saloon
Was still marked twelve and eighty.
"Now *here's* a lovely little job," he said,
And beamed with pride –
"Ten thousand genuine miles from new."
"We've kept *ours* low," we cried.
A WEARY look came to his eye
His face lost all its fun.
"Now that's a BAD MISTAKE," he said
"THEY'RE BETTER IF THEY'RE *RUN*."

We'll BUY, of course, and double quick –
It won't do to meander,
But how we wish that sauce for goose
WAS ALSO SAUCE FOR GANDER.

Dorothy J. Bacon,
Buxton, Derbyshire.

SMUDGE

Oh I remember once a face,
And thund'ring feet at frightening pace,
The flying ears' black silky sheen –
A happy vision now unseen.

The welcomed victim's mighty groans
As heavy paws increased their moans.
The joyful bark subduing soon
To throaty gurgle's softer croon.

A "tumma roll" was your desire,
Or sitting quietly by the fire
On Daddy's knee, black head erect
With Professor's curls, like Judge Elect.

Oh you would dream, stare into space,
And try to count each family face.
Once satisfied that four were there
You'd flop contented in the chair.

Then rustles of a bag would make
Your slumbrous eyes a brightness take.
Black nostrils then would moist and flare,
And interest animates your stare.

51

Those eyes which for a falter wait,
Denote an almost trance-like state:
From bag to mouth, from mouth to bag,
Cause mouth to slaver, jaw to sag.

No crumb, no drop fell unarrest',
So sorrow fills your little breast.
With heaving shoulders you then turn
From us, resigned to brood alone.

When workdays fill our weeks so long,
On Persian carpet you belong,
With human voice an echo till
The hour of five, you break the still —

Some inner harmony of time
Reveals this moment all sublime:
With two paws on the 'sill you 'wait
Familiar clickings of the gate.

At table I can see you watch
Adored Queen devour her tea.
You steal a glance demure and shy
But when She looks you turn away.

When finally Her favour's won
You throw Her paws and paws and paws.
Reserve, confusion all are gone
In mad delight, and muddy claws.

And She, the Queen, has not the heart
To 'draw Her hand from yours to part:
For with that cold and clasping pad
She feels not angry, only glad.

Oh I remember once a face
When illness swept on it apace.
When midnight hour's sweet silence broke,
Through sobbing howls your spirit spoke.

Oh I remember too, one day
Recovery's dawn edged Death away:
For shakily you made advance
With marrow bone and wobbly stance.

So thin, you entered through the door,
The bulging bone your thin mouth bore,
Green jersey hung on your small frame,
With bubbly nose you shiv'ring came.

And when a decade passed away,
Another malady's decay
Assumed a serpent's form to flay
Your faithful flesh relentlessly.

And then that cold and sunny day,
Before they took your life away,
You sat awhile beside my bed
And tranquilly I stroked your head.

That same morn' on the railway steps
A rushing form did intercept me,
Lively, black and full of life! –
A phantom resurrected life?

But no! I bent to clap your coat,
And flesh and fur still met my stroke.
The clock of fate did us deceive –
Your life received an hour's reprieve.

And now a portrait hangs in state
Above the dying ember's grate
Un-needed, for our memories fill –
A willing servant serves us still.

Miss Irene Baird,
Prestwick, Ayrshire.

INNOCENCE

A child undefiled
Lies curled, in the womb of the world,
Of whose untried innocence
The transience
Is grievous joy –
Is joyous grief.

For to be aware is to begin
To be wise. To know no sin
Is to do no right;
Only in the knowing
Can we begin – showing
Evil that his presence is not desired.

Marjorie Baker,
Bexhill, Sussex.

THE UNDEFEATED

I love to "talk" and be with them
These people that I love;
Yet most folk, never give a "thought"
No more than clouds above;

I have named them, "undefeated",
A "name" so well deserved;
For character-and-bearing
There is no other "word";

That could faithfully describe them
These human gold, of earth;
You can "range" all "odds" against them
With all that is per verse;

But through power, of mind and spirit
They'll strive for all their worth;
And a difficult position,
They'll over-come, with mirth;

Whatever "challenge" comes their way,
They know they can "win" through;
For not a "stone" they'll leave unturned
That might their "work" un'do;

How they must "daunt" the weaker-souls?
Who soon are down-at-heart;
And never seem to "stay-life's course"
And feel doomed, from the start;

So if you have the knack, to "beat"
Those who'd bring you "down"
Thank Him, who has endowed, you thus
With a "gift" so profound.

Henry Ball,
Huntly, Aberdeenshire.

THAT WONDERFUL LIFE

The world was full of ugly sin
And so God pondered on how He could win,
The souls of men back to Him.

No suit of armour would He don,
Or spear or sword would He put on,
Instead He'd send His only Son.

The baby was born on Christmas Day
In a stable, among beasts and hay,
And in a manger the tiny form lay.

"Jesus" was the little boy's name
And He grew up to be a man of fame,
Healing the sick, curing the lame.

He spoke to the crowds of God's wonderful Love
    and taught men to pray to His Father above;
He would sit by the lake or climb on to a hill,
Spreading the Good News of His Father's will.

Alas, some men despised Him, not wanting to listen
    to the message of Love from His Father in Heaven,
So He was betrayed by one of His friends
And hung on a Cross by nails in His hands.

But He rose again on that glad Easter morn
And spoke to His friends, showing hands which were torn;
Then the whole earth rejoiced, the victory was won.

So forty days later with His special friends
    He climbed into the hills to bid ast farewells,
And there in a cloud He ascended to Heaven
To reign with His Father in His glorious kingdom.

But He left us a promise, if we do His will,
That His Spirit will guide us and comfort us still,
And men shall again be united with Him.

And so we must strive in our lives day by day
    to listen to God and follow His way,
'Cause it's only by living the way Jesus taught
That we can share His wonderful Life, so dearly bought.

Mrs. Joan Ballantyne,
Carlisle, Cumbria.

AN ENGLISH GARDEN, SUMMER '72

The roses stand wall-backed, close in a row
the wind rushes at them it hurts them so
to know they are doing their level best
to keep a "head" in the freak "tempest".

Geraniums, in scarlet like Guardsmen near-by,
two-tiered in pots lift their heads to the sky
sway back for a closer contact with the wall –
lest they should fall.

Away in the distance the Rose of Sharon
a species so low scarcely heeds the rain's coming
or the winds "kow tow" but for the lives of others
drops her "rain tears" on the grass crying,
wind, oh wind, please pass! just pass!

Vera E. Ballard,
Reading, Berks.

IF

If life held no pain or sickness
How could we experience good health?
If the world was free from poverty
Would we then appreciate it's wealth?
If we never had any temptations
There would be no need for victory,
And no-one would have ever been
To the cross at Calvary.

If the sun shone night and day
Would we know how it feels to be cold?
If life held no mysteries
Then what could time unfold?
If there was no darkness
How could we see the light?
If no-one ever made mistakes
How would we know wrong from right?

If there is no second birth
How can the first one end?
If there is no heaven
Then to where did Christ ascend?
If sin held no forgiveness
The Bible just could not be read,
If there was no wooden cross
My friends, we would be DEAD.

Ann Barclay,
Cardenden, Fife.

LITTLE FRIEND

Oh! little robin red breast!
Your song awakes the dawn.
Sweet and so melodious,
Night's sleep has slipped and gone.

From bed so snug and cosy,
I creep to window pane.
In nightgown and soft slippers,
Just to hear your sweet refrain.

Surrounding trees are leafless,
Forked branches tower to sky.
A world swirls with snowy flakes,
As a pillow white to lie.

A scene so dreamlike, so picturesque,
All hearts as young will sigh.
To gaze from frosted window panes,
As tiny flakes flit by.

Ah, there you are! on limb of tree,
With chest a boastful red.
My, you've been a busy chap,
Whilst I was snug in bed.

Minute footprints dot the snow,
Where boundary lines are known.
And woe betide the stranger!
Who covets a kingdom's throne.

But now you rest sedately,
With cap of powdered snow.
Small, and yet so warm!
With tiny chest aglow.

If only, but alas I can't,
Stand here the whole day long.
Entranced by beauty Heaven sent,
Enraptured by your song.

My thanks sincerely little friend,
For gladness deep to stay.
My home is yours and welcome,
Until you fly away.

William Thomas Barclay,
Glasgow.

57

THOUGHTS AT THE TIME OF ELIZABETH
THE SECOND'S SILVER JUBILEE

The strife, the strikes, the desperate struggling
Of the people has never seemed to wane.
These have been symptoms of our age
In Elizabeth the Second's reign.

Can nuclear power be turned from arms
To good use, allaying our worries and fears?
This has been a major problem
Thro' Elizabeth's twenty five years.

The homeless, the battered, the violent, the sick,
The truants, delinquents, old people alone.
Have we been pre-occupied, lost all our caring
Since Elizabeth came to the throne?

Problems enormous education and politics,
Finances, Europe, starvation and crime,
Earthquakes and floods, international disasters
All in Elizabeth's time.

High rise housing breeding neurotics,
Encroachment on Green Belt, detergents rampage
And pollute our rivers; can this be progress
During Elizabeth's age?

Advances in medicine, inventions, engineering,
Prowess in sport, in the arts and in school.
Indeed we've achieved but at what cost
Throughout Elizabeth's rule?

Eternally night passes and with the dawn
Comes light, changing views and bringing us nearer
Hopefully to saner and calmer solutions
In Elizabeth's second era.

Mrs. Irene Barlow,
East Chinnock, Somerset.

REFLECTIONS

They shimmer and shiver,
Reflections on the river.
A bird swoops and calls "hello",
To itself mirrored below.
The reflections darken,
With black clouds above reflected below,
And harken, to the groans of thunder,
And the sun has lost its glow.
Now the river is shattering,
With the heavy glass-like drops,
But the farmers they're happy,
"Cos it's good for all the crops".
The thunder it's now crashing!
And the lightning comes bright and fast!

Now an hour has past,
And the sun returns its glow.
Reflections reappear, on the glinting river below,
To shimmer and to shiver, as like an age ago!

Mrs. Diana Margaret Barnes,
Westhill, Skene, Aberdeen.

ALWAYS

Always I will stay with you,
Until the butterfly in winter comes,
And nestles in the snowy drifts,
I will stay with you.

Until the robin comes in summer time,
And whispers gently to the rose,
I will stay with you,
Until the snowdrops bloom in APRIL,
The crocuses in MAY.

Until the tide does not leave the shore,
And the sun and moon meet in unison,
I will stay with you,
For ever I will stay with you.

Mrs. Phyllis Barton,
Meols, Wirral, Merseyside.

PLAY SCHOOL

Play School starts today, and little hands are busy,
Their active minds will sometimes make,
Their poor teacher dizzy!!
But they are all learning – being taught how to share,
Building – clay mixing – painting – reading – learning,
How to care for one another,
In an unselfconscious way.
Being taught self reliance,
On their own feet how to stand,
These up and coming citizens,
Of our "Beloved Land".

Mrs. Margaret Baxter,
Stockton-On-Tees, Cleveland.

THE WIND

The wind it howled outside my window,
It sounded like a lost child crying,
It echoed down the chimney, filling the room with its cry,
It sounded so sad, it hit the sides of the house, with invisible force,
The trees bent to it like it was their master,
The grass was flattened by it,
The flowers in my garden were uprooted
The sky was dark, everything looked gloomy,
The trees brushed their branches against my window, like long fingers,
Trying to reach out and get me,
The wind grew louder, it sounded like it was screaming with all its
    strength,
My house sounded like it was haunted,
I thought it would never be over,
I thought the world would end,
Everything was silent. only the wind howled,
It dominated the house,
It seemed to echo from all the walls,
I longed for the time when the wind would go,
And peace would be here once more.

Miss Christine Ann Beevers,
Leeds, Yorkshire.

AGE

Life's like a picture book, of past events,
Turning each page, until age is spent,
Then one looks back to glance at the past,
Did we choose right way? Each day,
Playing part of this world?

Was it a while of achievements complete? or
Off the track went our feet?

A baby is born, the world is there,
Loving eyes up and stare,
To open space.

A blank page starting to write,
What kind of being? this tiny mite?

Parents are there, to help bend or sway,
Developing a mind, a little each day.
The child can then expand its mind,
To betterment of mankind.

Showing a way not to drift or caring about,
Wonders are there to seek out,
When leaving this world maybe have found? and shown,
Loving kindness to those around.
A message to those, coming afore,
Leading to God's glory once more.

Edith Annie Bennett,
Paignton, Devon.

SUCH MERCY, SUCH LOVE AND SUCH GRACE

The man gazed down from Calvary
His eyes were fixed on me,
I felt guilt and bowed my head
In shame I turned away.

It wasn't me who put him there
Having nothing to do with him.
Why should the guilt seer through my heart
What had I done to him.

61

Should I turn my back on the innocent man
Who did nothing deserving death.
Why should I worry, he meant nothing to me,
Yet guilt overpowered instead.

Tears streamed down, I trembled sore,
Just couldn't understand.
Why should I let him upset me,
Why! who was this dying man.

"Jesus King of the Jews" the notice said,
But why should he bother me
Sinful men had put him there,
It had nothing to do with me.

The man looked down from Calvary
He fixed his gaze on me
Compassionate eyes were filled with love,
I knew! He was dying for me.

It should have been me, he took my place,
It was I who deserved to die.
Instead he took away my guilt
As I stood there and cried.

He died. but came to life again
He overcame the grave.
King of Kings and Lord of Lords
Such mercy, such love and such grace.

Mrs. Agnes T. Beveridge,
Methil, Fife.

VISIT TO BELSEN CONCENTRATION CAMP (1973)

A morning shimmering in blinding light,
The sky an ice blue frieze,
Our whispering tyres eating up the miles
Beneath the charcoal branches
Of the troop-like trees.
Houses, secretive behind their firs,
Disclaiming memories of jackboots, spurs.
Sunlight mocked all morbid speculation
As we arrived – emotions yet unshaken.

The yawning iron gates
The neat, high walls
Might well have sheltered stately home or park.
Instead, a slim stone monolith confronted us,
An understated exclamation mark!
We bowed our heads to read upon its base –
"To all who died within this place".

Within the Hall – the Documentary –
We saw the photographs;
A bloodless battlefield.
A sculptor's ghastly work-shop.
Naked rejects littering the floor,
With sunken eyes and cheeks and concave torsos
Hollowed out but not by Henry Moore!
Ten thousand dead – unburied dead!
And thirteen thousand dying,
When relief at last arrived.

Horror far too great for grief,
Premeditated – vile beyond belief.
We wandered up and down the criss-crossed paths
Among the well-mown bulging mounds
Which hid man's inhumanity to man.
Where mucus-coloured grass was loathe to grow
In case someone should eat it! –
As they did, you know!
Here, where thousands shelterless had lain
In blistering heat, in hail and snow and rain,
Suffering degradation worse than death.
Where prayer and supplication were in vain.
For pity, mercy were not just with-held
But attributes which some had never felt.

Inscribed at intervals upon the walls
The various names of many nations,
Austria, Hungary, Poland, Checoslav,
All who shared the sickening holocaust.
No melancholy half-mast flags hung here,
No bugled Last Post echoed on the air.

The sun still shone on our subdued departure,
Hills and woodlands stood serenely round,
A supernatural silence seemed to hang
About the listening watchful trees –
And no bird sang.

Grace Charlotte Bingham,
Scarborough, Yorkshire.

63

WESTMINSTER ABBEY

The glory and the pride of England's Kings
Still haunts the speaking stones of Westminster;
Dark shadows hover there and interplay
With the soft beams of sunlight; but today
Thinking no sadness brings
For now the peerless dignity and grace
Of our great Queen exalts this hallowed place
To a new splendour; pure in heart and mind
She yearns her peoples everywhere to bind
In love and harmony, as we no less
Pray Heaven her hopes to bless.

Edith Birch,
Plymouth, Devon.

REFLECTIONS

As I sit in pensive thought,
I realise what an awful lot
Of other people there must be,
In this world apart from me.

Each and every one a force,
Is born to live and run their course,
The world is not just my life, true
But each adds to their own,
And others too.

The reason for life is beyond you and I,
And just as elusive, is why we must die,
But live our life, and die we must,
Return to the immortal dust.

The chances are here for all to attain,
If only we knew, it won't come again,
For once we are dead, we cannot then say,
I could've, I should've, I will – one day.

David Black,
Redding, Falkirk, Stirlingshire.

INFLATION 1976

Ochone! Ochone! Ochone! Ochee!
Jim Callaghan is Britain's leading M.P.
And he did declare, that certain gent
That increases maun, be five per cent.
Aboot this statement, we ur no ower joyed,
Fur tae get higher wages, means mair unemployed,
The prices o' food, fair maks ye wunner,
An' tae see the costs soarin'
Jist gies ye the scunner.
The poon' has reached, an all time low
Sae whit can ye buy, ur whaur kin ye go?
Folks say strikes, ur maistly tae blame,
Fur some men waant money, fur steyin' at hame.
And vandalism and crime, is oan sich a high scale,
There's nae bloomin' room, fur the prisoners in jail,
But weemen's equality, is aboot the last straw,
And man noo is fightin', wi' his back tae the wa'.
It's faur mair serious, than ony buddy micht think,
Fur soon he'll be taakin', his place at the sink,
Ochone! Ochone! sich high inflation,
Whit hus happened, tae this bonnie nation?

Mr. H. Black,
Glasgow.

LUNCH DATE

Will you come to lunch with me,
If next Friday you are free?
I'd love to see you Mabel dear,
But first I'd better make it clear,
I can't afford the price of meat,
So don't know what we're going to eat,
These days I'm trying to get slimmer,
So don't eat much before my dinner.
I can't make anything from rabbits,
Because I hate their nasty habits,
My pastry never rises high,
So hopeless to attempt a pie.
I 'phoned, the butcher for a duck,
But so far I've been out of luck.
Some people say ducks are all grease,
So we'd better just have bread and cheese,
Accompanied by vitamins A & B
And if you're lucky C & D
Won't you come to lunch with me?

Mrs. Helen J. Blair,
Aberdeen.

THE LASS OF BAL-AN-OR

I'll tell you my story so please lend an ear;
Just picture the scene when the summer was here.
I was panning for gold by the stream I adore,
Mid the heather-clad hills of my own Bal-an-or.
I heard a voice calling as though in a dream;
In wonder my gaze wandered over the scene.
By the stream stood a lass – heavenly I declare;
Like an angel she was, with the gold in her hair.

Sweet innocence blossomed in bonnie blue eyes;
Her smile made me dream I was in paradise.
Just the touch of her hand brought a rapture divine,
While in heaven I strayed when her sweet lips met mine.
That night as the gloaming swept down through the glen,
She left with a promise to call back again.
But the months have gone by since she failed to appear,
So I sigh for the lass with the gold in her hair.

The bloom on the heather has faded and gone;
The winds blow so cold and the days are so long.
But I still linger on in the hope she'll return,
To the lad that she loved by the Bal-an-or burn.
Oh where is the fair one who captured my heart?
Oh where is the fair one I loved from the start?
Has she gone from this earth shall I see her no more?
Will she never come back to my own Bal-an-or?

Neil Blake,
Kilmarnock, Ayrshire.

WHAT IS LIFE

What is life?
Is it just a routine?
Is our life just there for the sake of living?
Or has it got a purpose?
An unknown purpose?
Or does someone know the purpose?
We live our lives without thinking,
Without giving a single thought as to why we are here.
There must be a reason,
A reason that someone, somewhere, knows of,
But does not share that reason,
Until it is too late.
People die, wondering what their lives were for,
So what is life?
Does anyone know?

Miss Ailsa Blight,
Kendal, Cumbria.

AGONY

This child is mine, a cry from the heart,
It's so unfair that we should part.
I brought him up as best I could,
I dressed him well, I gave him food.
Many's the night I paced the floor,
Then laid him down and closed the door,
I gave him all I had to give,
But what I couldn't give was birth.

Mrs. Mary Bogan,
Barlanark, Glasgow.

THE LANE THAT LEADS TO HOME

The beauty of the lane remains,
Although the trees are bare.
November mists and driving rains,
Obscure each garden that I pass.

But well I know with Spring's first kiss,
Daffodils will raise their heads
Around mauve crocus beds.
While wallflowers and drifting lilacs,
Will scent the home-ward air.

The grass seems greener by the path,
As I reach the door.
Which in my youth
I gaily entered,
And to where our children
Hurried home at four.

I've been away too long,
No more I want to roam,
The magic spell of Love rests here
Autumn has come,
And I've returned
to HOME.

Phyllis Bonser,
Alvaston, Derbyshire.

A LITTLE SHELL . . .

A little shell
Of humanity
Emerges –
Warm,
Heart beating,
Soft, –
For a moment.
Then, the tiny, frail thing
Dies.

Why did it enter this world
For everyone to see,
Only to disappear again
Into infinity?

Yolande Bourcier,
Beaconsfield, Bucks.

HEAVEN OR

The swallows have gone to bed,
The world grows cold and dead,
The moon comes creeping out of a silver sheath,
She sees nothing 'cept the darkened hours of grief.
People crying, someone dying,
Someone's lost a love.
Young and old and all alike
Weep silent in the sleepless night.
While others writhe in pain,
Lovers have gone ne'r to return again.
And people pray to God above
To send to them the dark envelopment of sleep.
The very young sleep peacefully,
They know not the turmoil of an older day.
Someone's dying, babies crying,
One is born to face the morn,
The other has release
From all the problems of this life
To a happy Paradise.
While some live on through Hell.

Mrs. Eileen Brand,
Thornton, Fife.

DYING

Boats moored in harbours,
Sail through my mind,
Planes in their hangars,
Fly past my eyes,
Cars locked up for the night,
Drive round my brain.

Trains with no drivers,
Make tracks in the sky,
Angels stand still,
But continue to fly,
Why?

The world moves on,
All around me,
While I,
Stand still.

Mr. Gerald Richard Branigan,
Crieff, Perthshire.

DAFFODILS

The daffodils, so straight and tall,
With colour yellow meets us all,
The centre with a deeper view,
Shines to greet us with a hue.

The gardens are, so full of glee,
To have such golden daffodils dancing on the spree.

The passing breeze just nods their heads,
So pleased to see them in firm beds,
The colours of a deeper shade,
And then a lighter too is made.

With trumpets large, and some are small,
Yet God has made them one, and all.

The pleasure that the Spring has brought,
Our eyes to see, bird, flower, and tree,
Renewing their life from mought.

Miss Edith Mary Bray,
Shrewsbury, Shropshire.

ATLANTIS – THE UNKNOWN

Down, down you sank in swirling, boiling seas,
Lost to creation, buried by the waves.
What caused your mighty land to crack,
Whose hand threw down the bolts of doom.
Who brought the storms that tore down cities proud,
Who raised the sea to flood your island fair?

Were you the cradle of the world,
Land of the Sun, ruled over by ten kings?
Were you the dawn of paradise,
Your wealth and knowledge lost to all?
Did men sail outward from your shores
To settle in some other lands afar?
Was knowledge left behind for us to seek
That we, so blind, can never comprehend?

Sleeping on the bed of ocean deep
Did you, Atlantis, ever see the sun?
Or are you myth, a dream of long ago,
That man once spoke of, ere his day was done?

Jennie Brown,
Axminster, Devon.

HIBERNATION

Two Herons fly
Horizontal motion
Natural, unhurried
Coasting across grass,
Fields and marshland,
Thick with the bullrush.

One train, following a set path
Hot and slow
Jarring and uneven
Two paths of horizontal motion
Crossing,
Away from the sea
The window glass, stained with sweat
And mist, slowly trickles downwards,
In vertical motion.
The Herons flap to a halt,
Out of view.

How many flights enacted?
How many train journeys are made?
How many times will the Heron,
Fly in horizontal motion?
And for how much longer,
Will the train,
Run from,
The Sea?

Malcolm J. Brown,
London.

THE LIGHTNING BOAST

I am a streak of lightning,
Flashing 'cross the sky
I strike at all the cables,
Cutting off supplies.

And in the night, I just might,
Hit a plane or two
A house, a car, a bridge,
A ship and all its crew.

It's such fun to see dogs run,
In terror and in fear
And folks in fright, a ghastly sight,
Afraid that I'll come near.

I lunge and plunge, I aim and maim,
Forever spoiling the sportsman's game
The golfer on the tee,
The runner, the footballer and the referee.

It is no boast that I'm the most,
When all is said and done
Fircest, bravest of them all,
(Well!) except MAYBE the sun.

Robert Brown,
Alexandria, Dunbartonshire.

AT THE CALF SALES
(*Oban 1972*)

Noblesse Oblige . . .
An infringement of his rights
in the small damp sawdust ring
as the young black bull bellows
from his thunderous, humerous cringe!
The hard, hot-hammer beat of the Auctioneer,
monotonous rasp of a thin timbred voice
in expectant and wasplike: "One hundred guineas Gentlemen?"
"Na'e – do I na'e hear more?" drumming
"Can Y' na'e think o' Spring upon Spring
and the new calves?" The young Hereford bull roared,
I kept quite still
it was merriment to dare, the thrill
to own, here . . .
Bidding began again: "One hundred – One hundred and four . . ."
I sat hard on a high tiered sawdusted bench
between a squelch of dung
and moved with the strong rhythmical equations, stench
sting of the Emporium . . .

A classic this
if one ignored beefburgers at my elbows,
multi-flavoured chips, odd cans of beer,
worn linaments with the tweeds of money,
mellowed happy-fat snores from quiet farmers with sunny
smiles, shrewd in having bought and sold, now bored!
A fair drift of manure with a spiral of smoke rings
a cow's soft lament from a distant dog's barking;
the hot, cursed remorse of a loser; and a solid content
in the intense tight circle of bidders railing the ring,
heads a' scratching, elbows bent to the double sting
of finger-poised waiting –
a raised cigarette – such secretive baiting

St. Bruno Flake? or was it the Condor Moment . . .
Scents of hill farm, good malt whisky and honey,
good money following hard on good money!
I had lost the quick count
a' spell in breath taking . . .
a-catching of crooks mellowed and horny
with the bull long since caught
sold at One-fifty – or was it Sixty?
Mallet with farmer's sticks brisk
then a golden prance into the ring
of a small Highland calf, a pedigree, I sat a'dreaming . . .
If I had one acre, one croft and a burn,
if I once rode a horse could I not milk a cow?

Noblesse Oblige . . .
Too old in the tooth?
I must have nodded my tartan tammy-topped head
for sheep in their hundreds pastured
when a resonant voice said:

"MADAM, do I then take your bid?" . . .

Twixt the thud of the bidding and the mead I was tethered
in heather-filled meadows, furze, mid low-Highlands green
from breeds of cattle and exile long tarried I plead:

GENTLEMEN, forgive me please
If when in haze of mist, rich Autumnal sun
I, with white-faced Romney Marsh sheep
was totally lost in this whimsical Highland
Oblivion . . .

Auctioneer, forgive me please,
Discount my bid
This infringement of calf rights
for in three storey high tenement I live! . . .

Stella Browning,
Elstree, Herts.

AN UNTITLED POEM BY DIANE BRUCE

Solitary moon, high,
Immaculate in your bountiful lonely plane
Far above the storms of life,
I cannot stretch to touch,
I only linger on the irridescent beauty,
Glowing, arbitary, colour of truth.

This evil world, no home
I – morose, sceptical, cynical.
You may laugh upon me moon,
Perhaps one lunar tear will fall.
Solve the hurt without the pity
But now you drift away and hide.

All my expectancy, falsehoods
Days are swept away with patience,
The dynasty will be my grave
But I will orienteer through renaissance
And survive above the others
To love and live with my blue moon.

Diane L. Bruce,
Darlington, Co. Durham.

A REVERIE

A Fairy danced into my room and lighted on my chair,
"You look so sad," she said, "Come on I'll take you anywhere."
"Let's go to Fairyland," I said, – no sooner said than done,
We flew through clouds of cotton wool, and on, and on, and on.
At last we reached the golden gates, the loveliest ever seen,
We went inside and, on her throne, we saw the Fairy Queen.
Her hair was silky, fair and long, her eyes a glorious blue,
Her dress was made of spiders' webs, her wings of gossamer too.
She waved her wand and I was dressed in shimmering clothes of white,
We danced around the fairy pool until the dead of night.
How sad I was when it was time to say a last goodbye,
And fly again back to my room, where, with a heavy sigh,
I hoped that one fine day another fairy passing by,
Would call me and transport me to that playground in the sky.

Barbara Brunton,
Arbroath, Angus.

FIRELIGHT

The golden firelight in this room
Reflects the gleam of daffodils
On polished wood. Tall shadows loom
Like guardian angels round the sills.
The glittering tiara of night
Enchants the unveiled window pane
And mingles with the splendid light
That blazens from the hearth again.

A whispering the silence breaks,
I know not if it is the wind
Or some sweet sound a winged thought makes
On secret journey from the mind.
Where gently drifting fireforms are
Rare gems of memory brightly shine,
God's smile resplendent in each star
His blessing on this room of mine.

Mrs. Ada L. Bull,
Long Eaton, Nottingham.

LIFE

Life should be a joy,
Like a pearl, beautiful, glowing,
Perfectly formed,
Which you want to bring out each day.
Enjoy and let others feel the beauty,
Use it to its full.
It may fade and turn yellow
If put away too carefully
For a rainy day.
Life is for living
Not just for getting through each weary day.
But for grasping, reaching, feeling
For the beauty and fulfilment
You can find along its way.

Life is a puzzle, a maze,
A trick of birth.
Can we cope while still on earth?
It's hard sometimes to persevere
With troubles and moans and other's fears.
If we take some time each day,
To hold that pearl,
And think and ponder
How precious, how rare.
It is ours for the taking,
Holding and keeping
Not to be lightly wasted away.

Annette Burgess,
Aylesbury, Buckinghamshire.

SCOTTISH THROUGH AND THROUGH

Do kilts in many colours swinging in the breeze,
Remind you of a Scottish burn, shadowed by the trees.
Do bagpipes when they're playing, make your heart leap as they play,
And remind you of your Scotland on a warm and sultry day.
When you walked beside the pipers, just a child, yet full of pride,
Never thinking you'd depart from there and travel far and wide.
If the sight of many tartans makes you want to dance and sing,
And the sound of bagpipes playing, makes your heart leap and take
    wing.
You can never leave Auld Scotland, for in travel it's with you,
Though miles and years you'r parted, your still Scottish through and
    through.

75

And though you say your happy, in this land so far away,
Is there not a secret longing to come back to here one day?
Does the sound of someone singing a Scottish song you know,
Make a lump come in your throat, and you long then just to go?
To leave this land you live in and return to Scotland's shore,
To be back with all your ain folk, and never part no more.
If the sight of many tartans makes you want to dance and sing,
And the sound of bagpipes playing makes your heart leap and take
wing.
You can never leave Auld Scotland, for in travel it's with you,
Though miles and years you'r parted, your still Scottish through and
through.

Mrs. Dorothy Fergusson Burns,
Alloa, Clackmannanshire.

SIGHT

The most wonderful sense of all is sight,
Just think if we could'nt see, darkness or
Light.
Could'nt see sunshine or rain, gladness or
pain, or a little bird fly –
Soaring up in the sky, or a puppy at play with
eyes full of love that just seem to say – come
on let's have fun or a walk in the sun,
If we could'nt see flowers or plants or trees
Or washing out hanging to dry in the breeze.
If we could'nt see animals great or small or
leaves turning red and gold, during the fall,
Or the rainbow in sun after rain or the face
of a loved one at peace after pain, or an
animal pleading with eyes full of trust, or a
little child sleeping, the sleep of the just.
Just think if we could'nt see faces we love,
Our family, our friends and the blue sky above,
A butterfly's wing or a clear waterfall.
All these are the reasons I think most of all
The most wonderful God-given sense is sight
and I pray that some day when my work here is
done, my eyes may be used to benefit one, who
is blind, and may see, all the things that
pleased me.

Mrs. Patricia Burns,
Dalry, Ayrshire.

THE NORMAN PARISH CHURCH OF MIDDLETON

From your lofted pinace you gaze upon the town, the hands of time
   have done their rounds
And o'er the years your tranquil face, has gently toll'd the parish
   bounds,
Ten times one hundred years your call brought worshippers to prayer
And curfews rung from barrowed heights instilled a peace and comfort
   there.
What sights and times your sundial sensed, and dramas you have seen,
Did man enact the years as you maturing scene by scene.
The curtain rose fore Williams day, stout trees used for your shell
Then Norman stone and Tudor stone and adorned glass to tell . . .
The story of your own sons deeds on Flodden field the brave
The very same you nurtured from peasent crib to grave.

What tears you shed when rustic charm gave way to cotton mill
Your woods and parkland were all raped excretia fouled wince rill
You saw rush-bearers from the farms, Molly dancers and their ilk,
The manufactories man built when cotton replaced silk.
You heard sung cant of voice in prayer you heard celt accent too
You saw the lambs of God to slaughter go on that field at Peterloo.
What nuptuals have been rung, what joy each Easter morn,
The rejoicing at the harvests, goodwill when Christs reborn.

A monument to all that man aspires to be
You bear the passage of the years with mild serenity
The saving cross you flaunt embracing all who came
To St. Cuthbert or St. Leonard, hallowed be thy name.
So may the curtain of lifes play, when all the acts are through
Proclaim the dignity of man whose skills portray in you.

Mr. John Burton,
Middleton, Manchester.

RETROSPECT

Why do I think of what could have been?
Endlessly think of what could have been?
Can I not plan and dream for something else?
I try – but just one moment –
One split second, and a face appears:
A place flits through my memory –
And I am torn with hidden tears.

And all my trying is in vain –
I am back to thinking of what could have been . . .
Again.

Why does the green leaf
Grace the tree
After summer's gone?
Why is there still belief in me
After Love's passed on?

Audrey Caie,
Glasgow.

LIFE

I see us all owning *3* state of minds
A morning one an afternoon one and plus
An (evening one as well). Can I just
remind to the morning mind state. You
travel on a bus or a train the human face
stares into (space.) Some even hiding
at the back of a newspaper. Come afternoon
a kind of some revival in relations, but the
evening state of mind sees the human being
at their grandest. The cheerio, the laughs
exchanging events of the hour.
I'm trying to illustrate what some
do find in reality, now that's life.

As presented by individuals.
And contrary to what some folk
suggest in (life) none of us
can be in the same frame of mind consistently.
We get the claim that Mr. X is always (one way).
I look at it, like this,
In a changing world it's almost impossible, this approach.

Mr. J. Callaghan,
Glasgow.

THE GRIEVING ON ME

The step from my source to the sea,
Leaves little room for boasting
But, mine is the spectral way,
The wake of a ghostly hosting.

And mine is the hidden way,
Secret my vigil unseen,
Remembering former joys,
Reliving ploys that have been.

I have seen the gallowglasses,
The massing of the kerns,
The wraiths of famined men revealed,
Congealed in slender ferns.

Heard war wolf's wailing, lifting,
Bullets drifting, sifting sedges,
The heart-stopped hush of ambuscade,
In brooding shade of hedges.

How they strode through the stirring years,
Hiding fears in the brave smiles of youth,
Who stumble now, discouraged now,
Who foretaste doom, in death of truth.

Thomas P. Callaghan,
Coatbridge, Lanarkshire.

LAMENT OF A SENSITIVE EAR

The sound of civilisation plays an overwhelming part
In the onset of those blacknesses that swallow up my heart,
Unheedingly it penetrates each molecule of air
First maddening, then numbing every sensitive thing there,
Shattering the delicate fibres of my mind, the
Clatters, bangs and jangles, the incessant grates and grinds
Of everyday suburban life stride onward undeterred,
While I all nerves and curses, must seek some retreat, unheard.

The thick skin of the noisemonger is quite impervious
To sounds of subtle nature, that are fair melodious,
Fine music, for example, or the soft and tender words
Of a sympathetic friend, or the lilting of the birds,
But even these I see are not safe from man's pure greed,
So they're caught and put in boxes, with scarcely holes to breathe,
And then the volume turned full up, so that the end result
Is more caos, and to the originals, insult.

Each brash tumultous stream of still increasing resonance
Goes surging across countryside on its satanic dance,
Till with one blow every living thing is under flood,
A sea of clamour, where before a golden silence stood.

Ruth E. Callan,
Hull, North Humberside.

79

TOWN SPARROW

Cheeky fellow in waistcoat brown,
Lives quite happily in Town.
Treetop home or old drain spout
He finds lots to talk about.
Everyday when I throw bread
He makes sure that he gets fed.
Blackbirds come and starlings too
But Mr. Sparrow pushes through.
While they are scrapping with each other
He gets his piece and then another.
When I come back from shops in Town
Mr. Sparrow in coat of brown,
Flies close to me to see "Who this is"
Then he's away to tell his missus
That the "Big creature without wings"
Who feeds them lots of lovely things,
Is home again "Hurrah she's here
Make haste and fetch the kids my dear."

Winifred Cambridge,
Aspley, Nottingham.

BENNY LYNCH

A waif was born in Glasgow town
In a slum of a Gorbals street,
'Gainst poverty and slumland
He fought to find his feet.

It was in the Great Depression
Folk fraught with hunger's pinch,
Few came through – as well we
knew,
Yet, one did – Benny Lynch.

Benny Lynch – your life was hard
You battled on to fame,
The boxing world was yours awhile
Until,
John Barleycorn came.

The demon drink demolished you
When no opponent could,
T'was sad to see such a
talent go,
And no one understood.

Angus John Cameron,
Glasgow.

LISTED BUILDING

Old house crowned by attics, mined by cellars
fathoms deep. Seaward windows, where men kept vigil for
invading fleets, now blind and bricked against the more
tenacious menace of the storm. Crumbled steadings,
cobbled yards, grass grown asleep.

Rogue gardens sealed by thorn form giant pomanders
of briar, pierced flowers and tangled weeds; Paradise
for butterflies and birds. Meeting place in twilight
hours for ghosts who seek an echo of the peace they found
there once. And on the skyline, reactor chimneys from
atomic power, spell sombre warning that human nature changes
little, though civilisations cease.

Marion Cameron,
Heads Nook,
Near Carlisle.

DUNFRAOCH HOUSE

Up upon a hillock, as quiet as a mouse,
Overlooking the Loch, is Dunfraoch House,
There's a haven for birds at the back,
And a copse all around,
And a field in front of that,
And a stream with a beautiful sound.

To the left there's Loch Etive,
And Ben Cruachan so tall,
And a forest beside the former,
But that is not all.

The field has Highland cows grazing,
And the stream a few oak trees,
And the flowering rush is never free,
Of a swarm of happy bees.

So it was in that house,
I spent many happy days,
Wanting to thank the owner,
And her many happy ways.

For t'was in that tiny copse,
That I sung many a song,
About my love for Scotland,
And Dunfraoch House I'll love for so long.

So when I left Taynuilt,
Tears came to my eyes,
For I was leaving Dunfraoch House,
After many sad goodbyes.

Never shall I forget,
The beauty of Taynuilt,
And the hospitality of,
The owner of Dunfraoch House.

Miss Lindsay Anne Campbell,
Cottingham, East Yorkshire.

THE TRAVELS OF A HOUSE-BOUND POET

The gently rising hills are speeding by,
Stately pines in streamed glen hide the sky.
Passengers nod sleepily, unaware
Nature's film, oft changes scenes out there,
A mist-bound loch, stance of curious sheep,
All passes by, while they, unheeding, sleep.
A river foaming white flecked to the sea,
Follows the train that holds the ghost of me.

Now let me leave the scene of highland glens.
By the gentle Avon my spirit wends.
A stately swan swims slowly to the shore
Where Stratford Town lies steeped in days of yore.
Yet there reclines amidst this splendid scene,
Gauche, in a deck chair, a sleeper, serene.
Swiftly, let me, from this gross sight, away
To gaze upon the ancient town I stray.

Enough now, faster than sound I arrive
In Edinburgh's fair City, may her beauty survive.
All visiting her, have been heard to declare
One may not sleep midst this historic fare.
A miraculous rise to Arthur's Seat
From a leisurely stroll in Princes Street,
The fine vista here the eye beguiles.
I hear an organ swell, I'm in St. Giles!

I thrill, as those great chords echo again,
Oh! that those diapasions may never wane.
Alas, a clock's sweet chime returns me home,
So now with television must I roam,
And if perchance my eyelids must compete
With no historic splendour, just a repeat?
No faux pas, then, to merely close my eyes,
To rest after travel, is being wise

J. Irene Cantle,
Sunderland, Tyne and Wear.

FIRE

Little hands came,
They reached up high,
For their owner's game,
Little did they know their owner would cry.

"Tommy, Tommy a match, a match,
It will be fun,
Come on, try and catch,
But I have won."

"Get another, get another,
It will be such fun,"
Said her brother,
"But I have won."

But as she took another,
It touched the box,
"Nice spark," said her brother,
But it caught her socks.

I'm sorry to have to tell you their fate,
But on that sad day,
Their mother was late,
So remember this moral –
Please, I pray –
NEVER PLAY WITH MATCHES!

Miss Miriam Carmel (Aged 10),
Wembley, Middlesex.

THE WOODCUTTER

High bird fine messenger from Him
Do you cry over serried logs?
If so take heed
For below the woodcutter nears the final tree.

But there is no need to worry
Experienced eyes will be attentive
And the woodcutter will be slain before
He strikes his final blow
And the high bird will come to rest
To peck the virulence from his heart.

From the final tree a forest will grow up
Covering over every stump
No symbol of him will be left
And his soul will fade.

Presently though progress will scratch
At the spot where he lay
To start man's line anew
His fingers will search and search
But from above the high bird
Will give an icy look and warning cry.

His reign is through and he is dead
The earth will soak up no more tears
Let nature raise her head once more
Man's feet on earth will no more tread.

Peter Carr,
Newbiggin-By-The-Sea,
Northumberland.

GUESS WHO?

The Clydebank Police are a great bunch of people
From Chief Superintendant to youngest Constable
There's a certain Sergeant who shall be nameless
Who always blames me, though I am blameless.

Like Bruce Forsyth he's the man in charge
But unlike Bruce he's a little but large
He helps collect money to take us all out
For lunches and teas and a big glass of stout.

It's Sergeant Wa . . . oops who marshalls the troops
Shouting "Wheelchairs in front we're off to the Co-op"
Zimmers come next at a very fast pace
Tripods and sticks last but that's no disgrace.

We spent all our money, it was gone in a flash
When off to the Yoker Club for high tea and a glass,
While the Sergeant looks on with a smile on his face
Thinking "I'll have you Carson you're a drunken disgrace."

I have friends in College, Miss Roberts for one,
I think she knows I do this for fun,
If you've guessed who it is tell the public at large
I'd better shut up or I'll be on a charge.

We thank St. Stephens helpers, a great little crew
Like Mary, Beth and Helen to name but a few,
Without them we ladies wouldn't know what to do
Till we nod and we wink and we say To . . . ra Loo?

Elizabeth Carson,
Faifley, Clydebank.

CAMBODIA

Spare pity for the helpless mite,
With upturned bowl in tragic plight,
Emaciated beyond compare
The large brown eyes can only stare.
His little world, in moments, shattered,
The threadbare clothes all thin and tattered,
Not for him the eager chatter,
Tomorrow, somehow, does not matter.

Into our keeping is given this blessing,
A child's happy laughter, little guessing
That smiles and banter can come too late,
In a war ridden world so filled with hate.
To hazard a guess is futile
As to what the future may bring,
At the moment, his passions lie dormant,
Yet, the wasp has a venemous sting.

Constance M. Cattell
Leeds, England.

SEASIDE MEMORIES

I love to walk along the beach,
To feel the sand, beneath my feet.
And watch the waves, recede with the tide,
While children, enjoy a donkey ride.
Father in deck chair, oblivious in sleep,
But mother her watchful eye doth keep.

Out on the horizon, the ships come and go,
While in the fair ground, people swing to and fro.
Traders all busy, selling their wares,
Nobody seems to have any cares.
I look o'er the ocean, so big and so wide,
And think of the people on the other side.
Are they so happy, are they so free,
To walk on the beach and sit by the sea.

Mrs. Elizabeth Chalmers,
West Boldon, Tyne and Wear.

STRONSAY

A ship on an endless journey,
Forging lanes through the eastern swell,
Her head dips deep but never founders
The crew are always safe and well.

This old stout craft mellows with age,
New cargoes richer than those before;
The crew rest sure they'll never hunger
Like some wretches in days of yore.

Through winter's gales she shrugs the blast
That lashes hull and decks with fury
From the eastern or the western breaker,
No chance for her to run to lee.

Her sodden decks all scarred and bare
From Thor and Neptune's wily pranks;
Transformation comes when early spring
Brings warmth and freshness to her planks.

Through summer months she sails serene,
No clawing breakers to stem each day
Which threaten to drain away life's blood
Like the wolves at throats of their prey.

In seas of liquid jewels she turns
Heading still east into dawning days;
Surging on beneath cumulus sails
Heaving sunset wakes of golden days.

Through thirty bounteous years and four
I've known ships cargoes and the seas;
Some day in distant mists obscured
I may return to sail with thee.

John R. Chalmers
Aberdeen.

THE SCOTTISH HIGHLANDS

My heart is in the highlands and there 'twill ever lie
yearning for their beauty as all the years roll by
haunting memories taunt me as now I'm faint and weak
that I'll no longer see those scenes my heart shall ever seek.

Strangely brooding mountains frowning at us through the mist
lone lochs whispering softly, stand fast, waiting to be kissed
by warming sunlight dancing over waters clear as glass
reflecting beauty in their depths, as we gaze down from highland pass.

Lofty trees in splendour mass around the lakeside shores
fairy glens and shady woods surround each scene our heart adores
we see again within our minds each vibrant, wondrous view
muted all the glorious colours, shades of every hue
climbing o'er the banks and braes and over all the hills
can there be more loveliness and shall there be more thrills.

Each season of the year brings its wonder to our heart
snow and ice in purity its glory doth impart
spring and summer's golden warmth spread the pine-woods scent
could I but see that perfect place – would that the years relent.

That heavenly light of Isle of Skye a'shimmer over all
yon Cuillins grandly gazing down, protecting as they call
return and listen to the legends of that lovely, fairy isle
Bonnie Charlie fled from here and history lies in every mile.

Glory of the highlands, our heart-beat quicks its pace
home of all perfection – we spy the mighty eagle in his race
around the shores of Torridon, king deer will stand and stare
remind us of his elegance, in case we're unaware.

The highlands, proud, majestic are, as they have ever been
can heaven be more beautiful, rewarding us with regal scene
my heart aches for the highlands, I count myself more blessed
for I have seen your beauty, I have tasted your eternal rest.

Doris Chambers,
Newcastle upon Tyne.

THE QUEEN

A regal woman in every way,
blessed with a lot of common sense.
Proud, yet humble, a little severe
taught to wave her hand when others do cheer.
Examples she sets to the island she loves –
born of a Scottish mother – now sits on the Throne.
Troubled times, industrial unrest,
Family times are the times she loves best.
Palaces, castles, lots of intrigue,
men around her, her word they should heed.
Parliaments, politicians, nobles and lords
let them offer the Queen their swords.
Serve her well, for she does her job.
Many envy her, one can tell –
but Elizabeth, Queen of our shores
you have many who will pull the oars.
Rule the country like a ship,
often on it you will find the sick,
but never weakening regal Queen, times will come hard,
Britons will roam
far away from their island home.
But Elizabeth they will never forget you
or how you ruled the nation, just and true –
if only you had a bigger say
then Parliaments could go away.

Fred Spencer Chesworth,
Preston, Lancashire.

LAMENT NOT

Nostalgic thoughts come crowding in
Of laughter, love and rowdy din
Amongst the alleys, down the backs
Where children played their game of jacks
It never rained, the sun was there
Warm, secure they used to care
Romantic dreams replace the facts
With homesick thoughts, escapist tracts
Emerge, as melodies recapture days
Now treasured in a distant haze

Even queueing for the dole
brings stirrings deep within the soul
Recalling comradeship in strife
And how we made the best of life
Alas, memories distort fair inquisitions
And leave behind rose tinted visions
Of skies so often overcast by sorrows
Which at times amassed
To form a whirlpool of despair
T'was then you wondered, did they care
So treasure thoughts of yesterday
But build on them a new today
Nostalgia is a changing scene
And should not spoil tomorrows dream.

Judith Helen Childs,
Milton, Ontario, Canada.

EMPTINESS OR LONLINESS? EACH IS DESPAIR

Emptiness or lonliness, each is despair,
Your feelings are numb, and yet you don't care,
You can go to a nightclub, and watch folk dancing around,
You know that there's music, but; your deaf to its sound,
Your trying to be cheerful, but you try in despair,
Is it? emptiness or lonliness, you really don't care.

When you get up for work, you know you'd rather be at home,
Your feeling all unsettled, and so terribly alone,
And you are miserably depressed, never wanting to eat,
So you retire to your bed, knowing fine well you won't sleep,
Everything around you looks so dull, and painfully bare,
It could; be emptiness or lonliness, but what do you care.

Friends try to help, but you just turn your back,
You've got to face facts, and it's that! courage you lack,
You know this pain will take time, and when the time comes along,
You will begin to feel happiness, and want to forget what went wrong,
Was it! emptiness? or lonliness? or! was it, despair?
Now that your getting over it, you don't even care.

Mrs. J. Chilton,
Hexham, Northumberland.

THE ARTIST

God gaed tae ye that magic touch
Tae express yersel wi' paint an' brush,
Pit upon canvas an' board
The inward thochts that ye hae stored,
Like partin' o' a simmer's day
Or winter's clouds sae dark an' grey,
Whatere may be yer pensive mood
Transfer it on tae cloth an' wood.

That temperamental artist's notions
Can visualise the scenes an' motions,
Create in oils or be it crayons
Sam crazy wannerin's o' the brain,
Across the mind flit like a bird
Creatin' samthing maist absurd,
Or samthing that haes nae relation
Tae ony stretch o' 'magination.

Noo dinna ye let go that gift
God gaed tae ye, yersel tae lift,
Abeen a' ordinar aucht-day things
Tae realms whaur untauld beauty clings,
Sae ye on canvas can impart
Communicate wi' creative art,
An' express yer ain free will
Wi' pride in magic artistic skill.

An' may the warld at future date
Enjoy samthing yer han's create,
Artistically beyon' compare
That radiates beauty iverwhere,
In a corner writ apon
Artist's name is seen, anon.

John Clark,
Peterculter, Aberdeen.

BLESSINGS

Sometimes when feeling sad and low,
We grumble and complain.
We feel the whole worlds on our back,
We've every ache and pain.
We haven't time to stop and look,
At crippled, deaf, or blind.
We just go on complaining,
Till some other grouse we find.
So let us count our blessings,
Say a prayer for each new day.
And thank the Lord he made us,
Complete in every way.

Shirley Clayton,
Ossett, West Yorkshire.

A MEMORY

T'was in a dream he came to me
So handsome and so tall,
His black hair like a raven's wing,
To him I gave my all.

I gave my life to share with him
A life of love and bliss,
He promised to be true to me,
And sealed it with a kiss.

All this was very long ago
In sunnier, happier years,
When we were young, and hopes were high,
There was no time for tears.

Now I can only think of him
As many times I sigh,
For the years we spent together,
He was too young to die.

Edna H. L. W. Coates,
Edinburgh.

A LIBRARY LAMENT
(On Cataloguing a Friend's Library)

I've been "Inside Africa" and "Through Kashmir"
Challenged Everest, and strolled up "Brighton Pier".
I've read all the Histories,
Investigated mysteries,
Read all the Catholic Poets,
And a boat and how to row it.
I've read all about babies,
And how you can't cure rabies.
Puzzled over Jung,
And the workings of the lung,
Boggled over Freud,
And "The life of Lady Boyd".
I wish by the scribes I was better employed.

I know all about wine and how to ferment,
I could even recite an old Scottish lament.
I know how to sew or put up a tent,
And I've learnt from the Bible our troubles are sent.
I know all about Psycho-schizo-neurosis
And how to make pretty flowery posies
I even know why we get colds in our noses!

I've learnt how to sit in the lotus position,
And how to define correct composition.
I know all about Rome, and investment, and cats,
And how to prevent bed-wetting in brats.
I even had a look at a "Book of World Drama",
And saw a picture of the Kaiser's West Indian Amah.

There ain't a thing in the world I ain't learnt:
And my learned opinion's all books should be burnt.
The cause of our troubles is the spoken word,
When they're put in books, they're well interred.
R.I.P.

Janet Morag Clendenin,
Giffnock, Renfrewshire.

ANOTHER DAY

Another day has just begun,
Another day of life.
Another day of age and fear,
Please God end all this strife.

Another day of fear, for some,
Another day of sorrow.
Another day, another death,
A thought of yet tomorrow.

Another child gone off to school,
Another thought of love.
Another fear of coming home,
That child of God above.

Another longing for some peace,
Another wish and prayer.
Another Ireland will there be?
With hearts to love and care.

Mrs. Margaret Coleman,
Kirkoswald, Ayrshire.

TUNE FOR OUR TIMES

I never thought that after,
Fourteen years of married bliss,
It would come to this,
You even send me photos of your lover,
I can't decide,
Is it really her, or her mother?
We were so close,
Now we're apart,
I cannot tell where to start,
No more quarrels, no more fights,
No work-weary days and happy nights,
We won't grow old together now, my dear,
Solicitors and Legal Aid,
Are now my lot,
Perhaps I should make a plan,
To find myself another man,
Or better still, perhaps a lover,
Ah, but still, I can't be chewed
I find the mere suggestion, rude.

Mrs. Anne Elizabeth Colledge,
Washington, Tyne and Wear.

94

FOR EVER AND EVER

This is an age of progress – with dynamic force and speed,
One wonders where we're getting to, and where it all will lead.
There's space-craft, planes and missiles, flying thro' the air;
Computors, Electronics . . . one wonders if we dare . . .
Look forward to the future, in this scientific age,
For t'would be a very sorry sight – if another war we wage.

There's multi-storey car-parks, speedway tracks and football grounds:
Sky-scrapers and monorails and then the undergrounds.
Of course there are the motorways, filled with "racing cars" . . .
Restaurants and cafes, bingo-halls and coffee bars.
This world of ours goes chasing on, and time just seems to fly,
And often it is easy – to forget that God is nigh.

And yet, through all the changing scenes, God – with His Guiding
    Hand,
Faileth not; His love is sure; firm as a rock it stands.
O wondrous, O yes wondrous Love, on the cross at Calvary . . .
Tis just the same today as then, God's love for you and me.
Forgive us Lord, when we forget – Thy greatness and Thy Power . . .
And keep us in Thy loving care, each day and every hour.

Jean Collins,
Leicester.

THE KISS

Clearly, I remember
The first kiss;
Virgin lips
On virgin lips,
Cold nose
Touching my cheek;
Startled, broke away,
Couldn't find a thing to say.
Clearly, I remember
The first kiss
But cannot remember
The Miss.

Mr. Joseph Connerton,
Beverley, North Humberside.

TO A RAM THAT BROKE OUT OF HIS PASTURE

Ye ranting rousting, heady tup,
To leave the farm that brought ye up,
And break through fences like a thief!
Ye should have known 'twould bring us grief.

Ye should have known ye hasty brute,
Society 'twould never suit
If every man left house and home
And anxious wives, to godless roam.

And then, to cap your breaking frolic
With rowdy fighting, like chol'ric
And half-drunken man!
Ye might have been no pure-bred ram!

Ye woolly bastard, thus to slay
Auld Henry's tup, and me to pay!
I marvel that ye'll watch my face!
Go on with you, you're in disgrace!

Mrs. Margaret Alice Conium,
Hereford.

MIGRAINE

Temporary blurring of my sight,
Before my eyes, flashes of light.
Pain, on the right side of my head;
Which sends me cringing, to my bed.
Vomiting, again, and again.
Long time before the monster's slain.
With its fury appeased, at last,
Long hours of dreamless sleep are passed.
For the beauty, which, round me lies,
Oh God! How precious, are my eyes.

A. I. Constantine
Long Preston,
North Yorkshire.

LOVE AND MARRIAGE

Love's like a fire that is burning when romance is fresh and new
And the heat from the fire is a comfort, so long as you tend the flue.
But a fire that's ignored will grow dimmer, without fuel a fire will die
    fast,
The embers will turn to ashes and love will fade into the past.

If only you notice the symptoms and see that the fire's burning low
Then add a good armful of fuel and soon it will flourish and glow.
The fire in our grate was fast fading, in fact it was almost dead
But we caught it in time, added fuel, and soon it was glowing red.

We brought everything out in the open, t'was important for us to
    reveal
The thoughts that were just like a canker, one must know how the
    other may feel,
We decided our love for each other strong enough to begin once again
So we packed up the life we'd been living and gave love a chance to
    remain.

Now listen you lads and lassies who contemplate wedded bliss
Go ahead with your plans despite this, you never know what you might
    miss.
Marriage is always a gamble, many win, though some end in tears,
And though at this stage mine was shaky it has lasted for thirty years.

Helen M. Corbett,
Portstewart, N. Ireland.

SCRAPS OF CONVERSATION HEARD
(*from an anguished four and a half year old*)

The little girl, came running in full of joy;
She stood on her hands,
Her thick long brown hair, carpeting the floor.
She had been staying with friends
And knew that daddy would be looking for her,
"Where is daddy?" she inquired
"I want to kiss him better"
His presence was dearly required.
"Come darling" said mummy, taking her thro' the door
I must tell you of daddy
"His love and devotion we shared together, he was our life my love"
"Now he has gone, we must love each other"
"He has been taken from this life; he loved with care
To another place – someday we'll see him there"
The cry came: "a deep agonised cry", of grievous grief and loss
A cry too "searing of soul" for such a tiny tot.
The little girl came in, with quiet tread
Saying to her friend "don't make a noise! my daddy is dead"
They won't let me in the bedroom; the handle is off the door
But I could climb thro' the window – 'tis not far from the floor
"I'll see my daddy" I'll kiss him better
He would'nt want to leave me till I get bigger.
I'll climb thro' the window, kiss his eyes, his ears, his nose
I'll comb his hair and tickle his toes
How! he will laugh! and say "Hell doll; your sweet self has made me
    well"
But they have closed the window and put on the catch
He is all alone – all shut up and lost
How! can he be happy? how can be laugh?
Without his little sunshine, without his little lass.
I must ask my nana "if little girls die too"
"For I could die today or tomorrow would do"
My nana says "Tomorrow will make me bigger and stronger"
"Tomorrows I'll be a woman: a little girl no longer"
Then I'll nurse my daddy as he lovingly nursed me
And I would live to see him grow, a new branch in the family tree.
Someday my sweet, your son you'll hold
A reflection of daddy, for you to love
"God bless you little girl" and protect you on lifes way
That your path will be straight and narrow
Till He brings you to your day.

Mrs. Elisabeth Corica,
Liverpool.

PLEASE DON'T

Please don't send flowers
Which only last for hours
Until the wind comes.

Please don't make speeches
Which bore all it reaches
Until the rain comes.

Please don't cry for me
Which everyone will see
Until the night comes.

Please don't sit and think
Which only leads to drink
Until the dawn comes.

Please don't pray and mourn
Which only makes you forlorn
Until the end comes.

Please don't think of reasons
Which only last for seasons
Until the snow comes.

Please don't ask why or where
When you don't really care
Until the doubt comes.

Please don't plant flowers
Which only live for showers
Until the picker comes.

John Charles Cornish,
Bodmin, Cornwall.

MY CARAVAN

Just one more look before I go
As I stand and shiver, I close the door
The snow is deep, the trees are bare
Once again winter is here.

I close my eyes to reminisce
I thought of all the things I'd miss
The happy talks, the fun and games

The birds, the flowers, the shady lanes
All at once I turned and ran
I'd said goodbye to my caravan.

April showers they bring a song
For now I know it won't be long
My friends the birds came by today
I heard them sing as they flew away.

The trees in bloom, the flowers too
I knew just what I had to do
Straight through the forest, down the lane
I quickly made my way again
I laughed, I cried, I walked, I ran
Back to my love, my caravan.

Martha Clark Craig,
Rugby, Warwickshire.

T'WAS SAID TO ME

T'was said to me, when I was young,
You'll be old yourself one day,
And I recall being quite amazed,
At the silly things people say.

Me – be – old with wrinkled face,
And hair of silver grey,
And blue veined hands upon a stick,
A tapping on my way.

To me that ne'er could happen,
To other folk maybe,
But I would stand outside the pall,
And escape that destiny.

But time went blithely on it's way,
And fate laughted secretly,
For here am I, still young in heart,
In age – a century.

And so it is with wrinkled face,
And hair of silver grey,
And blue veined hands upon a stick,
I slowly tap my way.

Mrs. Ethel Crawford,
Sheffield, Yorkshire.

TOO LATE FOR LOVE

Pity not the missing limb gone absent without leave.
No sorrow for a crooked spine adrift from vertical,
or wheel-chaired spinsters twisted arm, searching wayward sleeve.
Too late to pity broken minds seeking beds already full.
Your love and friendship needed once, now not at all.

Pity not the sightless one who once had eyes so blue.
No sorrow for a cancered lung that strives to spread its fruit,
or new deaf ears, once guiding hands to tune piano true.
Too late to find the time to talk to one who is now mute.
Your love and friendship needed once, now not at all.

Pity not the wayward youth whose antics end in jail.
No sorrow for the pregnant girl just into her "teens",
or besotted drunk, now methylated, with clothes that rot and smell.
Too late to cleanse out L.S.D. and spurn its abstract dreams.
Your love and friendship needed once, now not at all.
    – now not at all.

Roy Cresswell,
St. Albans, Hertfordshire.

MY GIFT OF ROSES

Petals like velvet all clustered around,
Looking at these, new beauty I found.
Long stately stalks, and leaves, lovely green,
Now be very careful, there are thorns in between.

The scent of the roses, the lovely array,
To me this discloses God's lovely display.
Of roses so tender, so nice and so sweet,
And a beautiful treasure so dainty and neat.

I will treasure for ever this thought dear of you,
And be like the roses in all that I do.
I will try and show beauty wherever I be,
And give as much pleasure, as you gave to me.

Mrs. Blanche Critchley
Bolton, Lancashire.

A GUIDE DOG'S THOUGHTS

They tell me I am special
With a special job to do
They say they've given me to you
To help make your dreams come true.

Through me you'll listen to the trees
gossiping in a summer breeze
Smell sweet flowers and new morn hay
Walk along a sandy bay.

Feel the softly falling snow
Face the winds with face aglow
Sit at the fireside of a friend
Walk without fear around each bend.

Dear Master all I ask is this
I want no other "doggy bliss'
To guide you through what e'r arise
I give you now my heart and eyes.

Jane Wilson Cross,
Welling, Kent.

AULD LANG SYNE

The little robin by the barn
The holly berries red,
Somewhere a sprig of mistletoe
To hang up overhead,
    Cobwebs wet and sticky
    Clinging to the thorns
    Dried up cones and withered leaves
    Blowing in the storm.

Shaggy boughs all shank and bare
Withered grass in tufts,
Thistles brown and hard and lank
Keep their stature up,
    Sparrows in the corn yard
    Gather close in flocks
    Sheltering from the sharp cold wind
    Blowing from the north.

People dashing to and fro
Wrapped in furs and hats,
In the darkening afternoon

Struts the pheasant cocks,
 In the farm fold warm and snug
 We hear the cattle cough
 Their breath ascending to the roof
 As they gather round their trough.

Lights go on at evening all along the Firth
These are signs that winter's here,
Autumn's had enough
Soon, the Christmas Carols blending
On the midnight air,
Soon the sounds of revelry
Heard from everywhere,
 Soon then music, dancing
 Hogmanay is here
 Auld Lang Syne and handshakes round
 Close another year.

Minnie I. Cruickshank,
Darnaway, Morayshire.

OUR LOVE

The leaves were green upon the tree
The day I first met you
Before the leaves had turned to Brown
I knew I loved you true.

If you could love me in this way
How happy I would be
To have your love be evergreen
As the leaves upon the tree
My love for you will never fade
But evergreen will be
It will grow stronger every day
As we stand beneath the tree
Protected in the gentle shade
Telling of our love, the Joy it's made.

Many days have passed
Since the day I first met you
The leaves have turned to brown
Sealing our love so True.

Violet E. Crumpton,
Sherwood, Nottingham.

PET HAMSTER

Squirrel-coloured, furry, full of sleep,
Curled inside a smooth-wound nest;
Sleeping in the day, nocturnally
Venturing from his day-long rest.
Darting, patter-pawed, at evening,
Slow, pink yawn revealing rodent teeth;
Discreetly washing, paws on parchment ears,
Soft brown fur soft-shading down to cream beneath.
Squirrel-grasp of food in tiny finger-paws,
Twin-engined bomber, pouch distended,
Slave to age-old instinct, hoarding,
Fears of starving never ended.
Captive, now, for generations,
A plastic wheel his life's endeavour;
Ringed by curious human faces,
Pattering round his little, whirring wheel for ever.

J. E. Cubbin,
Ipswich, Suffolk.

MEMORIES PRECIOUS

Remember, oh how I remember,
That cold disarming, bleak December,
That sorrowful Christmas, in thought I tremble,
The memories unhappy, harrowingly, ensemble.

Softly as tears well up in my eyes,
I remember the heartache, the grief when Mum died,
Tearfully I tremble, tender memories mine,
I miss thee my loved one, I miss thee inside.

Sadly on that be-fated morn,
The tragic news descended upon one and all,
Our lives fell apart, sad hearts now mourn,
For the tender love we can but recall.

Hair golden, soft as a cloud,
Voice gentle, sincerity glowed,
Petite, almost fragile, gently endowed,
So young at heart, smartly a-glow.

Her gentle manner, christened with love,
A mother of love, cherished, adored,

Angelic features, sent from above,
As calm as an autumns early morn.

I remember, remember how life used to be,
Mum, Dad, Peter, Sue and me,
Life happily revolving around Mum, hectic but real,
Love and understanding, perfection to be seen.

But sadly good things don't last forever,
Eventually, inevitably, they're merely remembered,
Gladly, my memories will remain with me ever,
And the love so felt will last forever.

Elizabeth Jane Curtis,
Porthcawl, Glamorgan.

THE VIKING WARRIOR

A big, strong fierce and fat man,
About six feet tall,
With his powerful brain full of nasty things
He annoys you
A brave face
His eyelashes go down with a straight look
Quite a sneaky look.
Green eyes
Yellow-white hair blowing in the wind
And his beard flaps into his hair
Sword, axe with blood on the end
Sharp and gleaming when the sun shone
Knife and helmet and armour to guard him
Stealing, killing, burning and fighting
The islands of Britain
With his torch of flames flickering.

Miss Lorna C. Dairon (Aged 10),
Isle of Tiree, Argyll.

HOW LONG?

Every night I lose My dear one, I lose him once again,
The tears soak my pillow like heavy drops of rain,
When dawn is breaking, I face my loss anew,
The tears lay upon my cheeks, like on the rose, the dew,
At noon-time, I acknowledge that I'll see my love no more,
Never again will I hold him close, the one that I adore.
At eventide I accept the lonliness, all those hours to fill,
Remembering the happy times when he was with me still,
Then, once again, the darkness comes, to hide my anguished tears
How many more such lonely days? How many lonely years?

Louise G. Daley,
Hartlepool, Cleveland.

NIGHT

Night spread her velvet jet black gown
The gleaming, glittering, glinting crystal ball
Shone shimmering and shining
Reflected in the rippling running stream
Shadows limply fell long and lean
The trees silhouetted still and silent
Snow gently drifted down,
Casting a spell,
Changing the land,
To an enchanted expanse
Of white fairy tale country
Far away crooked stone images slept
A fox slyly crept, sensitively listening for danger
As he slunk along the ground
Slipping skilfully into the hen house . . .
A squawk rang out!
Shattering the silence
Outside the warm scarlet blood
Dripped into the crispy freshly laid snow
Like ink on blotting paper.
The chickens anxiously cackled gossip,
After hearing the scream.
The owl hooted a long weird call
And glided down.
His ever ready sabre talons
Sharp and deadly
Plunged deep into the flesh of a helpless tiny creature
The scuttling movements were killed
And the ghostly spirit
Flew away to his high up look out post.

In satisfaction sat majestically
Swallowing bones and all
His amber eyes quivering
Eyeing the ground
The sun's wintery dim rays
Lept along the horizon
As day came into the world's mansion.

Helen J. Daniel,
Darlington, Co. Durham.

SAINT TERESA OF THE ROSES

On the Island of Marcassa,
Stands Teresa of the Roses,
Stories tell us this is the place,
Where the gentle Saint reposes.
The Statue can be seen for miles,
Each rose hewn out of stone,
Carved by Monks in long gone days,
She is beautiful and alone.
The earth is made of rock and ash,
No blade of grass will seed,
No flowers no trees, will ever grow,
No birds ever come to feed.
Once a week on Sunday morn,
Mainlanders come for the day,
They row across in small canoes,
Hear Mass, sing hymns, and pray.
One evening when they'd all gone home,
Young Shenra, hidden and fast asleep,
Was left behind, he awakened,
And noisily started to weep.
Then down from the stone came a maiden,
And tenderly knelt at his side,
He could smell the sweet perfume of roses,
When she kissed him as he cried.
Then the people returned and marvelled,
That such a small child was alright,
But he laughed and told them the story,
Of the lady who came in the night.
"She came out of the stone and loved me"
Maybe its true, who knows?
For held in this tiny small boy's hand,
Was a beautiful dark red rose.

Mrs. K. Darcy,
Cleveleys, Lancashire.

TUTANKHAMUN

Tutankhamun, Tutankhamun,
Taken from your Shell,
Was this place your heaven,
Or was it just your hell.

Your vital organs removed,
Your soul untouched, unsoothed,
Was your face so beautiful,
On your coffin lid,
Or was it so distorted,
A face that should be hid.

Bones in your casket rotting away,
Fumes in your casket endless decay.

Remember me! Remember me!
The soul you have forgotten,
The soul you left for centuries,
The soul you left for rotting.

Miss Carey A. Davidson,
Glasgow.

TREES

The trees in winter standing there,
With branches brown and very bare,
Or maybe weighted down with snow,
Waving wildly when north winds blow.

Now it's Spring and trees are green,
Bird's building nests now can be seen,
And buds are growing on the trees,
Blowing gently in the breeze.

Then summer brings the blossoms gay,
Birds are singing all the day,
Apples green and cherries red,
Hanging gaily overhead.

Summer passes, Autumn's on,
Leaves are falling, fruits are gone,
Soon snow will be falling down,
And change to white those trees of brown.

Mandy Davidson,
Alness, Ross-shire.

THE QUEEN'S CORONATION

Come from the East, come from the West,
and let us join together,
In this great year of happiness, forget
all strife for ever.

A symbol of our Empire Strong, a Queen
so full of beauty.
Has now a path to tread so long
endlessly for duty.

Let the bells ring out, let the people shout,
Come on let's all be gay.
For in our hearts there is no doubt.
This is a glorious day.

And soon she'll ride, and by her side
the Consort proud and tall.
His love will guide, whate're betide
To help to rule us all.

And when the crowds have gone away.
Our Queen is crowned in splendour,
Lets pledge ourselves on this great day.
Our services to render.

Rosina Davidson,
Baillieston, Glasgow.

LOVE POEM TO A MIDDLEAGED HUSBAND

I dreamed the dreams of a young woman
But awoke and it was now.

I awoke to know that the pot of gold
The future holds is now

Lucky me to realise in dreary middle age
I've still got time to use this truth;
To spread the word is now.

It could have been a taunting dream
In a geriatric ward.

But I woke at home with my dear love
And almond blossom on New Years Day.

Anne Davis,
Radlett, Hertfordshire.

LOVE IN WARTIME

In days gone by, when we were young,
My heart and I, how we did love,
A brave Adonis, young and fair,
Who came to camp whilst I was there,
No cares upon our shoulders then,
T'was war, and both in uniform, so proud,
And yet afraid, of sad things that could part us.
Things that happened every day,
Yet each morning felt so wonderful,
Knowing that someone cared, and,
In return, my caring, with a love that grew with time.
Later on, we married,
Still in a haze of love,
In time came three dear babies,
One boy, two girls to love.
Now, after thirty years and more,
In spite of ups and downs,
My brave Adonis, whiter now, me too, of course, but still,
It matters not the outward look,
What counts is what's within,
Of course we've had our quarrels,
As many couples do,
But I would miss him, were he gone,
And, I hope that he'd miss me!

Mrs. Dorothy Davis, Bridgwater, Somerset.

BORSTAL FREE

The Borstal boys are on the run,
Broken out to have some fun.
Tired of locked doors and strict timetable,
Flown like a bird while they're able.
Out of the grounds, into the country so free,
To do ordinary things like you and me.
Admire the scenery at your leisure,
The simple things that give you pleasure.
Strolling from that captive place,
Your parents reaction sheer disgrace.
Vowing never to be taken again,
Running now, down the country lane.
Frustration, panic, now where to go,
Heading for home, think again, No!
Nowhere is safe for a wanted man,
So enjoy your freedom while you can.

Colin Dixon, Irlam, Nr. Manchester.

110

TO MANKIND

With thee this day, our Lord we pray,
That we may seek, a happier way,
To end this feud, between black and white,
And may we find, the way that's right.

So that all can live, a better life,
In years to come, there be no strife,
No matter what, our colour be,
We should live, as all men free.

So may it be, that we can find,
A solution too, suit all mankind,
The coloured man, he's just like you,
He's fighting for a living too.

So please give him, a chance to say,
How he should live, in his own way,
We should not shun, or taunt or call,
Because coloured men, are champions all.

They fought with us, in time of need,
And very glad, we were indeed,
They never shirked, a task at all,
So many thousands, they did fall.

And let's just think, and remember this,
We have ours, so give him his,
The freedom he has, so long sought,
So please just give, this a thought,
And let us live, as our Lord meant,
Brothers to all, was Heaven sent.

Robert Dickson,
Musselburgh, Midlothian.

PAST AND PRESENT

I.

Take your steps carefully
when you walk in Scotland:
your path will lead you
along cliffs and gorges
breaking off
suddenly
into time:

111

vicious feuds,
peasants driven
out of insecure holdings,
a harsh religion
that damns the poor and the happy
invading armies
and massacres in the night;

the struggle with nature
wherever you fall,
storm and rain
breaking in
ever again
with the howl
and the wild light
of the furies;

interspersed with
fantastic beauty,
gripping loneliness,
and the mellow gleam
of the whisky
by the fire,

after the blood
has oozed away
and the sweat
has dried in the wrinkles.

The past is present:
in the living
and the dead,
in the towns
and the ruins.

II.

The clans had their feuds
on the backs of the peasants,
between the hills of Skye
and under the pinnacles
of Quiraing and Storr
where the Old Man
cries in the rain
and still today
shrouds himself in fog
so he doesn't see.

112

They ate
from the plates of the peasants,
guests all the time,
uninvited in their couple of rooms,
until many raised the white flag,
probably their only shirt,
under the assault of the sheep.
And they left their homes
with the lost peasants
from Sutherland
and all the others
who like them
came out of the fog
and disappeared as they came.

The feuds are over these days,
they wouldn't seize
an old man any more,
any old man,
to test a new gallows —
but they still eat,
so not much has changed:
and the free world in the west
lost for the poor long time ago.

Nothing of that is written
on Flora MacDonald's tombstone,
whose name was full of blood,
though she herself
was said to have a gentle nature.
But: she did eat well.

Not much of that you'll find
in the stories
about Bonnie Prince Charlie,
who fetched the peasants
from their lean hillsides
and chased them
into the bullets of the English,
then disappeared in the fog
to find safety
at Flora's side on Skye.

Juergen Diethe,
London.

A WINNER

I was standing one day at the bus stop,
  Waiting for number thirteen,
When round the bend, it came into view,
  All shiny, polished and clean.

It was the racecourse special,
  Bound for the local event,
Everyone was happy and jolly,
  All except one old gent.

To me he unfolded his story,
  I listened what he had to say,
He urgently needed some money,
  So the horses he'd decided to play.

His debts were too numerous to mention,
  His assets were little or none,
He was at the end of his tether,
  And now he was left all alone.

He backed every winner 'til the last one,
  And on that one he bet the whole lot,
Tho' his horse won the race, was disqualified,
  Now everything had gone to pot.

He returned to his room disallusioned,
  His problems much worse than before,
Stepping inside very sadly,
  He picked up a letter from the floor.

He opened it up very slowly,
  Wondering from whom it had come,
As he read his hands started to tremble,
  His One Premium Bond had just won.

One thousand pounds was the amount of his bounty,
  Life took on a different view,
He felt ten years younger and happy,
  It's surprising what Ernie can do.

Mr. L. G. Dobbs,
Preston.

Our Queen she was a handsome lass,
all be it six feet tall.
For reddish hair she had a flair
outside her palace wall
Sat she at home in Holyrood
a place of grim forboding
Whilst outside troubles piled up high,
her Nobles busy loading.
On ilka days she sat alone
an brooding long she wan'nered
What sort o' man her Darnley was
O' him she was fair scunnered.
For he and Knox gave her such shocks
to make her life a hell,
For nocht but pain lay in her reign
and dropped on hersell.
Plots and counter plots were hatched
the very walls to sicken,
Such schemes too often gang agley,
and ulcered tounges too clickin.
Yet still anon she kept her head
though not for very long,
the forces that surrounded her
were getting far too strong.
And so she fell to other plans
this strapping six foot wench,
there's nothing on God's earth against
I'll make my people French.
So she set too with feathered quill
yet still a wee perplexed,
to wonder if they'd boot her out
because they were sore vexed.
Then thinking of her Rizzio
the Queen she turned pale
to think that they should murder him
for playing her a scale.
Anon her mind kept wandering on
back to the pier o' Leith,
where some had cheered, a few had jeered
and others bared their teeth.
An on she thought o' dangers brought
to her wee son the Prince,
in dread o' that coup-de-tat
made Scotlands Mary wince.
She knew the kind, the scurrilous mind
to make her more unhappy

for light of day was to gain say,
just who was James's pappy.
Still – there at last the die was cast
the seal thereon and ready,
yet little did our Mary know
her plan was loose and heady.
A messenger she summoned then,
a man of high degree,
in safety you'll deliver this
to France's King Louis.
So off he went like a bow half bent
On Scotlands destiny.
Next grabbed a ship and made a skip
across the cold North Sea.
To plod his way to Louis court
in darkest secrecy.
There – stuttered what lay in his mind
whilst quakin at the knee.
King Louis read then reading said,
in this I quite agree,
go hence my man I like this plan
its contents fair suit me.
Go tell your Queen its no day dream
I fully understand,
and just to compensate ourselves
we'el whack off Lizzie's hand.
Still strife it grew at home anew
that merited a decision,
to be a Queen or worst a pawn
an object of derision.
Then came langside an ebbing tide
her life an crown to gamble
alack-a-day she fled that fray
her army in a tangle.
Then heading south near Solways mouth
she crossed the Scottish border
to leave behind with anguished mind,
her country in disorder.
Still memises kept on her heels,
Her Kingdom soon to shock;
The Thistle and the Fluer-de-Lis
had sped her to the block.
Still – history is a lying Jade
it skims the cream from pleasure,
it stultus acts to damn most facts
and deals in truth-short measure.

William Dorward, Hawick.

116

HERITAGE

Still they are there, deep under tranquil waters
Or fretted wave, and knowing not the sun.
These other beings call as in my childhood,
In answer, scorning age, my footsteps run.

And they? From out earth's womb came elementals,
Spirits of other times and other ways,
Dwelling eternally in caves of darkness,
Having no place in sunlit happy days.

In mists of time the Celtic people knew them,
Heart of their hearts, their love, their mortal fear,
Placating their wrath with gifts of gold and silver
And sacrificing all they held most dear.

(Was it the food that hungry people cherished,
Tears in their hollow eyes to watch it go?
Was it a child who, screaming, met the water
And, drowning, was consumed by those below?)

Still of the brotherhood, they are in mountains,
Held in the riven cleft or jagged peak.
Wild is their waking, thunder with the lightning,
And in the wind their eldritch voices speak.

Sorrow in life – they offer naught of comfort
To those who seek them, yet to these are all,
Born of the forest, loch or mountain –
Ever to these the spirit voices call.

Creatures of time – their hours of waiting vanish,
Now I am old I know there will they be,
With arms outstretched in welcome to their brother –
I part of them, forever part of me.

Mary M. B. Dougal,
Bathgate, By Edinburgh.

THE CAT (CASEY)

I walked into the yard in the early morning hours
The moon gleamed down on potted plants and flowers
And there you sat upon the wall
King of the Night!!
Tawny in the moonlight,
Golden eyes I knew by day
Slitted now, waiting for an answering call
To ancient rites, secret only to your tribes
And I felt "Who was I to think that I knew you"
I thought of jungles and of other larger cats,
And if in your mind (because I know you have a mind)
You thought "Poor Human, my race goes back to ancient times
When we were worshipped by your kind."
You gave no sign of recognition,
So I looked once more to the starlit and the moonlit sky
And left you to your meditation.

Jane W. Douglas,
Newcastle upon Tyne.

THE FALL OF O'HENRY

Six foot two without a shoe, stood O'Henry the bosuns mate,
With pig eyes red and a shaven head and a heart black with hate.
The strength of a bull in his shoulders full and a mean and dirty look,
He lived by the law of the tooth and claw and what he wanted he took.
I've seen men mean but none have been as mean as O'Henry I swear,
On that ship, was a tough trip for us lads under him there.

One night by chance we found a dance down at the mission hall,
Was a humble affair with a small band there but we were glad we made
the call.
Then silence fell with a laugh known well and O'Henry stood at the
door,
His eyes were red and sunk in his head and he dribbled and spat on
the floor.
He was drunk real mean and his eyes did gleam and his laugh was as
black as his heart,
As the bottle in his hand he hurled at the band and roared for the
music to start.

We all stood still for we'd had our fill as he swayed and gazed about,
"I'm here to stay, so what do you say, will any man put me out?"

Like an image of wood the pardre stood at the top of the wooden stair,
He looked small and grey but I heard him say, "I'll try for my duty is
there."
O'Henry smiled at this figure mild and laughed with a black toothed
grin,
"Yes come on down, dog collared clown and sure I'll do you in."

The pardre brave looked old and grave as he came on down the stair,
We stood dismayed and a bit afraid for this fight just was not fair.
There's a scream of girls as O'Henry whirls with a punch that's mean
and cruel,
But the pardre's fist just never missed and fell with the kick of a mule.
Then O'Henry sagged and the pardre dragged him to the nearest
chair,
Then without any fuss he turned to us and said to all of us there.

"A man of the cloth should not show wrath as I have done tonight,
There are times when a man must do what he can for what he feels is
right.
And you my friend, let's not pretend, you left me little choice,
For I feared my hand you'd understand much better than my voice.
I hope you've learned from the blow you've earned and the way your
jaw is aching,
That the joy of living is in the giving than rather in the taking."

O'Henry's paw went to his jaw and he said then after a pause,
"I guess you're right for when I fight I regret the trouble I cause."
We then felt shame and a bit to blame and all just a little sad,
For if we had stood as well we should O'Henry would not have been
bad.
But in retrospect, I strongly suspect, that the greatest lesson that night,
Was the faith of a man who will do what he can for what he believes is
right.

Charles Edward James Dowswell,
Edinburgh.

THE TIME AND THE PAIN

The time is the time when everythings fine,
your lung is alright, and your heart is in line.
The days are so good, and the sun is up high,
your feeling so light, like a kite in the sky.
You've no time to notice that child that goes by,
but a girl thats a beauty you say, where? O aye,
Its spring and its perfect for catching your eye.
Then everything stops like a clock thats just fell,
you turn, oh so silent you can't even yell,
Your brain takes a shudder and thinks, it's like Hell
You lie on your back with your eyes staring high,
up where you thought was that beautiful sky,
except at your eye lids that close automatically.
Then everything blackens, and days are so long,
and that pain that was there becomes a bit strong.
You think other thoughts to pass each new day,
and that pain it defeats you, and makes you aware,
that you no longer bear it, except to just stare.
So you pray to a someone, a friend, or your mother,
you might think of a neighbour, a relative, a brother.
and then a slight thought that your leaving alright,
with everything right and documents tight.
and then as your eyes begin to slow down,
just like a movie that starts its run down.
It turns blacker, and deeper, and softer, and fine,
and that is the end of that beautiful time.

Peter Dragoonis,
Rutherglen, Glasgow.

LONELINESS

I open the door and step inside
The walls they echo, but nothing said.
I put on the light and look around
Nothing human to be found.
I put on the kettle and make some tea
And wish just for someone more than me.
The tea it helps, but not that much,
I long and look for a human touch.
My work is done and now it's night
My only company the electric light.
I listen to the news of world wide
What a mass of humanity outside.

There am I quite alone
Wishing for someone to call my own.
I wonder, will the door bell ring,
Does someone care, if I'm out or in?
I leave the door, a little space
While having a bath, just in case
A friendly guest may come tonight
To ask if I'm well and will be alright.
I go to bed feeling sore
No one has called at my door,
I shut out the wind and the sleet
And thed to bed between the sheets
To sleep, I try, but with open eye
I'm thankful another day's gone by.

Jessie Dryden,
Pitlochry, Perthshire.

SOLITUDE BY NIGHT

Quiet and still is the night
High above the moon shines bright,
Sitting alone near the end of the pier
I see reflections on water, crisp and clear.

The lights on the water seem to glitter and dance
As I sit watching, near in a trance,
The night is quiet, not a sound to be heard
No people stirring, not even a bird.

Slowly and silently a boat makes to leave
For distant waters the nets to heave,
Its lights on the yardarms, both red and green
And steadfast crew, both eager and keen.

A clock in the distance strikes the hour
As the boat pulls out surging with power,
Soon again it is as quiet as can be
And the only sound heard, is the sound of the sea.

Mr. Iane Duncan,
Anstruther, Fife.

A WOODLAND TRAGEDY

Along the way I walk there lies a carpet
Woven of green and gold,
Russet and brown. Tall trees look down
And wave stark boughs as if to say,
"We made this carpet motley-gay."

Sweet is His autumn morn, and I drink
Deep the tang of frosty air,
And feel God's love, around, above,
And think no sorrow lives today
Whe ah! Morn's gold turns all to grey.

For just along my path there lies
A tuft of ruffled feathers, brown,
And I can see, ahead of me,
A little sparrow lying – dead
"And there's no sorrow" I had said!

Somewhere I know, in some tall tree,
A little brown mate patient waits
Or flies around from tree to ground
All tremulous. That there should be
On a blithe morn such tragedy.

Mrs. P. M. Eckersley,
Creetown, By Newton Stewart.

LIFE

Dreams we dream; the young must dream;
Hopes are high, sinews supple. We scheme,
Disappointment shrugged aside; we'll find a way
No need to hurry; up then down; we pay,
Feel the drowning, no rescue near,
Some to worldly solace, will it cover fear?

Pay your taxes, where's your rent,
Peace of mind if only lent.
See the trees yet only darkly,
Smell the flowers, see the sun, sometimes starkly.
Taste the rain, feel the joyful propagating,
Joys of lust; knawing pain; all negotiating.

Tired sinews growing brittle, the earth will soon be dust,
Is life wasted, just a hurried session; a must.
The apple tree, the touch of vellum, music of tears,
I tried the race for years, and years.
We within the herd were penned, then soiled,
Dreams, dreams, ambitious desires foiled.

When your life is judged in the morning light,
Wailing cries die; we're all lost in the night.
What matters now the deeds the brave,
Worldly touch of Mammon; the knave, his grave.

My soul, my soul, I need my soul,
Have I a second chance.
Or will the man within me,
Bring even this death's dance?

Vera Elliott,
Wallasey, Merseyside.

BABE WITH WONDERING EYES

Dear child, dear babe with wondering eyes,
Searching the ever changing skies,
Why do you stare, what see you there?
Is it some stately galleon fair,
A treasure ship within its hold,
A precious store of yellow gold?
Or do you see white horses run,
With flowing manes across the sun,
Or giant birds that softly go,
To distant mountains capped with snow.
Or coral isles in azure seas?
But no, perhaps 'tis none of these.
Is it perchance you glimpse awhile,
That other land where angels smile
And children who have passed this way,
In flowering meadows laugh and play,
Where mortal man immortal now,
Walks tall with quiet, unfurrowed brow?
Are you sweet babe to heaven so near,
That angel voices reach your ear?
Or is it just the wonder of the skies,
That brings such wonder to your baby eyes?

Mary Bryce Stewart Ellis,
Perth.

Through vicious minds I carry on
Secreting not a single tear,
Instead, unearthing what they've done,
To hurt me through the passing years;
And I am still wondering how they could,
Choose all the evil for the good.
Are "these" what Son of Man must lead –
Their hunger – blood, their thirst is greed:
The nail behind my back sticks out
Has all my suffering been in vain! –
My heart inside my body yields, – to wipe
Out – the Perennial pain.
Is this mankinds barbaric ways,
Then do their loving – I Disdain, for they
Cannot know to what extent
The words I spoke, Have all been Meant!
Not like your son do I hang here,
A six inch nail pierced through my ear.
But you saw it coming, by and by
And let it happen – Oh Father, Why? –
It's time to make my last repeal,
To see what savage man might feel.
"Am I your master, or a clown in
Purple cloak and thorny crown.
Do I make you people smile and
Was it such a funny trial;"
But time has passed and it is late,
And nothing on earth can change my fate:

I'm losing sense of all my mind
I'm first in front, and then behind, –
I see my throne in Kingdom come,
Father thy will hast been done:
My body dead, my head now hung,
The judgement on them now begun,
I'm going; yes – but not away
I shall be back, and see the day
That you'll repent to see me here
God Thy Father You Will Fear!

Julie Alexandra Eckford,
South Shields, Tyne and Wear.

THE ROYAL MAIL

On and on through cold grey dawn,
Past the Vicar's pleasant lawn,
Past the tall church steeple,
Past the town of sleeping people,
On through the golden fields
Where the annual harvest yields,
Past the farm it rattles and roars
While the farmer gently snoars.
Onward through a tiny station,
No this isn't its destination.
As the sun begins to rise,
Onward this monster swiftly flies,
Onward through hill and dale,
Carrying the people's mail.
The engine groans beneath the strain,
Many precious seconds gain.
The engine whines through such stress,
Yes this is the Royal Mail Express.

Kevin Andrew Evans,
Wooburn Common, Buckinghamshire.

ACROSS THE SEA

Across the dark still waters
A boat comes from afar,
Only following the direction
Of the small North Star.

My blood stops running
As it lands on shore,
Carrying twenty barrels
Or maybe even more.

Out of the dark gloom
A figure appears,
Bringing with it your
Worries and fears.

By a flickering candle light
Does appear this wonderful sight:

Twenty barrels of good old rum
Twenty bars of gold (a pretty sum),
Lace for the women
And wine for the gentlemen.

And soon they will have gone
As quickly as they came,
Coming next month
Bringing just the same.

Twenty barrels of good old rum
Twenty bars of gold (a pretty sum),
Lace for the women
And wine for the gentlemen
And wine for the gentlemen.

Laura Jane Fantozzi (Aged 11),
Macclesfield, Cheshire.

TREE

Crispness –
    Breaks!
On grey doom coloured stones.
Smashing like a plate of glass –
Into flickering colours –
    Shaking!
    Dancing!
    Flying!
In movements of Paradise
Making a rough abstract of a water-fall,
Crashing in powers –
    Falling –
Hitting with unknown senses.
Low bedding-sailing –
    Drifting –
    Skating –
In almighty colours.
Representing a beautiful tree –
    Sloping –
In a dazzled sleepiness.
It has woken –
After the yelling bird's cry,
"Waken waken do not freeze
Shudder branch and leaf of trees."
Dazzling and dreamy –
It sleeps once more,
Leaving behind a crisp silence –
Waiting in readiness
For powers to fall.

Sarah Farley,
Malton, Yorkshire.

LOVE

"What is it of which men have writ,
Since first t'was deemed to pen
The mind, its thoughts and so to wit,
Immortalise idem;
What hast the gifted eye inspired,
The master hand imbued,
The artist soul with fervence fired,
By few from choice eschewed;
What to the poor hast ever brought,
An affluence sublime
The rich so swayed to set at naught,
The lustre of the mine;
Full weak, fain strong, alike hast stayed,
Nor failed to gratify,
The restless spirit, once allayed,
Could'st aught but satisfy:
'Tis not the sickly warmth that gleams,
Within the shallow heart,
Instructing servile lips, it seems,
To play their kindred part;
Nor is it that mean sentiment,
Which glows so sweet awhile,
As Fate withholds her detriment,
So tarries to revile;
Lo! 'tis a greater, grander thing,
More noble claim by far,
Supreme in that it Once Did'st Bring,
LIFE 'neath an Eastern Star;
'Tis Love, th' incomprehensible!
Plants paradise 'midst care,
In woman irrepressible,
For yonder babe she bear;
'Tis Love perfects paternity,
O'er erring child prevails,
Creates that fair fraternity,
True harmoney entails;
'Tis Love 'twixt worthy man and maid,
That fountain ever pure,
'Twixt man and wife hast ever made,
The sacred bond secure:
For be we dull or be we gay,
Or be we sentimental,
The honest heart must needs give way,
'Fore this vast fundamental."

Gladys Helen Farquhar, Elgin, Morayshire.

127

AZALEA

A gift was given at Christmastime,
A mass of leaf and bloom,
A simple gift, yet one that cheered
The heart and banished gloom,
Thrice-welcomed as the Child it came,
Nor heard the cry "No Room".

Its pure and perfect loveliness,
Encouraged each new day,
And spoke of love unseen, unknown,
Of hands that fashioned clay
To give it root, and home, and warmth,
Its beauty to display.

But everything a season has,
A zenith reached, and then
A slow, relentless final fade
Of nature, as with men.
Accept, reject, decry, bemoan,
Earth claims her own again.

Refreshing Spring and Summer sun
Have come and gone twice o'er,
And men have fought and bled and let
Their wickedness outpour
On innocents, both young and old,
In air, on sea, on shore.

Yet some there are, whose constancy
Of trust and faith untold,
Hold fast the eternal virtues,
Believing as of old
That faith begets its own reward,
And, lo, again behold . . .

A leaf, a bud, and now a flower
Of soft and rosy hue
Unfolds its petals tenderly
And silently as dew,
Revealing the Creator's power
And giving hope anew.

Miss Mary E. Farries,
Hawick, Roxburghshire.

THE QUITTER

The man who quits has both brain and hand
as good as the next, but he isn't the brand
that would try to stick – with a courage stout –
to whatever he tackles, and fight it out.

He starts with a rush and the solemn vow
that he'll soon be showing the others how.
Then something new takes his roving eye,
and he leaves his task for another to try.

It rests with each man what becomes of him;
he must find in himself the grit and vim
that will bring success; he'll get the skill
if he brings to his aid a steadfast will.

No man is beaten until he gives in –
bad luck just can't stand for a cheerful grin.
The man who fails needs a better excuse
than the quitter's whining "What's the use."

Such a man who quits lets his chances slip
because he's too lazy to tighten his grip.
The man who holds on goes ahead, without doubt,
while a quitter can only go down – and out!

Mr. Archibald Faulds,
Paisley.

CHILDREN OF GOD

Look down upon us Lord, we humbly ask Thee
And lead us in Thy Path,
Show us light that our steps we may see
And spare us in Thy wrath.

We give Praise and thanks to Thee
And in Thee our trusts we place,
Give us strength to show to others Thy will,
While we pray that Thy will be done.

With our heads bowed and thoughts ascended
In homage and with prayers to Thee,
Often we felt the blessings which are descended,
As answers to our fervent pleas.

The songs of birds and the hum of bees
The ever flowing streams,
The beautiful flowers, and the fruitful trees,
We thank you Lord for all these.

As children of Thine we arise
With praise and glory to Thee,
For the joys you have given to those who have striven
Of peace within and love abound.

Mr. Isaiah A. Felix,
Ipswich, Suffolk.

ANVIL WEDDING

A match, to strike and kindle,
First glance, responds desire,
Carefree and so gentle,
A courtship, to inspire,
For all, a brief engagement,
The years, that lie beyond,
Their wedding day – may they be gay;

There's a proclamation,
Tacked upon a tree,
An open invitation,
For everyone, to see,
The 'smith will give his blessing,
On the day, not far away,
Their wedding day – complete bouquet;

He fashions, in the twilight,
A tiny, wisp of gold,
A bond, to last a lifetime,
When the embers, have gone cold,
The echoes of the anvil,
Will ring back here again,
On this refrain – their wedding day.

Tom Files,
Oban, Argyll.

SIGNS OF SPRING

Cloud suds fleck the sky's bright bowl,
Rinsing round its azure rim,
Dove grey, the humid feathers float,
Plucked and tossed at the wind's whim.

In middle air flap-happy rooks
Cavort upon its gusty surges,
Black feather-dusters flung aloft,
They scour the sky like spring-clean purges.

Cold, weary winter's grip has failed
And signs of spring gleam everywhere,
White daisies bare their hearts of gold,
Return the sun's bold, brassy stare.

New lambs, their catkin tails a-twitch,
Leap light around their stolid dams;
While young tups jostle and contend,
The ram his cud with sweet grass crams.

The hedgerows, slow to don green leaves,
Sport celandines' bright, varnished stars,
And trees, yet bleak, pump heady sap
To swelling crowns through living spars.

In Countryman, as spring comes round,
The sun's new warmth sparks life and hope,
Ruddies his weathered cheek with health,
Confers new strength by which to cope.

To Urban Man these signs of spring
Appear as Mother Nature's plot
To rouse in his denatured soul
Dissatisfaction with his lot.

Ian R. Ferguson,
Bournemouth.

The budgie flichts a' ower the hoose,
But kens fine whaur it's gaun,
Syne wi' a chirp o' pleesure
Settles on Blind Billy's haun;
The tither haun cums canny up
Tae mak a cosy nest,
An' the budgie coories doon, whaur
It's aye a welcome guest.

"Wee Joey luves ye!" is the cry
That maks Blind Billy smile,
"An' Billy luves you tae" he says
Caressin a' the while;
The budgie micht be black or white
Fur a' Blind Billy kens,
Fur a' his warld is gloamin – gray
An' no' like ither men's.

He's niver seen the gowden sun
Lave a cottabe wa',
He's niver seen the verdant buds
Appear in withered shaw;
He's niver seen a gowden curl
Atower a bairnie's broo,
Nor yet the glint o' buttercups
Like gowd amid the dew.

But yet there is anither gowd,
The gowd o' luve itsel,
A selfless luve, mair precious than
The pearl, in oyster shell;
Nae winner thon wee budgie's sae
Content in Billy's care,
Fur weel it kens thae gentle hauns,
Hae luve enfaulded there.

Marion Findlay,
Blackridge, West Lothian.

THE RIVER

Ripping, racing, rushing, rills
Hareing down from mist clad hills,
Tumbling, tearing, twisting, torrents,
Slashing falls with icy currents.

Smashing into deep black pools,
Chinking sunlight, gravel jewels,
Gliding swift by heather bank,
Risking leafy tunnels rank.

Soft and deep through fields of green,
Rushing rapids fine and clean,
Swollen now by other burns,
Suddenly the river turns.

Coloured by the smoky pits,
Stinking sewers, slimy slits,
Cowering, filthy water sulks,
Lapping liners, rotting hulks.

Steadily, slowly, pushing strong,
Tasting salt and then among,
Surging waves lifting far,
Mighty Sea, at last "Hurrah".

Jim Finlay,
Spott, Dunbar.

ODE TO THE BLACK PUDDING

This is an Ode to the Lancashire Black Pud
Known throughout the country as being so very good,
Ev em wi mustard, it makes em taste so nice
Bring out t' flavour, if tha' likes a bit a spice
There med fra pigs blood an such
If tha's more than one, its a bit ta much,
Mi mither used to boil 'em on cawd winter neets
When tha come ta fat in middle – that surely was a treet,
They celebrate wi haggis Robbie Burns Neet
So why not Owd Lancs Pud on Bonfire Neet?

Rosamond A. Fishwick,
Preston, Lancashire.

ON OUR ANNIVERSARY

Oh, how incredible it seems,
That I have realised my dreams,
And lived all of my life with you,
And done the things we said we'd do.

For thirty years, a little more,
You've loved me, made me feel secure,
When I've been afraid and sad,
You held me close, and made me glad.

You've given all that you could earn,
And asked for nothing in return,
Except my love, which I shall give,
As long as you and I shall live.

And after that because I trust,
That life hereafter is a must.

Mrs. Joan Fletcher,
Horwich, Nr. Bolton.

SLEEP

Message of warmth,
Flowing through walls of flesh
And mental substance;
Bring life to the sad body
Who seeks only contentment

Delay the callous dawn
For temporary eternity
And radiate spiritual meaning
In thoroughness of depth
In my innermost being

Sleep; conducing perfect thoughts
To emanate and waver
In unhurried suspension
Unaware of cold threats
From the advancing tyrant

Thwarted flight: the essence of life
Crushed to submission –
The brain awakes to the grey light
Of another day
Unaware of the flights of night.

Jonathan Flint,
Chester, England.

134

HOMING

Up and away, into the day,
Wheel across the meadow,
Wing upon wing, string upon string,
Of flight as straight as an arrow.

O'er tree top, circle sheep acrop,
Dip and glide together,
Home in sight, black and white,
None lost, all here, to a feather.

Margaretta Forrester,
Meir Heath, Staffordshire.

MY ISLANDS

Sand and sea weave a spell,
The waving pines also tell;
Of stormy days, star-kissed nights;
The whirlpool deep, the mountain heights.

Shores untouched by human feet;
Echoed sound of the breakers beat;
Cries of birds, heard, yet unseen
Through tangled ivies, murky green.

Misty hills and limpid pools,
Rainbowed flowers set like jewels;
Welcoming scent of burning peat,
Drooling taste of venison meat.

Some lonesome sheep, an empty Glen,
The crofter folk, the fishermen.
Sadly, softly, a lament is played,
Another clansman down is laid.

These are the islands dear to me,
Scattered o'er the Hebridean Sea.
Unspoilt, beloved, remote, they lie,
Slumbering neath a Scottish sky.

Mrs. Elizabeth Fowler,
Glasgow.

GUILE AND INNOCENCE

Woman, you have a beauty
As hard and sharp as a glittering diamond.
To me you are not worth your weight in gold;
Your heart is stone, and like a stone, so cold.
Your cunning face sends shivers down my spine
As with your sharp-nailed fingers you entwine
Yourself about me, a no-good, clinging, poison ivy vine.
You're rich in ice, but have no fire, vitality or life,
The all enveloping glow;
A spark of inner warmth would melt you,
My little queen of snow.

But you, my child, resemble the little fawn,
Quite wide-eyed in your innocence;
A little wild violet peeping at the world,
Gentle and shy and not intense.
I plucked you, nature's work of art,
And slowly as your leaves unfurled
You looked at me
Tentatively
And stole my heart.

Sheena Elizabeth Fraser,
Edinburgh.

THE VANDALS

The old woman looks out her window,
Her thoughts return to the past,
Of a bright and sunny summer's day,
And her a winsome country lass.

Oh happy times and wholesome leisure,
When a daisy-chain was a fingered treasure,
The computered age had never begun,
Just blossoming youth and nature's fun.

From her bottom flat in a concrete hell,
The bustling city sprawled to swell,
Suddenly her view it seemed restricted,
Her spectacles fell with fingers twisted.

On stooping down there came the crack,
A shattered window an excited dogs bark,
The teenage louts they ran and scattered,
It's only an old woman to them nothing mattered.

Two passers-by without resolve,
With footsteps hurry they're not involved,
The blast-out sound like angry thunder,
Tearing the still-house air asunder.

The startled old lady clutched her heart,
A searing pain and all was dark,
And passing on it's life's reward,
She returned again to that green sward.

Mr. William Fraser,
Whitburn, West Lothian.

THE TEACHER'S TASK

There they sit.
Eager and alert?
Ready to reflect, react, respond?
No!
Eager to disrupt, defend, deny.
They are not ready.

There they sit.
Drugged by the warmth
Of sun and central heating,
Double-glazed windows
And chalky atmosphere.
A film of dust suspended in the air.
Timeless.

There they sit.
Overdressed in the height of fashion,
Sullen and inactive,
Insignificant, wilting vegetables
Dying in their monotony.
How can I revitalise them?

Joanna Fullwood,
Shrewsbury, Salop.

SELF DESTRUCTION

This, they had me know,
Was what it was to be;
This strangely sane madness
Was a glorious creative flood
Swamped in neon sunlights.

But they couldn't see,
As their view was shattered
By its blinding dazzle.
And reality won't flourish from
A vision lost to artificial light.

Paul Gardner
Harrow, Weald,
Middlesex.

WOULD YOU BE FAITHFUL

HE   If you were a princess and I were a king
If I made you mine with this gold wedding ring
If I gave you my love, my wealth, everything
Would you be faithful to me?

SHE   If you were a king and made me your bride
I'd be honoured and happy to reign by your side
And with your problems I'd help you decide
I'd always be faithful to you.

HE   If I were a sailor in some foreign land
Parted by duty, would you understand?
Would you forget that gold ring on your hand?
Would you be faithful to me?

SHE   If you were a sailor and sailed far away
I feel sure I'd take comfort in tears every day
Don't ever doubt me dear, I'd never stray
I'd always be faithful to you.

HE   If I were a poor man and wore denim grey
Toil-worn and tired by the end of the day
Would you be content? Would you want to stay?
Would you be faithful to me?

SHE If you were a poor man I'd be by your side
In humble surroundings I'd gladly abide
With love such as ours we'd take all in our stride
I'd always be faithful to you.

HE If I were a sick man, confined to a bed
Would you regret those fine words you have said?
Would other hands help to soothe me instead?
Would you be faithful to me?

SHE If you were a sick man I'd tend you with care
In good times or bad times we've promised to share
There is nothing too great with my love to compare
I'd always be faithful to you.

HE Then you are my princess.

SHE And you are my king

BOTH Bonded as one by this gold wedding ring
I feel so happy I just want to sing
I'll always be faithful to you.

Jean L. Garlick,
Havant, Hants.

BRAILLE

Feel the rabbits china bones,
Warm flat fur
And twitching nose.
Feet that thump
Upon my knee.
Ears lie flat along his spine
Or stand erect in velvet line.
Warm and frightened, petrified,
He humps and trembles
In my hands, resisting me,
Then struggles,
With strong frenzied limbs,
And he is free.

Barbara Garner,
Wheathampstead, Herts.

THE ENTRANCE

If I were to come to Your door,
Your little door,
Would you let me in?

If I were to come to You,
Lustful and vain and full of sin,
Would You let me in?

If I were to come to Your gate,
Your little gate,
Full of anger and hate,
Would you open straight?

Let me come along Your narrow path,
And crouch upon Your hearth.

Lois Mary Gent,
Helensburgh, Dunbartonshire.

ARDNAMURCHAN

Dae ye mind how in the simmer, by the "shieling of the goats",
Where Mingary Castle guards the sound o' Mull,
There the clans of Ardnamurchan, held Loch Sunart by the throat,
In the days o' Auld Lang Syne, remembered still.

Dae ye mind how high o'er Salen, we climbed yon muckle hill,
Where the trees were sabin saft and twisted sair,
There we laboured hard through waters as they tumbled down the rills,
And the midges claimed oor blid, and brought despair.

Dae ye mind how in the mirk, before yon hellish storm,
Where the "Seven Men of Moidart" are at hand,
There once the "Prince of Scotland", set on his fateful road,
Like we who with each year, by fate must stand.

Dae ye mind Dalelia on Loch Shiel, "The meadow by the shore"
Where the simmer sun brought lightness tae oor heart,
There we dipped oor paddles bravely, in the waters crystal clear,
And the love we have together was oor part.

Dae ye mind how many years ago, how first we met and loved,
The laughter, tears, the sunshine and the rain,
There's been much we've shared together and many sights we've seen,
We'll go back tae Ardnamurchan again and yet again.

Alfred Gibb,
Atherton, Manchester.

140

God bless your Gracious Majesty,
In this year of Silver Jubilee;
For four and twenty years you've reigned,
And kept the British peoples free;
Free from the bends and shackles,
Of Nations who live in fear,
Great Britain thanks you, Queen Elizabeth,
With a great resounding cheer.

No blight of war has cast its shadow,
On your long and glorious reign;
Despite the internal differences
That brought loss, and grief, and pain,
May your peoples in the British Isles,
And The Commonwealth, over the sea,
Rejoice with you and your family,
In this year of Silver Jubilee.

In moral, spiritual, and family life,
The example you have shown the Nation;
Must fill the hearts of all your subjects,
With respect, devotion, and admiration,
In politics, industry, and religion,
Despite the various views of many factions;
You have always stood both firm and fair,
To guide Great Britain by your actions.

Your peoples in Britain and The Commonwealth,
Both here and over the sea,
Together with you, will pray that peace,
Shall reign and all differences flee,
God Bless your Royal Husband,
The Royal Princess, and Royal Princes Three,
May this year bring greatest happiness to all,
In this your Silver Jubilee.

Thomas D. Gibson,
Blackhall, Edinburgh.

TIME TRAVELLING

I like to travel through time,
It's no crime.
It really gives me pleasure
To see the Kings treasure.
I must have seen it all
The rich, the poor.
The giants who really aren't tall.
To travel through space
And leave no trace.
I can go where I like
Visit every sight.
But where will it all end
No-one seems to know,
What will God send
When there are no more seeds to sow.

Mr. George H. Gill,
Livingston, West Lothian.

SUFFOLK HARVEST

Golden squares
Of ripe corn tassels
Nudged together
By Suffolks fair lanes.
Rustling in time
To unseen conductor
Led by the hand
Of Summers breeze.
Nodding their heads
Changing direction
Patterns woven
In shadowy waves.
Dipping and stretching
In symphonic motion
Stilled in finale
By combine machine.

Jean Gill,
Felixstowe, Suffolk.

142

BACK IN OLD SCOTLAND

Back in old Scotland
Is the heather still growing
On the hills and in the valleys
of bonnie Glenshie?
Back in old Scotland
Are the waters still flowing
From the streams in the mountains
Then down to the sea?
Do they still sing and dance
On Stornoway Pier
While they wait for the ferry
From Kyle to draw near?
Are sweethearts still roaming
The Banks of Loch Lomond?
Oh its back in old Scotland
I'm longing to be
Yes its back in old Scotland
I'm longing to be.

Eddie Gillanders
Aberdeen.

A BIRD SINGS ALONE

On this bleak and freezing morning,
Tiniest bird to me is calling
From windswept branch of tree stripped bare,
Near my beech hedge, for breakfast fare.

Can one neglect this simple plead?
Dare I eat well and then not heed
The call of this my tiny neighbour,
Whose summer song did court my favour?

To-day a plaintive song I hear,
Almost a sadness, almost a tear;
As if winter might put an end
To partnership of bird and friend.

This puts me in nostalgic mind
Of palmier days when life was kind.
This little bird with endless song
Makes life worthwhile – takes me along.

A. R. Gilmore.
Newcastle upon Tyne,
Northumberland.

PARENTHOOD

Bent o'er our child in silent prayer,
A golden halo is her hair.
She folds his sweetness to her heart,
But in her eyes the tears still smart.
That I put there.
Help me, Oh Lord, to understand,
That in this love I had a hand,
That petty jealousy and strife,
Are no part of this small, new life.
She has not left the care of me,
For all her life is loving Thee,
And through Thee, us – the child – the man,
All part of one Eternal Plan.
Forgive me, Lord, it is enough,
That she is made of Angels' stuff
I cannot see through Your clear eyes –
I know she's only half my size –
Nor understand the Will Divine,
Her heart is twice as big as mine.

Mrs. Rose Helen Glennie,
Kilmarnock, Ayrshire.

THE DEATH OF JESUS CHRIST

Long ago in Jerusalem,
A man was mocked and scourged and beaten,
Then made to bear a heavy cross,
To the place of a skull,
Which is called Golgotha,
So long ago in Jerusalem,
That's when our Saviour died for us.

We mock Him,
We scourge Him,
We beat Him still,
With our lies,
Our cheating,
Our envy,
Our hate,
The things that make our lives so pointless.
If we could only rest our faith in Him,
Our burdens would be much lighter,
And our sins so far away.

Miss Catherine Glover,
Whitfield, Dundee.

LETTER TO SIR JOHN BETJEMAN

To: Sir John Betjeman,
    The Poet Laureate,
    John Murray Paperbacks,
    London.

The Head Mouse,
Mrs. Y's Pantry,
The Round Church,
Shrewsbury,
New Year's Day, 1977.

Dear Sir John,
You published the Diary of my ancestor great in your "Collected
Poems" 1958. Could you publish again in this Jubilee Year, the
progress made by C. of E's here?

There are lots of mice now and plenty of Staff, curates in cassocks,
hassocks and chaff.

On November 1st, *ALL SAINTS*, great or small, large bowls of
porridge are eaten by all,

Mime, music and dancing in Church today, masses of food and
little to pay –

Friendship, fellowship, freedom and fun, priests and people mix
as they come.

My forbear *warned* of the faithless rat, just coming to see what we
were at!

Of two field mice who had no desire to be baptized, invading the
choir!

"Out with the tinsel and the tree decoration" the Vicar *warned* in
his Oration!

"*In* with the Crib, the Babe on the floor, Mary his Mother, cattle
and straw.

For Midnight Mass every seat was taken – some of those seats so
long forsaken.

Next comes Easter, then Whitsun and in the "fall", a fill-up for
Harvest Festival.

Yes, a fill-up in September's fall, but August brought no food at
all!

I heard them say there was a *drought*, so to the flower Dingle we
crept out.

The pool we found was dried mud flat, above, our home, "Noah's
Ark" – Mount Ararat!

Biscuits and bread were thrown our way, then dawned the Shrewsbury Flower Show Day!

Pinky-mauve manna of candyfloss, the Tamarisk's sticky and
honeyed mass,

Pear drops, peaches and pomegranites, lilies, dahlias and
amaryllis –

This was indeed a "Fertile Crescent" – very plentiful and very
pleasant!

But from matters Clerical I have digressed, and back to "The
Round" we must progress.
Here, men use "YOU" and "WE" books, green quite nice, but
black "THOU" ones please for lowly mice.
"Give us today our daily bread", oh dear! I've nibbled the book
instead.
"Forgive us our sins as we forgive", it is so hard, a *rat* who says
there is no God!
Yes, the road is hard for mice and men, a little progress made just
now and then.
Yet, please Sir John do make it clear to our dear Queen in her
Jubilee Year,
That we'll go on trying and by God's grace, we will "make it good"
in this lovely place.
Your obedient servant.

MICHAEL

Mrs. Margaret Goff,
Shrewsbury.

THE SHIRE HORSE

The shire once did tend the land,
The shire, the plough and helping hand.
The shire tall, regal and grand,
No more do they till the land.
Gone now has the shire, plough and helping hand.

Mr. Irving Gold,
Sheffield, Yorkshire.

THE WHITE STAG

The Red Deer roam the mountains
On Arran's island fair,
There also was a legend
That a white stag wandered there.

The Duchess of Montrose had died,
And in that very year,
This strange beast on the hills was born,
Just then he did appear.

The spirit of the Duchess
The stag was said to be,
He roamed alone, and kept aloof,
Elusive, wild and free.

Now thirteen years had all gone by
The beast was growing old;
He frequented Lochranza,
Hunger had made him bold.

The villagers kindly gave him food
Repeatedly he came back
Until fear grew if turned away
Starving, he would attack.

From Lady Jean the order came,
To shoot the aged deer,
The keeper killed him with a shot
In a cottage garden there.

The stag is gone! – but tales live on.
The legend will not die;
And generations yet to come,
Will learn it by-and-by.

Mrs. May Gorrie,
Brodick, Arran.

THE LONELY MAN

Weak of limb, short of breath,
Waiting only till the death.
Forgetful mind, muddled brain,
Re-living all the past again.
Sat the old man in his chair,
Fleeting glimpses of despair.
Caring not too much for time,
Life had no reason or no rhyme.
There came a knock upon the door,
He slowly rose and crossed the floor.
"Please wait" he breathed with movements slow,
"I won't be long, so please don't go."
He opened up the front door wide,
And three little children stepped inside.
He wondered why they'd come to call,
But in their arms there lay quite small.
A tiny kitten wet and forlorn,
He felt a part of him ré-born.
"We've brought him back to you" they said,
And with those words away they sped.
He took the tiny mite inside,
Dried and stroked him with such pride.
He'd never owned a cat before,
And this one comes to his front door.
He shared his soup and drop of milk,
And soon its coat was just like silk.
Inseparable they came to be,
Shared many a dinner and a tea.
Despair and loneliness he'd had before,
Went like magic when he'd opened the door.

Marjorie Evelyn Gould,
Liverpool.

BEAUTY

Say it in a poem, in a story, or a song,
Tell of friendship, hope and love that help the world along.
Paint it in a picture, all the beauty that you see,
The river and the hill, the meadow and the tree.
Compose a piece of music of all the sounds you hear,
The whispering breeze, the buzzing bees, bird calls sweet and clear.
Say it, paint it, play it, with unrestricted zeal,
God in all creation, His beauty will reveal.

Say it when you're speaking, in your voice so clear and sweet,
The cheery word, the friendly smile for all you chance to meet.
Convey it with firm handshake, let friends know that you care,
That you are always willing, your hand and heart to share.
Show it with your patience, your calm amid the storm,
The deed that will encourage, and give hope where hope had gone;
Say it, show it, do it, with generosity,
God will be revealed within the hearts of you and me.

Elsie M. Gowling,
Crieff, Perthshire.

THE GATHERING STORM

The wind begins to rustle through the tall waving trees,
While the clouds travel fast, and set together with ease,
The sun quickly fades behind a thick blackened shroud,
And the water in the lake, reflects a big dense cloud,
Rabbits in the nearby field, burrow fast to a dry rest,
As the birds in the dull sky, make haste to their nest,
Ruffled trees in the meadow, bend, shaking far and near,
While cattle in the green fields, huddle together in fear,
The thunder in the distance, sounds with a threat and roar,
And the lightning in the sky, flashes with ominous terror,
Rain bursting from the heavens, pours down in great haste,
The streets and fields drenched, are soon water and paste,
Folk in the streets clasping their coats, run for shelter,
While the wind blows the rain, and all is helter skelter,
The stormy elements are angry, and spreading their spite,
Rains falling fast, and the wind blows with all its might,
Pretty flowers in the field, swaying and enjoying the show,
The empty river quickly filling, that was thirsty and low,
When all have drank well, the clouds drift and slide away,
The sun shines again, while the wind drops to gently play,
Rabbits leave their holes, and the foxes search for a feed,
And birds fly from the nest, to seek food their young need,
Soon, the blue sky returns, and white clouds quickly form,
We're no longer in fear, or hide from The Gathering Storm.

Charles M. Graham,
Thurstonfield, Carlisle.

Tip high,
Tip low,
Tip stop,
Tip go,
Tip move, tip flow
Tip fast
Tip slow.
Two and two are four,
Tip comes through the door,
Four and four are eight,
To run 'tis now too late.
Hear the school bell ring,
Hear the children sing,
A song comes from their lips
A rhyme about the tips.
Covered,
Smothered,
Now are they
No more to sing, no more to play.
No notice the tip took of our warning
It came just as the day was dawning,
Creeping,
Leaping,
Down came that mound,
Silently it came,
With not a sound.
And even now all is quiet,
By day, and by night.
But if you listen softly,
You can hear children singing
In the evening light.
Tip high,
Tip low,
Tip stop,
Tip go,
Tip takes, never borrows,
Tip snatched away
All our Tomorrows.

Georgina A. Graham,
Swansea, West Glamorgan.

THE TRAMP

His pack is light, his heart is free,
And the journey has no end.
No backward glance will seek a chance,
In lifes ambitious trend.

His wine is from the running stream,
Its crystal drops to spill.
His jewels, are scenes before him spread,
Surveyed from yonder hill.

And then with footsteps weary,
He finds a heather bed.
In slumbers deep, his dreams are sweet,
The night sky overhead.

A ragged figure sleeping, but,
Disdain him not to see.
The gifts of nature are his wealth,
And the road, his destiny.

Mrs. Jessie Graham,
Dunblane, Perthshire.

CRUACHAN

Loch Awe! Loch Awe! Just what ava'
Are ye dain' wi' yer watters?
Ye dam them up
Then pelt them doon
Tae drive yon turbines roon an' roon
Gie electric licht tae every toon
O' ony size that matters.

Not yet content wi' dain' that
Or jist usin' aince yer watters
Ye pump them up
Yon lofty Ben.
It's Cruachan, of course, ye ken.
It is a name that matters.

So when the rain comes drenchin' doon
A splashin' an' pitter-patters
On tree an' bush
On road or toon
We dinna wear a worried froon
But picture turbines whirlin' roon
An' usin' a' yer watters.

Barbara L. Grant,
Glasgow.

151

AN UNTITLED POEM BY COLIN GRANT

As an exile from my homeland my thoughts are ever near
The land that I was born in, the tongue I love to hear,
Although I may be biased, as a Scotsman, hear my cry
As my thoughts I put in writing, of memories gone by.

I can see the hills in Springtime or in their coat of snow,
The rishings of the burns and streams as to the sea they go,
The heather when it's purple all glowing in the heat,
A cosy winter evening with the smell of burning peat.

I journey down a river on a paddler old and grand
And hear the happy singing to the usual shipboard band,
I see the passing "Ladies", a liner or a tug,
The smoke out of their funnels, causing such a "Fug".

I stand upon a lonely hill and view the scene below
The setting of an Autumn sun that leaves a brilliant glow
But across my thoughts there flashes a scene quite up to date
Of Power Stations, Oil Rigs and lots of things I hate.

I long to turn back the clock to things when I was young,
To hear a Scottish Ballad as only it is sung
In Gaelic or in English with a merry Scottish lilt
To hear the bagpipes proudly played by a Scotsman in his kilt.

Colin C. N. Grant,
Finchley, London.

AN UNTITLED POEM BY FIONA J. GRANT

Bold in your beauty
In silent serenity
Peaceful but brave
In honour you stand.

Your limbs, they are bare now
And silent your branches
The breeze ripples through them
But calm, still you stand.

No chirping of sparrow
No warble of songbird
No nest in your great arms
At rest, now you stand.

Asleep now – for Winter
With frost in her fingers
Comes soon to attack
Your honourable stand.

But you shall awake
When Springtime advances
Once more clothed in colour
In beauty you'll stand.

Then warbling songbirds
From nests in your branches
Will proclaim to the wide world
How mighty you stand.

Till round comes the Autumn
To rob your bright foliage
And bold and serene
Once more you will stand.

Fiona J. Grant,
Aberdeen.

HIGHLAND HILLS

Heather bells are blooming on the wild hillside
Evening sun is glowing, shining far and wide,
The small croft on the hillside,
The village in the dell,
These are things of Scotland
We know and love so well.

The Highlands in the Winter,
The Highlands in the Spring,
The Highlands in the Autumn,
All make a man's heart sing
The Highlands are a beauty
Which all folk can behold
The Highlands are a treasure
Worth more than any gold.

Richard Gray,
Glenrothes, Fife.

EMOTION

Why dost thou cry fair lassie, hast thou loved and lost,
Why dost the tears run down thy face, and from thy cheeks are tossed.
Why dost thy sobs wrack thy frame, thine eyes swollen are red,
Thy hair awry, face crumpled up, I've plucked thee from thy bed.
Hush now don't cry I prithee, come into my arms,
Let me wipe thy tears away, once more to see thy charms.
There that's better cuddle in, thy heart near broke in two,
Sleep my bairn nightmares are gone, thy Father watches you.
Hush now, sleep my little dove, once more thy face serene,
Nestle in like wee small bird, dream a sweeter dream.

Mr. Thomas Gray,
Bishop Auckland, Co. Durham.

SHADOWS

Tall grows the grass, where once we fought,
The misty hill looks down on field below.
We who are gone, do we count for naught,
To you or you, as your children grow.

Lush grow the meadows, where once we crept,
Silent, like shadows, with blackened face.
Green grow the trees, where once they wept,
Yesterday was it, a different world, or different place.

Soft flows the stream, where once we crossed,
With silent prayer, and quickened breath.
Was it here, this lovely place, where we were lost.
And was it here, or there, that we saw Death.

Bright shines the sunlight, where once it was dark.
For our hope, to our faith, we cried.
MIST . . . Was that our voices . . . HARK!
It was here, we lived, we fought, and died.

Gone now the scene, light grows dim,
And yet, in this quiet place of dreams,
Are shadows, "Rusty", "Chalky", "Spike", and "Slim"
Nothing happened here . . . or so it seems.

Mr. F. E. Greenwood,
Manchester.

154

IONA

They wait, perched on the rocks, gazing towards Iona.
Chattering bird-like, scattered like bright confetti
Down to the lapping water, the rickety jetty.
The ferry chugs, The light, salt, scented air of the Isles,
The shining air, touches the waiting ones
(Their jewel ahead, serene and opalescent).
The ferry carries another jostle of souls,
The pilgrims sail to Iona, Columba's island.

To Iona, over the shining sea, aquamarine and sapphire
And by the boat's edge clear, transparent jade;
White sand, glassed green, shell-scattered, tentacle-veined, with
   seaweed shadows waving.

To Iona, to the calm, grey Abbey
With the cornfield close to the sturdy walls,
Misty gold, amethyst rocks and shadows – still, still as the held breath
   of September
Or the deep-buried dust, the white dust of Duncan.

To the peace, the peace enwrapped in the sacred Island,
Deep, deep as the quiet earth's dreaming eternity's womb cradles the
   lost vision . . .
Columba's dawn – a pale gleam on the sea – his hill revealed, the cool
   air stirring.
Columba's dawn on Iona – a bird singing.

To the Island, haloed in shining mist
Dazzling the burning eyes of dying kings,
This is the shimmering path the saints have followed,
Launching in faith their fragile coracles, tossing on curdling waves to
   reach Iona.
The chanted prayers swell and sink with the sea.
The gulls' cry pierces the sun's shroud,
The crown falls – only the earth remains,
Blessed, enfolding earth of the Holy Island.

Pamela Griffin,
Bucklebury, Berkshire.

A POEM FOR CHILDREN AT CHRISTMAS

Little children softly say
Thank you God for "Christmas Day"
For the parties and the toys
Make us happy girls and boys

But so very long ago
When all the earth was white with snow
Then a tiny Baby small
"Jesus" came to save us all

And he showed us how to live
To love each other and to give
So let us do our very best
And Jesus Christ will do the rest.

Joan Mary Greaves,
Doncaster, S. Yorks.

DAWN

A thin grey mist o'er spreads the sky,
The mountain peaks are lost to sight,
Low in the East a faint red tinge
Comes to hasten the flying night.

Slowly at first the colour spreads,
Shedding o'er all a softening glow,
Chasing away the mists above,
Telling of dawn in the world below.

Now in the East a deeper hue,
The peaks flush red in the crimson ray,
The birds burst forth in joyous song,
The rising sun proclaims the day.

Margaret J. Haig,
Bangor, Co. Down.

EMPTY THINGS

The park is empty
The birds cannot sing
Boats are moored-up
Shored-up
Hollowed-up until spring
A silent lover rests
Crying for the autumn leaves that fall
To the nip of the chill wind fingers
Returning home from work
To watch the sun go down
Over
Towers of concrete
The play-grounds limp
Children's screams
Are the hollows of dreams
No Kings and Queens
White chargers
For Knights nights
Spent
Gone forever
Alone the lover.

Donald Hale,
Cheltenham, Gloucesters.

EMBRYO

Curled up in a watery nest,
Little mermaid there you rest.
Can you hear my big heart beat,
As you kick your tiny feet.
Really do you feel my joy,
Are you girl or are you boy?
It seems now you rule my life,
Two are one there is no strife.
Untiring little embryo,
The time has come for you to grow.
Will you be born with certain grace,
With a smile upon your face.
The world is yours upon this day,
Don't give the gift of life away.

Mrs. R. Hall,
Guildford, Surrey.

MY DAD'S BEER

My Dad tried to make some beer,
And the result I dread and fear,
Instead of sugar he put in salt,
And put in a corndolly instead of malt.
Instead of yeast he put in dough,
And the next thing Ho, Ho, Ho,
Instead of putting in water,
He through in his eldest daughter!
My Mum told him never,
Never to make beer again,
Not now, not ever, never again!

Miss Karen Hallmark,
Bolton, Lancashire.

WHERE IS THE BROTHERHOOD OF MAN?

The world's gone sour,
With abuse of power,
And Man is reaching for the stars;
With boastful error,
He launches terror,
And has not learnt from all the wars.

Whilst folks are starving,
Tyrants are carving
With bombs their claim to other lands.
Armageddon approaches,
But, deaf to reproaches,
They take over states with greedy hands.

Permissiveness, disorder,
Make mock of law and order,
While theorists say that we must spare the rod.
Religion is derided,
By those who are divided,
In ignorance of the Fatherhood of God.

Blood-stained flags are flying
And freedom is dying,
Forgotten is the Golden Master Plan!
Where is the reason,
Where is the hope
Where is the Brotherhood of Man?

Mona Hamlet,
Blackpool.

MUSIC

The music of the earth has always been,
Since first the Master-mind, with mighty hand,
Set her in motion, axially revolving,
In her appointed place.

No other ears might then have recognised
This complementary note in the music of the spheres,
As, like an ever-spinning top, the latest-born of all creation
Added her voice to the universal harmony.

Silence there never was, before Man came
With his attendant noise.
For, from the first, the unpolluted waters
Sang with bliss to wash the naked shores.

Then came the storms. What music is like rain,
Rolling peals of thunder their sonorous organs playing,
Or the spontaneous joy of those young streamlets,
Carolling along their paths to the enticing seas?

The sun engendered life, and soon the trees
Made dirge-like moan, in Winter's icy grip.
But when sweet summer came, they sang in unison,
Leafy susurrations of pure happiness.

For now they housed the birds, whose diversity of hymns
Resounded in compulsive praise of the Cosmic Plan,
And so became Man's true, instinctive guide
To a whole new world of music.

By inventive skill he learned to imitate their songs
With voice and instruments, ingeniously contrived,
Until the cornucopia of sound
Quite overflows with soul-enchanting minstrelsy.

Mr. L. S. Harrison,
Radburne, Derby.

THE VIENNA WOODS

One Viennese hour –
Stark jewels of a city
Seen from a height, and
With my imagination
A silent symphony

From old baroque churches,
Soaring dark spires and buildings
Around waves of time less movement
In a ribbon of river,
Threading, dividing
And dancing with light
Cold alpine winds blow
As I gaze at the sight –
Lifting thoughts upward
Into the night.

Mrs. Suzanne Harvey,
Sheffield, Yorkshire.

DRESSING THE WELL

Stone Age
Our tools are of stone, and we're often afraid,
our world's full of danger and cold.
But today we caught meat, we've shelter and fire,
the joy of the day spreads from young to the old.
But from our precious meat we cut the best slice
To give to the water god his sacrifice.

Druids
Men of mystery, lone priests of the green woods,
Our past's lost and clouded in years.
Our knowledge surpasses all lesser of men,
and we can trade best on their ignorant fears.
But we bless the streams, with green leaves and flowers,
So the gift of water will always be ours.

Today
The twentieth century's now growing old,
and we know all there is to tell,
Yet still each year we fetch flowers and green leaves,
and make a sweet place of our well.
And as through the village the procession wends,
We thank the same God for the water He sends.

Mary Hatton,
Stanmore, Middlesex.

A SMALL BIRDS SONG

Oh! bird what vigor in your tune,
You fill the air with song;
Such lusty note from one so small,
Compares with mighty throng.

Do you, to your loved one sing,
Or to rival challenge throw;
Perhaps you sing to thank the Lord,
For the place where nestlings grow?

What err the reason of your acclaim,
You shame a wretch like me;
Who, until you warbled loud,
No joy could see.

Now your joy with me shared,
Much lighter seems my load;
A blith tune bubbles to my lips,
As I step off down the road.

With such as this, man is blessed,
A song when life is drear;
When sadness seems to overwhelm,
Wild songster comes to cheer.

The weary miles made shorter thus,
Once uphill, now near flat;
God has made this a pleasant place,
Him praise, with joy, for that.

James Hay,
Dundee, Angus.

NO MANS LAND

What punishment we mere mortals suffered,
Blundering wildly in the trenches,
We walk mechanically along to death,
For there, a Nazi stands, with rifle poised,
He fires, and another body lines the ditch,
The next man walks on for there is no time to be sentimental,
For this is War.

The smell is disgusting.
Men, once eager to fight for King and country,
Have been reduced to shreds.
They scream, but their blood adds inches to the mud.
All around the shells whine.
Youths lament at lost souls but they carry on,
For this is war.

Oh why can't somebody end this?
The wounded men, lying bloody and paralysed,
Scream, for want of proper treatment.
One man lies delirious,
Others have gone insane,
Deaths are numerous but on them pity cannot be spared,
For this is War.

I fear now that I too, shall die,
For gas is becoming frequent,
And I am getting slower.
I fear too that I am delirious,
"Lizzie, Lizzie where are you Lizzie?"
"Sir, have you seen my Lizzie?"
And all is still, silent, deserted, but strangely peaceful,
For now, I'm in heaven.

Jennifer Hay (Aged 11),
Nairn, Scotland.

CHAMELEON

The quality of life, like wine,
It comes in many grades.
To lift you up to heaven,
Or sink you deep as hades.
Its symptoms oft are fleeting,
Like the rainbow in the sky.
The sudden showers, the burning sun,
The tears, the laughter and the fun.
It's all a part of lifes great game,
For rich and poor, it's just the same.
For love has many meanings,
And twice as many grades.
The only one which matters,
Is the one which never fades.

Mr. Mervyn Henderson,
Port Glasgow, Renfrewshire.

THE WEE BLUE CERD

Thae traivel cerds is just the thing, tae let us get aroon,
So oan the buses an the trains, they sure are a boon,
We wake up in the mornin, an we spring right oot o' bed,
Fur that wee cerd thats in oor purse, maks us awfy gled.

Gaff fur the bus we run lik stoor, tae huv a day in Toon,
There we huv a cup o' tea, an a walk awe roon,
We like tae wander roon the shopes, no that we've much tae spend,
But its nice tae see the fancy claes, wae the modern trend.

The sights ye see in thae big stores, the kind o' folk ye meet,
How they venture intae Toon, really his me beat,
Tae know if they are man or wife, that ye canny tell,
The men huv long hair doon their back, an think that they look swell.

Wae ear-rings, beads, an bracelets, shoes wae heels sae high,
How lassies waant a man lik that, ah often wonder why,
Their wives they wear the troosers, and at his side she'll trot,
Her troosers burstin it the seams, nae slim line she has got.

If ye canny beat them join them, is whit they often say,
A widny like tae look lik that, naw, naw, al stye this way,
Their wee bit weans must wonder, which waan o' them is Dad,
They'll likely think it is the waan, thats in the troosers clad.

If oor grannies could come back agane, they sure wid get a fright,
They'd think that we hid awe gone mad, if they seen such a sight,
Waan thing aboot oor grannies, they sure knew how tae dress,
Tae know if they were man or wife, ye didny need tae guess.

Its been an awfy winter, we've been frozen tae the bone,
'Tween froast an snaw an slippy roads, nae wunner that we moan,
Ye see oor blood is awfy thin, we canny staun the caul,
When the waarmer days are here agane, that'll suit us all.

So roll oan Spring an Summer, an we will no be slow,
In steppin oan thae buses, tae the seaside we will go,
We'll surely get a tan this year, the forecast is guid we've heard,
We're no fur sittin in the hoose, thanks tae "the wee blue cerd".

Annie Hendry,
Eaglesham, Glasgow.

THOUGHTS ON MY FATHER

When just a boy and still at school,
Rheumatic Fever made me ill,
And through the night, I'd wake and cry,
'Daddy turn me please."
His answer always was the same,
"Alright Son I will,"
I will ever look back with a thankful heart,
For Memories like these.

Each morning he drew the curtain,
Not to view the dawn,
But to see if any daisies had dared,
Flower on his lawn,
The only enemies he had were the flowers,
That "Rabbie Burns" loved so,
When among his grass and roses,
They did decide to grow.

He always blithely left the house,
To start his work at eight,
If he wasn't there by seven
He considered he was late,
A rose in his skippet bunnet,
String tied below his knees,
His piece box in his pocket,
I will always remember these.

The gentry on the golf course, and
The tinker in the lane,
Ah aye mornin, grand day,
They all got the same acclaim,
"You'll no be as guid as yer faither,"
I didn't need to be told
For after they made my father
They threw away the mould.

He walked so gently through this world,
He trod on no-ones toe,
And was treated well with due respect,
Where ever he did go,
He very rarely went to Church,
But a truer Christian I've never seen,
Because he simply did not care
If you wore blue or green.

He never lost his temper,
His nature it was placid,
And the way that he was put upon
It sometimes made me livid,
Then he would turn and stare at me
To see if my mouth was shut,
And then he'd start to dress me down,
In his strongest words "God's Truth" tut tut.

When lying in my hospital bed,
Bedecked with tubes, and feeling in another land,
His gentle voice would pierce this thought,
With his "Aye Jim youre looking grand,"
Tell me please what could I say
I simply had to smile,
Then he would sit down, put his hand on me
And the pain would ease for a while.

His pocket watch he treasured,
They had been together so long,
When Big Ben's bell pealed six o'clock,
With it's truly massive gong,
And my Dad's watch was a minute past
He knew the one that was wrong,
These memories I'll keep and to me
They will always belong.

He couldn't take it with him,
So it has come to me,
And I will always treasure it,
Nearly as much as he.
It doesn't have a calendar or the
Zodiac sign of your birth,
But it always will be cherished
For I know it's proper worth.

I love my family dearly and I know
I have their love,
When people ask "Would you do it again"
I say "Yes as sure as God's above"
My Wife's hard work and kindly ministrations,
Have brought me through much pain
Though I can't see for the life of me
Just what she has to gain.
When I've to leave this painful shell
I pray my family don't grieve
Because I know my Dad he will be there
And He'll have a hand on my sleeve.

You may say I'm laying aghost you may
Say I'm playing a part
Though sometimes he may be out of my head
He'll never be out of my heart
You may say I am being presumptious
You may say I'm just being quaint
But I'm sure no trace of doubt
All my life I have known a saint.

James Middleton Henry,
Saltcoats, Ayrshire.

A SHEPHERD'S LOVE

What thoughts lie behind those sad brown, faithful eyes
Which now alas, have closed for their eternal rest?
It seems but yesterday, no larger than a soft dark ball of wool,
You tumbled, fought and played with boundless energy,
No different from a child in first warm years of happy carefree youth.

Maturity came early to your small, strong willed frame,
So eager for the work of each new day.
It mattered not the season's weather, warm or cold;
You raced away across those friendly hills, to answer my poor whistle
As is it was the clear command, a sergeant major rifled to a clockwork
    squad.

Even the sheep, mindless creatures that they are
Appeared to understand your firm but gentle will
And I suspect that on those countless times when,
At a Trial's end, we stood together to receive the accolade,
It was well nigh imppossible to tell, which was the proudest, you or I

And when the limbs grew tired, too old for outside toil,
Your joyous bark of welcome was such music to my ears,
As I returned each evening from the hills around our croft.
Our nights were spent in close companionship before the homely fire,
You listening to my hopes and fears, success and failure of our simple
    life.

I place this stone with ever loving hands
Upon this, first resting place of early morning sun
When rising from the grasp of yonder soft green hills.
This favourite sacred spot, a resting place where you will always be.
Lie peacefully old friend. Your memory is ever in my heart.

Colin E. Herriman,
Ashtead, Surrey.

THE QUEEN OF THE SEAS

A hundred thousand horsepower
A hundred thousand and more
From the dawn on the South horizon
With her classic prow to the fore
Comes the Queen of the race of seamen
Came the Queen of the British fleet
And the hearts of the British soldiers
Start to beat with a faster beat.

Southward wallows the convoy
With the African shore to the lee
And Northwards leaps the Queen ship
North to the land of the free
Ten thousand men of British breed
She carries regally
Proud eyes of a Scottish soldier
See the skills of heredity.

On she drives from the far horizon
Serene, unencumbered, unspent
A host of eyes upon her Grace
This, the Queen of environment
O favoured one of the oceans
Bathed in milk by Neptune's decree
Wilt thou even deign to notice us
To acknowledge such as we.

She is seen in the breathless silence
From her course just a moment to fade
And with the grace of an elegant lady
She bestowed us her accolade
From the depths of unknown emotion
From the heart of each man and boy
Rose the wave of a vast acclamation
Like a paean of holy joy.

Speed on then with our devotion
God preserve you in Liberty
You remembered the secret between us
Of our common nativity
A hundred thousand horsepower
Unfettered and not as we
Speed on to the embattled Island
With the souls of the sons of the free.

John Urquhart Heron,
Helensburgh, Dunbartonshire.

DEFINITELY THERE IS A PATTERN

I look at the bluetits somersaulting without care
I look at the sparrows ribboning the air
I look and I wonder, at the strength of their candour
Oh misery me with all my work and no play
How I would like to change places and go far away.

I look at the squirrels, so playful a streak
I look at the rabbits, inquisitive and meek
I shake with a feeling and an urge to presume,
A little brown striated warbler with a gorgeous green plume.

I look at a hare, having no secret affair
Manners perfect, swanking with air
Sitting and straddling by a babbling green brook,
I sit and I wonder
Opening and closing are vivid blue wings
Colours so beautiful, I feel I should sing
So I try to imagine What could have Imagined such things.

There above me was moored a cloud, a separating trail of shirred white
    vapour
Then through the lilac air enchantingly, came an exceptionally large
    and throbbing hum,
all along the low bushes bees were having fun
Chimed with a heart of ardour, breaks out a linnet's call, gaily reciting
    each small syllable
it controls, winging through the air, penetrating for its pair, its trite
    tethered soul implores
Plus a sonnet of small cries, ever reaching upwards ever upwards,
    moving like a sigh
So many sounds without our sphere, expounding carefully, impressing
    on our minds, still there
is a duty, yet albeit to fulfil

Plainly are heard, when the shifting mind explores, beyond our senses,
    beyond our toil, here
it is, that there appears, a stretch of land, another shore.
The qualms of a nation are waging wars, in shades of black, a raging
    sore, no fearless track
will lead us back, the temple of our wrath grows cold as we enroll our
    peerless hearts, to
enslave our ego parts, with eager charts we ford the storms, we dream
    to dust each foreign
thumb, we incarcerate each lacerating thorn, if we fail we are forlorn
Now is born a jewelled host, a pleasing courage tape for us to follow,
    a yearning to inhabit each

But a braided blotch of gasping, rasping whispers, perforates, etching
   out and breathing, new
notches in our minds, an uninspiring sallow colour, follows us behind,
   clutching furiously,
cutting deep, drawn to sever, a painful thrust, a blemishing stain, a
   horrid sorrow.

Springing into view come I to a crimson lake, unfolding roses already
   laminating, kindling in
the sun, persistingly executively, loafing advertently, are running small
   white butterflies,
Pacing across this crimson park, parsing, clausing, drifting, entombed
   in a saffron envelope,
their thoughts in kind are sped in mind, to deliver anonymously, a
   contemplative autonomy
slants and animals seemingly alike, mellifluously harmoned, ex-
   hibiting insight, an impressive,
incessant, imbued, activity, an evergreen exhortation from some
   excellent obedience, a small
sign perhaps, pertaining, perhaps, to an Evergreen, Effrolene, Ener-
   vating, Expanding, Exhalation.

Miss Barbara Hewitt,
Edinburgh.

THE CAPTIVE MUSIC

"Listen," they say,
"Is there not magic
In the violin's sighing strings?
In flute's clear piping,
Harp's cascade, and in the mellow
Deep romantic notes of the cello?"

"And is there not grandeur
In an organ's surging swell?
In Cathedral choirs,
The clash of percussion and brass,
And in bagpipes, wailing over Highland grass?"

"Yes," I reply,
"But is there not magic too
In the crystal rippling of a mountain stream?
In blackbird's song,
Tall meadow grasses whispering in the breeze
And in the lulling, lazy humming of the bees?"

"And is there not grandeur
In thunder rolling among mountains?
In crashing hail,
The west wind roaring loudly through the trees,
And in the wild raging of the stormy seas?"

"For is not music captive in all sound?
Captive, since that first boy blew upon a reed,
In all the instruments devised by man?
Captive, since the first breeze blew across the earth,
In all the instruments produced by nature?
Captive alike in song and laughter surely music dwells.
And sometimes, when the world is very still,
Listen! Is there not music even in silence?"

Margaret Heywood,
Bournemouth, Dorset.

PRESS ON

Can you see yonder tiny flame aglowing
Beyond the sombre distance dark and bare?
Say, can you see it growing, ever growing
To lead you from the cavern of despair?

Then wherefore stand you meekly hesitating?
Take up your load and struggle ever on,
Believing that the long, dark night of waiting
Must end before the brightness of the dawn.

For every good and worthwhile undertaking
Still meets with opposition from the mass;
Press onward though your heart be almost breaking . . .
In time they'll step aside to let you pass.

Today the mass unthinkingly impedes you;
Tomorrow they'll applaud you all the more.
Press on and follow where the glimmer leads you . . .
And may the goal be all you're hoping for!

Alexander Hinds,
Mauchline, Ayrshire.

GOD BLESS 'EM ALL
(*A tribute to the U.S.A. upon its Bicentennial*)

God Bless America, bless 'em all,
Andrew Carnegie, and his Hall,
John Paul Jones and John Wayne . . .
Boston, Detroit, Chicago, Maine,
King Kong, and Fay Wray,
Chinatown, Harlem, Independence Day,
Apple Pie, and Hershey Bars,
The mighty Boeings and Plymouth cars,
Donald Duck and Mickey Mouse . . .
The Apollo Theatre, White House . . .
Davy Crockett and Elvis "P",
Hugh Hefner, Robert E. Lee;
Judy Garland and Marilyn Monroe,
Tallahassee . . . Idaho,
Jim Bowie and J.F.K.,
Gene Kelly . . . Doris Day.
For Martin-Luther-King, a silent prayer,
For he taught us all to love and care;
Count Basie and his band . . .
The Yankee Stadium, Disneyland.
San Francisco and L.A.,
Thanksgiving . . . time to stop, and pray;
The Empire State and Capitol Tower,
General McArthur and Eisenhower,
With Daughters fair, and Sons so tall . . .
GOD BLESS . . . America . . . BLESS 'em all!

Iain Hines,
Feltham, Middlesex.

IGNORANCE IS BLISS

Three children: one life,
A life of hardship.
A life of decay,
A slum child's life.
Or is it ?
Perhaps it's better to be ignorant
Of the other man's life,
The life of high schools, taxes, child-stress,
These three children,
With dirty faces,
Dirty knees, hand-me-downs,

They are unaware of these things.
They don't have leather shoes,
Or modern new clothes,
Nor do they have a lovely house to live in . . .
They have one thing . . .
Happiness,
Around them stand the decrepit
Houses, the begrimed panes and windows,
Crumbling bricks, but . . .
The three children are ignorant of this.
They're happy in their own world,
A slum child's world.

Miss Diane Hitches,
Sheldon, Birmingham.

BOUQUET AND BLOSSOMS
(He met her at the Singer Store, and that indeed was that . . .)

Janny and Michael
I wish you success –
Wonderful cycle
Of rare happiness –

Fortune the bringer
Of ev'rything fine
Song of a Singer
(A special new line) –

Lockstitch and bobbins
With magic of old
Rosy red robins
And threads of pure gold . . .

Sunsilk and clippers
No longer to roam,
Firesides and slippers . . .
And music . . . of Home . . .!

. . . Congratulations, Janny,
        and the best to you both . . .
1977

Mr. W. Hobbs,
West Ealing, London.

172

MEMORY

Life, on its urgent journey, leaves
Behind the blissful drama of the past,
And on the plains of despair the
Light of memory is cast.
Within the realms of tomorrow lie the
Laughter and the tear, which makes the
Hour and the day of the bygone year
Take hopes and dreams, make them your
Aim, for future to weave and touch
The heart with memory again.

Barry R. Hodges,
Sheffield, Yorkshire.

CHRISTMAS ROBIN

I can't see you in the darkness,
But I know you're in that tree,
Waiting for the usual titbit,
Then your thanks – a song for me.

Friendly bird, endearing Robin,
Nightingale ne'er sang so sweet –
What would Christmas be without you,
With red waistcoat trim and neat?

Long ago in Bethlehem stable,
Heeding not the risk of harm,
You fanned the brazier's dying embers,
To keep the infant Jesus warm.

Legend says the flame so scorched you,
That since then your breast stayed red,
On Christmas morn I'll bring, not breadcrumbs,
But some Christmas cake instead.

Mrs. Mary Hogg,
Aberdeen.

VISION

No tears would come – these might have brought relief,
No sleep to soothe the pangs of bitter grief.
My mind was dark – dark as the blackest night,
Filled with anxiety for the plight.
Of one young wanderer, still so dear,
Then suddenly I knew Our Lord was near.
Close by my side,
In pity he looked down and though no word he spoke,
My chain of anxious thought he broke.
His presence brought new hope and solace deep,
Lulling me into calm and gentle sleep.

Mrs. Jean Holden,
Edinburgh.

THEORY OF SCIENCE

Art created man
Created art,
Science intervened like a festering wart,
Science was the servant of art
The master,
But now the reverse
. . . What a disaster.

Science has taken the charm out of life,
Put back the bomb
Confusion and strife,
But that doesn't matter
. . . Everything's clean
And for anything that's not there's a machine.

The scientists developed precision and sanitary,
But . . . not thinking
Forgot man's sanity,
Now man's mad
Through loss of his style
But the computer knows it's down in a file.

Exactness produced pollution
. . . The pill,
Also the "H" bomb
. . . Ready to kill,
To see why science is in such a mess
Look at the scientist in precise thoughtlessness.

Mr. Christopher J. Holliday,
Bradford, Yorkshire.

ALLEGORY FOR A POET

Into a mineral man old fires have forged him
To brood beyond the birth of rivers,
Heron aloof and tall; an outcrop glooming
Over fields of sunward thrusting grain.

King upon crag, so fast in isolation
That young badgers foot his turf like lambs,
Under a burn of sun by the brown tarn
He watches the waggons rollick home.

He has rejected exaltations of lamplight
Round rooms blithe with children.
The lewd sallies of Harvest Supper
Appraisals under market crosses.

Only to hill-bred winds which veer through seasons
South unto North inclines his summit,
To absorb their one cadence
Into a rare music.

Whenever the valley windows kindle and see,
And tractors snarl against the dog-waking morning,
His sea-grey stone looms over sure fields
Warm in the cloak of the winds charities.

Stuart Hoskins,
Bristol.

ONE WAY TICKET

The steeple clock is striking six,
The people start to wake,
Mrs. Smith to feed her chicks,
Mrs. Brown her bread to bake.
Jim and Joe go off to town,
Their wives go back to bed.
Yet in the street but farther down
An old man's lying dead.

He must have died while he still slept,
Though none would hear his call,
No loving ones a vigil kept
He had no friends at all.

He lived alone and made no fuss
So no one seemed to care,
He never bothered any of us
Although his house was bare.

Mrs. Smith said, "I never thought,"
Mrs. Brown, "I wish I'd known,"
Jim and Joe some flowers bought
For the man who died alone.
If only we would look around
Then others we might see,
One day the one that's found
Might just be you . . . or me.

Mrs. Lillian Howe,
Hartlepool.

A LITTLE STRANGER

A stranger came into my garden
On a lovely summer's day.
A hedgehog, all prickly
Scurried on its way.

To the shelter of the flowering hedge
Near where the badgers play.
But the angry Blackbird
Cried: Go away Go away.

The seagulls circling overhead
Dived to the loch nearby,
Among the little ducklings
Fishing for the fry.

The dogs they came asniffing,
Pounced on a busy mole.
But the little stranger hedgehog
Had found a warm snug hole.

Mary Hudson,
Garelochhead, Dunbartonshire.

OLD LADY

I'm sitting in my armchair,
At last the chores are done,
Now the night is falling,
Soon the dark will come,
Thinking of today,
It quickly becomes a dream,
All too soon the days pass by,
Much quicker than they seem.

Listening in my solitude,
To cars that hurry by,
Thinking to myself . . . how soon,
Precious moments fly,
Times when we were together,
No time for thinking then,
How I wish with all my heart,
Those times were here again.

I took for granted company,
There were lots of things to do,
I took for granted everything,
Even my dear one you,
Now I sit here all alone,
Waiting for night to fall,
Longing here deep in my heart,
To hear my darling call.

I'm just a little old lady,
That's what the neighbours say,
Alone sadly forgotten,
Well I have had my day,
Now they enjoy their happiness,
Company and sweet content,
Yet one day they could sit lonely like me,
And wonder just where time went.

Joyce Hudspith,
Stanley, Co. Durham.

ON THE TRAIL OF THE BUFFALO

I am following the buffalo.
His trail leads across
Plains, alive with my dead.
I see ahead
A mound wherein lies
A warrior now mourned
By the echoing death cries
Still blowing over these plains
Now left, bereft
Of buffalo.

I am following the buffalo.
His trail leads to a strange,
Tall and mysterious place
Where every face
Is blanched by the stifling air
Pressing against me everywhere.
As I run, my naked feet feel the pain,
I must escape, to touch the earth again
Now hidden, forbidden
Beneath this false floor.

I am following the buffalo.
Riding across the open plains,
Searching through the concrete maze,
In a daze
Knowing he will feed and shelter me
Yet still the stronger be
If there were only him and me.
But the trail is now fading
And I am weak
From seeking.

I am following the buffalo.
We two could have survived
That which others cannot bear –
A freedom, a balance now rare
Between man and nature, but now
His trail is disappearing
As I search desperately, fearing
I have lost
As much as he;
And I will follow.

Dorothy Hughes,
Mabelthorpe, Lincolnshire.

178

THE INWARD VOICE

I am lost, I cried out aloud one day,
And I know not which way to go.
Nay, not so, a voice within did say
The way you must go, I will show.

Take the road that is right and spurn what is wrong,
And to those who don't love you, do good
Be childlike and gentle, be wise and be strong,
And to those who are starving give food.

The way maybe uphill, but if you will smile
And rest when the day's work is done
You'll find it all so very worthwhile
And life will be wholesome fun.

And so my friend, if you have lost your way,
Take heed of the voice within,
Try and do some good deed every day,
And the Master's "Well Done" you will win.

Albert Hull,
Ferryhill, Co. Durham.

THE GIFT OF SPRING

Panting breath on the keen night air,
Cool winds whisping
A young girl's hair.

Glorious sunsets light the sky,
The honk of geese
Just gliding by.

Yachts in the evening browse along,
The hooting owl,
Nightingale's song.

Musical twitters in the eaves,
Soft breeze rustling
The new grown leaves.

The fresh good smell of waking earth,
This welcome Spring,
The world's rebirth.

Miss May Hulme,
Port Glasgow.

WINTER INTO SPRING

Trees that have lost their leaves,
Cold icy winds that blow,
Holly berries bright and red,
Lots and lots of snow.

A robin with his breast so red,
Hopping to the door for bread,
A rabbit's footprints in the snow,
As he hurries to and fro.

Wintry mornings drear and dark,
Log fires burning bright,
Ponds frozen in the park,
Long cold dark nights.

Now at long last Spring has come,
And the sun's rays warm the air,
Birds are singing, flowers are springing,
Seems there's magic everywhere.

Long the banks of a babbling brook,
Violets and primroses peep,
While in the woods anemones grow,
And all the world seems sweet.

Gardens filled with daffodils,
Sight my heart with pleasure fills,
Tulips too, so gay and bright,
I could gaze from morn till night.

Pussy willows by the stream,
Shining in the sun's bright beam,
On the farm the lambkins play,
A nest of kittens in the hay.

I am wakened each new morn,
By the blackbird's note at dawn,
At evening still he's singing sweet,
I wonder if he ever sleeps.

Mrs. Mary Hutchison,
Bankfoot, Perthshire.

CAPTAIN SCOTT AND ANTARCTICA

These may well be the last words I utter,
My lips are all parched, my voice is a mutter,
The icy clouds, the sky they do blot,
These are my last words, I, Robert Scott.

I sit in our camp, with snow all around,
Snow above, snow below, snow on the ground,
Soon will my friends know, what it is like to die,
And dead we will be, 'fore the moon leaves the sky.

'Twas a long way for us to reach our goal,
To the swirling mists of the icy South Pole,
And unto Antarctica, there are many ways,
And we reached our goal, only beaten by days.

Another eleven miles to the next food depot,
But our progress has been naught but slow,
I know we won't reach it, for soon I'll be dead,
So I write in this diary, hoping it will be read.

Amunsden of his task is free,
'Tis he who will go down in history,
Nobody cares about second place,
'Tis better I die than to face the disgrace.

The task to the Pole has been my doom,
This snow-covered tent will be my tomb,
If men again try this track, if they dare,
Don't be like me, take more care!

My fingers have frostbite, and my brow,
Is burning up I know not how,
My companions are dead, why can't I be like them too,
God knows the agony I'm going through!

I have one more thing to say, 'fore my time will end,
One small message I wish to send,
Look after our country, and one more thing,
More important than all, God save the King!

Ian Spence Hutton (Aged 12),
Bowburn, Durham.

THE SOUNDS I LIKE

Chirping birds and Church bells ringing,
The congregation and choir all singing,
Waves all splashing on the rocks,
So restfully the clock tick-tocks.

The chugging as a train is going,
Dogs all barking, cattle lowing,
The whistling and hissing of a kettle,
The clanking, banging beat of metal.

The tapping of the gentle rain,
Hitting on the window pane,
Of all the sounds I like so well,
My favourite is the home-time bell.

Miss Carol Ann Hyslop,
Kilbarchan, Renfrewshire.

FOR ENGLAND AND ELIZABETH

This brave man Sir Francis Chichester
Around the world did sail
In a boat made by English men
Alone, afraid, in wind and hail.

He called his boat the "Gipsy Moth"
A fine boat we know
Around Cape Hope, the Horn
Then back to Plymouth Hoe.

Great crowds were there to greet him
Ships big and small
To see this brave man step ashore
Greet the Lord Mayor and all.

For all the world knows he is strong
To do battle with the sea
Just like Sir Francis Drake
Strong men of the sea.

Elizabeth of England
Our true and graceful Queen
Knighted this brave man
Conqueror of the sea.

Isabella Iley,
Boldon Colliery, Tyne and Wear.

AS I WRITE

Yellowing leaves of a
Man planted poplar
Shimmer in the clear
Winter sunlight
Which dries the ink
As I write.

High straight lined clouds
Are motionless in the blue clear
Windless atmosphere
Of winter sunlight
Which sweats my hand
As I write.

Wind blown water waves
Ripple around the roof pools
Reflecting the yellowing poplar, blue sky,
And the winter sunlight
Which burns my heart
As I write.

Robert Vincent Ingham,
Warrington, Cheshire.

DONALD

He was not with us very long
his life was but a short sad song.
Loved in life he's missed in death
our memories are all that's left
of happy moments, joyfully shared.
I wonder if he knew how much we cared.
Living with his coming end
knowing that soon we'd send him
off to meet our God, where, safe in his
house, he'll wait for us,
our Donald.

We made him like the other two
our middle child, whose gone and
left a void that's hard to fill,
we think of him and miss him still.
To see the wonder in his eyes
a brand new toy, a great surprise
His zest for life was short but full.
We told ourselves it cannot be,
there's some mistake you wait and see,
all will be well
with Donald.

The eyes are objects of expression,
they show our joy, reveal depression.
His darkened pools expressed his pain
his waxen face devoid of colour,
smiled bravely from the mass of tubes,
the drips that fed his wasted body,
buying time, till time would stretch
no farther.
And so it was he slipped away,
quietly and with no pain,
relieved of it by man made potions
farewell brave Donald.

M. W. Inglis,
Aberdeen.

AN OXFORD NIGHT

In the west the sun is setting
O'er the Isis where the rowers
Strain to be first at the Folly.
And the swans with regal bearing
Drift past cruisers at their moorings –
In the shadows courting couples
Speak in whispers to the moonrise
And a lost and lonely poet
Wanders by and by.

At the lock he stops to wonder
At the love that binds creation
Through the sapphire tinted water
To the silver of the night star
And his eye betrays a tear
Rolling gently in its coolness
With his pen he points a finger
At his heart now fondly beating
With his heart he points
To love.

So he journeys on the towpath
Finding all yet seeking nothing
Wishing only that the moment
Could be plucked from time's progression
Then as dawn removes night's mantle
Brushing out her golden tresses
Smiles to see the laughing figure
Who is dancing near the river
Who is lost yet found existence
Who is found yet lost
No more.

Robert James Inglis,
Summertown, Oxford.

185

MY FRIENDS THE HANKIES

You're always there
15″ square,
Irish Linen
    peeping from my Sunday Best
Breast Pocket . . .
      or
crumpled
    thrust down warmly
in the pocket of my "strads" or "jeans"
awaiting withdrawal
    for . . .
    tear staining
    proboscus cleaning
    lipstick wiping
    stain removing,
greasy finger marks erasing;
    you have been seen
trying to put a shine on unpolished boots,
(after the "Bull" was over).
    It has been said
you were even discreetly tucked inside some bathing trunks,
to create a false impression . . .
    Ah! the tricks that you are forced to perform,
      where nature has been less than generous
        with her gifts . . .
        "poor things"
You take the place of oily rags,
or bandages,
and head-squares for the bald mens'
cricket watching heads at Lords –
or Rule Brittanias Sailors on the Norfolk Broads.

Initialled, flower encrested, germ infested
    Handkerchiefs –
lie stagnant in my wardrobe drawer,
Boxed, and given with Love
so many Christmasses before;
  I'd need a thousand noses more or less
  to make the most of you, my friends –

I'm a handkerchief millionaire
    when I compare
    with my youth –
when
  a wipe of the cuff
  was enough!!

Mr. David Iredale,
South Shields, Tyne and Wear.

THOUGHTS

The Creator's manifestation,
Call it what you will,
Eludes truthful explanation,
The riddle is with us still.

For some, Genesis provides an answer,
For others, Logic ends in nought,
Yet, "The Truth that is within us,"
Awaits our own purity in thought.

When God gave Life to matter,
Did He enclose within selected Form,
A potential Spark of Science,
A divergence from the norm,
And watch Earth's evolution,
For aeons; Darkness fighting Light,
Until, His Spark-engendered Genus,
Evolved Homo Sapiens,
The winner of the fight?

In my thinking, speculation,
Of Man's uphill taking shape,
Is of secondary importance,
To the path Man NOW should take.

Purpose is served by increasing numbers,
Who exercise a rightful plan,
Expanding Knowledge; ever growing,
Within the Science God began.

But, if in self-assurances,
Man ignores God's Vital Spark,
Fire may consume its Phoenix,
To sterile ashes,
Floating in the Dark.

Mr. Alec Jackson,
Worthing, Sussex.

TERMINUS

Bathed in the light of the dying sun,
Beneath the paradise tree:
There he had lain since time had begun
And none was as old as he.

He heard the world around him weep;
It would never again be free.
Soon young and old alike would sleep,
Yet none was as old as he.

For in the east in a mourning town,
A boy thought that time held the key.
Time's home he searched for, up and down,
For none was as old as he.

At last he found his hiding place
Beneath the paradise tree:
Blood red light bathed an old man's face
And none was as old as he.

The boy approached in wondering awe
Of the sight beneath the tree.
The dying sun gave a mighty roar
And Time was at last set free.

Catherine Jones,
Wakefield, West Yorkshire.

D.I.Y. ON THE NATIONAL HEALTH

Super-duper education.
All we hear from dawn to dusk,
O-A levelled rectification.
All to earn an honest crust.

If we could but see the reason,
For this academic thrust.
As the birthrate figures smoulder.
Wards foreclose – is life so just.

Taxed are we beyond redemption.
Working hard from dawn till night,
Just to earn an honest living,
Alas, the end is out of sight.

If we could but turn the clock back.
To see where trouble made its mark.
What use is further Education.
Without a D.I.Y. Health Chart.

Doris M. Jackson,
Crawley, Sussex.

ALLEY CATS

Yowling in the alley,
Fighting on the roofs,
Scrounging in the dustbins,
Under horses hoofs.

Sniffing in the larder,
Worming under gates,
Playing in the gutter,
Licking empty plates.

Lapping dirty puddles,
Jumping onto walls,
Waking, sleeping people,
With their raucous calls.

Claire Louise James,
Altrincham, Cheshire.

THE COST OF LIVING

How far does your wage pack go today,
How much have you left when you've paid your way.
The rise in the cost of living is so great,
How much longer can we go on paying at this rate.
We cannot afford to go on a spree,
Nor have a family day out by the sea.
Take the working man's pint of beer for a start,
Now he can't manage to go "on the cart".
The housewife's budget is hard to adjust,
We cut out the luxuries and just get the "musts".
Life has no longer got the zest,
We cannot go out now and buy the best.
From shop to shop we walk every day,
To save those small pennies in every small way.
Take this inflation, it must end one day
But what's going to happen when we can't pay?
Whatever else goes short, we must eat, that is certain
Who is the one, that will pull down the curtain.
Without the working man this country is lost
He's the backbone of Britain whatever the cost.
So whatever the future may hold for us all,
We must all pull together, we must never fall.
We all keep striking for higher wages you know,
But is this really the best way to go?

The more that we earn, the more we pay out,
It must come from somewhere without any doubt.
But one thing is certain, that day will come,
When life will be easy, and we can have fun.
Let's stop this bickering and reason a while,
Won't it be lovely when we can all smile.
Just tighten our belts and go hell for leather,
Don't stop, and hold back, and then wonder whether.
We always fight best when our backs to the wall,
What's stopping us now, it's all there, for us all.

Mrs. Irene M. Jones,
Birkenhead, Merseyside.

COMPETITION POEM

Highland island, amongst your dewny mere,
Of the purple of the tourist, with the sparkled summer sun,
Gloating down; to a thousand loch coaches. And that
Wooly little shepherd, camera cute and Baptist still,
Sober as the sombre grey, that, yellow weeded, swivelled about
The sun, below his feet.
    And now the leaves have fallen,
    And the ice is blowing bite,
    To every single marrow,
    In the downpour of the night.
    And now in every corner,
    The sheep are wombing lambs,
    Bleating for their father,
    And father to the rams.
Sighing, crying, the stag misted peaks, screaming to the
Horizons valleys, bundling, waiting for the suffocating
White, of the freezing snow. There was the shadow, and of
Ben by his side, through the falling, bitting screen, head
Collared white, to the stone snook corner, where the wool huddled
To nurture warm each other. Where are your sweated cameras
now, elbowed in a sheep? To wait for Spring, and a thousand
more as these. But where is your heaven; in the Summer, to
crook on a lean, and stare and smile at the sheep in their cars?
    But now, as you see in the glass of the sky,
    A tiny mouth opens, life flickers an eye,
    The worry is over, right there in his hands,
    A smile glows his mind in milk and honey lands.

Mr. P. G. Jones,
Rhoshirwaun, Gwynedd.

ON ROBERT BURNS

A gifted man was Robert Burns,
Who with a quill could write of ferns,
Of mice, and Scotland's countryside
And of Jean, his lovely bride.

A farmer's son and ploughman gay,
Born and bred in Alloway,
He grew to be a bonny lad,
But made his father very sad.
The man sens'd Rabbie nurs'd a gift,
But could not name it tho' he'd sift
And search his mind – and Rabbie's too,
To seek out what the lad could do.
Alas! The father passed away,
'Ere Rab's great gift came into play.
'Twas rhyming of the written word,
Of mountains, Lochs and feathered bird,
Of pretty maidens and their tresses,
With or without their summer dresses.
But brand him not an evil-doer,
Tho' dark his record as a wooer,
For Rabbie was as slak-ed fire,
Without the joy of man's desire
Since love to him was life, required
To keep his genius inspired.
His fame it spread like fire wild,
From man to man and likewise child,
'Til all of Scotland knew at last
That here was poet unsurpass'd
In Quality so rich and rare,
Of words and phrases plucked with care
From simple thoughts and open mind
To pass with joy to all mankind.
Sad loss it was to Scottish folk,
When death enwrapp'd him in her cloak,
To take this man of men to heaven
At tender age of thirty-seven.

The hills of Scotland – Grassy green, to be remembered must be seen.
But if your heart, for home it yearns, just read the works of Robert
    Burns,
For therein lies a man's endeavour, to mind you of your land forever.

Ronald Joyce
St. Giles, Lincoln.

THE WEE BLACK HEN
(*In memory of James Sutherland last miller of The Whaligoe Meal Mills*)

O'er there below the hill ye'll find the Foligoe Meal Mill,
Ae young man was ae miller but noo it stands still,
Frae morn tae nicht he toiled amangst ae stoor,
In ae auld days when a were poor,
A'body liked him a his fellow men,
Richt doon tae ae crofters wee black hen.

One day when busy in ae loft,
He spied below an auld boy frae a croft,
Fillan each pocket wae corn frae a bag,
Nae thocht o' whether it belonged tae Will or Wag,
Till noo ae blame was centred roon a hairmless moose,
But noo ae miller kent so he watched ae hoose,
Awa back there ae hens were fo o' glee,
Ae crofter he was doon on one knee,
Feedan all ae ducks and geese A'body had a piece,
And ae wee black hen.

Next day a repetition o' ae day afore,
A thing was greedy and wanted more,
Noo ae miller whose name was Him,
Says tae himsel "I've had enough o' him,"
The third day cam he watched frae ae stair,
Saw ae auld body samplan mair,
Jim gave oot a yell frae ae hatch abeen,
Ye wid hae thocht ae gluff wid have turned a chiel green.

Ae cute lad openan his palm said very calm,
"Man its a real fine puckle ye have here,"
Noo empty handed he went back tae his but and ben,
Ae ducks, ae geese and ae wee black hen,
To them he had to explain from where he had obtained ae last grain,
Wae a splutter and a flutter they flew at him,
For cheatan an honest man like Jim,
Grabbed him by ae collar skelpt him wae a hook,
Quackan and cacklan "What will we dae wae ae crook,"
Said ae wee black hen "Let's thraw his neck for pinchan frae ae
Miller an anither mans seck."

The auld man promised to mend his ways,
And this he did to the end o' his days,
        Honesty pays
A weel loved brother is hard to replace,
Mine I'll remember for the rest o' my days.

Etta Bremner Juhle,
Ulbster, Caithness.

SCAFELL PIKE

The man set forth at the break of day, when dew was on the ground,
His pack was slung upon his back, he moved with barely a sound.
The sky above with alto filled, the air was calm and still,
King Sol had not yet climbed the sky to remove the morning chill.
The man walked from the grassy slope onto the stony path,
Maybe the Derwent's other route in times of stormy wrath.
His boots now crunched the stones beneath as he strode on his way,
He whistled as he walked along during the youth of day.
The Golden Orb was now in the sky, but hidden from his sight,
Behind huge stones and rocks massif, behind nature's might.
Over rivulets and streams the man passed with his tremendous stride,
His pace was swift and effortless, his body seemed to glide.
The cloud was slowly breaking now to show some daubs of blue;
In the great bowl of sky above a lone raven flew.
The craggy path did steepen now and the man began to climb,
The sun flashed above a rocky crest with the passage of some time.
The man's pace was swift as can be, but his breathing laboured now,
The aclivity still steeper ran, the sweat was on his brow.
Higher and higher, yet higher still this man did trek and climb,
With more and more laboured breath, with more sweat than grime.
The sun became a dazzling orb, so hot even to the man,
It sapped him of his energy and slowed his climbing plan.
After resting awhile he felt afresh, he bounded to his feet,
He jumped from rocks and boulders and stones, this mountain would
   not him cheat.
He soon was standing on the peak alone on its very summit,
Surveilling "Gable" and Wasdale Valley and surrounding screes that
   plummet.
Peaks galore in the distance stood, one still with a cloudy plume,
The rest stood stark, foreboding rocks with barely a flowery bloom.
The heat for a while was quite intense, but a breeze soon sprang to
   task,
The man he had to quench his thirst; he drank quickly from his flask.
It now was time to be homeward bound from this place he did like,
So finally he went his weary way, down the track of Scafell Pike.

David Russell Keedy,
South Shields, Tyne and Wear

A NEW DAY

Birds on the wing,
Hear them all sing
Their songs of the joy of living.
People on earth
Devoid of mirth
Have lost the art of giving.

Spring on the way
A beautiful day,
What more could one ever wish for,
Nature so grand
Goes hand in hand
With the good things always in store.

Lessons we learn
From the trickling burn,
How to peacefully go on our way,
Love in the heart
Is always a start
To a happy, worthwhile new day.

M. Keedy,
South Shields, Tyne and Wear.

DREAMS! DREAMS! DREAMS!

Life is composed of dreams, even when we are quite small.
And still goes on when we grow tall.
As we lie in our beds,
All sorts of fantasies go through our heads.
As a child of three or four, we wonder just how a fairy
Comes through a door.

These are the pleasant dreams that makes us love our childhood,
Just wondering and hoping to see these mythical things in reality.
Like life, there is always the "Giant of Terror" whom we don't wish to
    meet,
Yet in our childish thoughts, think maybe it would be a treat.

Next the stage of more make believe,
As at Christmas our fathers and mothers miss their code of honesty,
    and do deceive.
Santa Claus is coming soon, he'll be riding his sleigh over the moon.
As we snuggle down in childish delight,
Thinking of all the nice things, that just may be more than a "might".

And so the next phase goes on.
When we have grown between small and tall.
Our thoughts now, are past all this deceive and believe.
And know that soon we shall finish school.
Hoping we have made good,
Even though we know,
At times we have broken a rule.

Out into the world we must go,
Make believe now, for us, is not so.
Although still in our minds there is a little of it left,
As again in bed, we imagine being the boss of our work.

If a boy, then a Captain of the ship we'll be,
Even though we've only been six weeks at sea.
Should we be the other sex, to be perhaps top model, we'll rise.
Or even as a Beauty Queen we'll win a prize.

This boy has now grown to a man,
And managed to do the best he can.
Or this girl to woman has grown, and hoped she has stood the test.
Perhaps the "girl of his dreams" lies by his side,
Or her "Knight" is at her side,
A baby in a cot, gurgling and big blue eyed.

And so for him and her, most dreams have been dreamt.
But, for the little one, he's back where his Mammy and Daddy began.
As soon he'll be lying in his cot, and beginning to plan.
And this is what we all have found,
Just keeps this old world going round and round.
... This thing, called dreams.

Violet Kenworthy,
Newcastle on Tyne.

WASTED DAYS

Hand in hand you led me through a dream,
And the world you built clasped me in its pretty claws.
And made me live a lie.
I lived and dreamt and ate and drank that dream,
And cared not as I watched the hum-drum world go by.

But once distant clouds moved closer
Bringing with them whisperers cautious whispers
With which to fill my ears.
Oh if I'd listened to their words
The cruel hand of scorn might not have slapped me down,
And would not now be making me work my hand
Or waste the ink in my pen,
Or the months I have left,
Before forgetting you and
Starting to live again.

Ann Kiesler,
Selby, Yorkshire.

SEEING THINGS FROM MY WINDOW

As I look out my window
A play park I can see;
The children playing merrily,
As happy as can be.

Some are on the see-saw,
Some are on the swings,
Some are sliding down the chute:
You'd think they all had wings.

And noo I see a laddie
Running roon' and roon',
Chasing a wee lassie –
But she's fell and hurt her croon.

Noo, he's run tae pick her up;
To comfort her he tries:
He takes his hankie oot his pooch
Tae wipe her tearful eyes.

Then he takes her by the hand
And makes a daisy chain:
When he hangs it roon' her neck
She turns and smiles again.

Now, there's a lesson tae us a' –
Whenever there is trouble
Just take each other by the hand:
T'would be a different world.

Mrs. Isabella Kilpatrick,
Carluke, Lanarkshire.

LIFE

Life is such a precious gift, an easy thing to lose,
Yet still we moan our time away, we wish to pick and choose.
A better lot, we always want to change the life we've got,
Can't be content with what we have, we want what we have not.

"If only," or "I wish I could," are common words to hear,
We sit and wish our life away, the passing of each year.

Goes unnoticed, then we find that life has passed us by,
We've nothing to show for the years we've lived, and nothing achieved,
   when we die.

So instead of sitting wishing for the things you haven't got,
Think of all the things you have, you'll find they're quite a lot.
The many beautiful moods of nature, a babys' innocent smile,
These gifts from God, the many things that make life so worthwhile!

Marjorie Lynne Kinnear,
Stanley, Co. Durham.

THOUGHTS ON A STARRY NIGHT

Moonlight, starlight, lamplight,
Images above me,
Shadows thrown below me,
My Spirit flies at night.

Perhaps far out in space,
There dwells in mystic place,
A being seeing all,
Our rise, our pause, our fall.

For eons Man had praised
Himself. Perhaps one day he'll know
That, when his cities razed,
There is nowhere to go
But up, to flee to space
To seek that mystic place
And bow his head to Him,
Say, "Please forgive my sin,
My crimes, my murderous deeds,
My small and petty greeds."

Moonlight, lamplight, starlight,
Twinkling far above me,
I turn but cannot see,
Salvation from our plight.

Alan Kirk,
Montrose, Angus.

THE SADNESS – OF AMBITION

Just another glass of wine –
No harm in that – I'm lonely – he's gone.
Gone with his brief case – clean shirt and tie,
Leaving me to wonder why.
All he talks about is his Boss –
The need to be there on time,
Okay he's right – the bread winner of the family
No crime.
Provides me with lovely things –
Carpets wall to wall – Automatic washer –
Just the flick of a switch –
Why did he marry this God damned bitch?
I'm sick of perfection – why can't he be,
Suddenly wanting to grovel to me.
Then I could be loving and kind,
Appease his heart – his soul – his mind.
He is perfection – but what am I,
It doesn't ease my heart to cry.
To analyse my emotions – what do I seek,
To put things right – another drink.
That feels better – all of a sudden I don't care,
For the hell of it –
I'll pour one over his treasured chair.
The clock strikes – one – two – three – four,
Only another twenty to go – then he should be home,
Saying "God I'm tired – why do I roam"
What shall I do with twenty hours –
Does no-one in this street care.
I'll pour myself another drink –
I'm good company, don't need to share.
Now I feel mellow – no longer wishing for a different feller,
I shall now relax in his Special chair,
Something not allowed when he is there.
But God damn it – he can't see me,
He's married to a Company.
So I'll sit and drink my lonely wine,
Until the chair and bottle becomes my shrine.

Eve King,
Ryton, Tyne and Wear.

AVALANCHE

Virgin snows,
White glistening
Smooth.

What atrocities
Have you committed
With your hugging,
Choking,
Smothering blanket?

How your vision
Ill becomes you,
So innocent,
Whipped cream.
But your graveyard
Menace, malicious
Slumbers
All the while
Beneath its white blanket.

When the earth
Shrugs you aside,
Like some irksome garment
You tumble
Head over heels
Caught in a holocaust
Of motion,
Your rumble and thunder
Reeks and rages
Destruction
Then the power
Descends,
So smooth again.

But the light
Of day
Gives you away
The steely gleam,
Cold as death.

David Kirk,
Cumbernauld, Glasgow.

GRAN

Most city dwellers of my vintage
Can boast the memory of a rural gran:
Some intrepid old lady, out digging
Her artichokes at eighty-three.
In black silk dress and boots with laces,
Never catching cold, expert at making.

A devilish wine from flower or berry,
Or a lardy cake, rich as sin.
For us, nostalgia draws sweet faces
In a borrowed frame, sentimentalising
No doubt, forgetting to paint in
The rheumatic hands and the scars of life.

Or the flesh that hung from shrivelled bone,
Terrible against white sheets, at the end.
Still, even if, in reality,
Her skill came from need and her drains would send
Us running for some nice disinfectant,
Time is a powerful deoderant.

So, for all my practised modernity,
I can still grieve with a child's grief
When I walk on bricks that made her cottage
(Greenhouses recall where she stored the jam).
My sorrow is absurd of course, for what has gone
Is not one old woman, but a lousy Age.

Pauline Kirk,
Woodley, Reading.

FOUNDED ON EXPERIENCE

Oh these four walls that lock me in
And these four wheels that chain me down
And all lifes pains that take my smile
And make my face a frown.

How can I be free of this plight?
Oh tell me how I can be free!
There is no other way out I fear
That these two eyes can see.

For these two hands are much too frail
And these legs are far too weak,
To even take the weight of me
'Till I remember that baby meek.

Then I think of that old, old story
Of the babe in the manger long ago
And I see God in all his glory
Up towards Heaven go.

And he plants his love within me
Like the farmer sowing his seed
And I'm honoured to have his mercy,
I just a simple weed.

Now his love is my strength, my power.
My foe is also a true friend
And I must try to love him
'Till my life is at its end.

So you see all you so called smart people
Who sing of loving each other,
You must first receive the love of God
Before you can give it to your brother.

Agnes H. Kirker,
Newtownabbey, Co. Antrim.

THE EASTERTON PIPER – *A folk poem*
(The folk poem, a long and honorable tradition in Scotland, is written to be spoken or sung)

Piper Johnny pipes no more,
His wind has gone and his bones are sore,
But for all his years, now eighty five,
His eye is keen and his mind alive,
And the howling gales fight at the painted door
Of his lonely croft near the Carron shore.
His ageing neice keeps the homestead neat,
Though many would say – "How obselete."
For to enter the portals of Johnny and Kate
Is to whisk you away to another date,
Where skirling pipes would seem to contrive
To carry you back to the forty five.
The lamp burns faint and the clock ticks loud,
Darkness hangs as the embers cloud –
The crock with the meal for the hens put past,
The spell for the rest of the night is cast.

There he is in a straight-backed chair,
The veteran soldier with silver hair.
"A crabbit old devil!" you well might say,
But he sits and thinks of another day
When Johnny Duguid piped for them all,
Those fair-cheeked lads, where many would fall
In bloody combat on French terrain,
Forward and back and forward again.
And the airs that he played were rent with cries,
And the last lament with the whispered sighs
Of dying men with the proud plaid strewn
Round their broken bodies by Battle hewn.
But home from the fourteen-eighteen war
Came the country piper to roam no more.
Nigh six decades have rolled past the door
Of the white-washed croft on the Carron shore.
When Easterton finally sheds its stone
And the last lament with the frost has flown,
Then out of the mists on the rise of the hill
You'll glimpse him standing, straight and still,
Playing the airs he knew so well
In the far off days when his comrades fell.

Daphne P. Kirkpatrick,
Greenfaulds, Cumbernauld.

LONDON 1952

On this cold and wintry day
The new young Queen was on her way
Flying to her native land
Her Ministers took up their stand.

A hush fell on the waiting crowds
The aircraft seen below the clouds
What will the years hold in store
For this our Queen, a girl no more.

A slender figure coming down
Her head so soon to bear a crown
The sacrifices she must make
The path of duty now to take.

A promise made when twenty one
To pledge herself to everyone
To follow on her father's reign
His selfless years of work and strain.

Britons gathered waiting there
Offered up a silent prayer
Look down upon our Queen this day
And help to guide her future way.

Mrs. Barbara Kathleen Laing,
Hawick, Roxburghshire.

AFORE THE COMIN' O' THE LAIRD

Sma' damp draughty and black wa'd hoose,
Wae never a crumb tae feed a moose
Flagstane flair in water lies
Windaes gowking at the skies
Hoo mony bairnies on yer brigstanes ran?

Sma' damp draughty and black wa'd hoose,
Wae never a heid tae feed a loose
Stark stanes that look sae bare,
Lichen covered here and there,
Hoo mony bairnies on yer brigstanes ran?

Sma' damp draughty and black wa'd hoose,
Wae never a cry tae boo a goose,
Alone and lonely noo empty stands,
Aerosol sprayed by hooligans,
Hoo mony bairnies on yer brigstanes ran?

Sma' damp draughty and black wa'd hoose,
Ye wad be the better for a moose,
A dirty heid tae feed a loose,
And wee bit gress tae feed yer goose
Aye, and bairnies that aince on yer brigstanes ran.

The countra'side aroond left bared;
Vacated by the anes that cared,
The anes that lived, wrocht, and shared,
"Afore the comin' o' the Laird,"
Alas! in peace in yon kirkyaird.

David M. Lamb,
Edinburgh.

KIDS OF TODAY

Like pins in the bowling alley they frequent
So alike is their make-up
Or following like sheep
An idol of pop who else to worship
There's no God they say
These kids of today

Saint's all have guitars is their infinite wisdom
And who are we to disagree
A world of psychedelic art
Boutiques, Discotheques each play its part
There's no God they say
These kids of today

So tightly wrapped in a world of their own
No need for God or spiritual things
Material requirements too easily available
Even knowledge of knowing the Bible's a fable
There's no God they say
These kids of today

A new language they've thought up
Geared up, or fab
Thinking they rule the world they have
Never to thinking how long its been here
There's no God they say
These kids of today

Somehow I know this phase will pass
That one day each one will need
Something to cling to, to find new strength
Of spiritual blessing they know not the length
Of help they can have then they will say
There's a God for sure
These kids of today.

Sarah Lambert,
Chester-Le-Street, Co. Durham.

A NEW YEAR

With God's good grace there will be Spring
When hearts are glad and warm
When all the best there is in life
Is excitingly reborn –
Reborn to what?

To grief and sadness, struggle and madness?
Or to the joy of doing and giving and having?
The choice is ours, as the ingredients we use
Are mixed to harmonise, blend or abuse –
The result should be summer
With all nature to work and rest
If we do not falter, but do our best –
Our best, how futile that can be
Without our Guide to help us see
Where our thoughts and efforts should be directed
For others to gain and members elected
To spread, like ripples on pond and lake
And build and reap for humanity's sake,
Then, when Autumn is here
With its golden glory and peace,
We can take stock of what we have done with the lease
Which the seasons gave us, and, who knows
It maybe that Winter will seem less dark
If, in the New Year, we aim to hit the mark.

Primrose Lane,
Honiton, Devon.

TO A SPIDER
(He was a tiny wee black spider, I met him while spring cleaning, so I
just had to stop and speak to him)

Hulloh! wee beastie boy yer clever
Hoo ye pit yer web the gither
Where dae ye keep yer ba' o' threed
Tae yaise it ony time ye need?

Hoo dis yer wee legs ever rin
Up they threeds that you dae spin?
Hoo a envy you swinging there
Ye hivnae a worry or a care.

Tae think the same man made us two
Aye, but he didnae gie me brains like you
And ye don't get butchers bills like me
Ye're favourite steak's a bit o' flee.

If a circus had an artist like you
Their seats would a' be pack-ed fu'
You wudnae need a safety net
Nae fear o' you brekin' yer neck.

Hoo dae ye wae this world cope
Could we see yer brains wae a microscope?
A marvel at yer tiny size
Yer geest a speck before my eyes.

No a'll no' hit ye wae ma broom
Hae the freedom o' ma hoose aroon
Hoo could a ever knock apart
A beast like you A WORK O' ART?

O LORD, this genius that you've made
Could pit ony human in the shade
Them hands o' yours dae never fail
He's perfect there in every detail.

They say we must be born again
Well, PLEASE GOD DON'T SEND ME AS A WEAN
Let me be my decider
Your gifted hands that made him, mould me
SEND ME BACK AS A SPIDER.

Mrs. Jeannie Laurie,
Kirkcudbright.

KING GEORGE VI'S DEATH

To us he gave no last farewell,
No loved one by his side,
So peacefully he slept away,
From life's engulfing tide.

God called him to His realm above,
His battles bravely fought,
The victory that now is his,
No glory ever sought.

The fifteen years he did reign,
Were full of work and strain,
Yet in his ever failing health,
The highest did attain.

A gracious wife stood by his side,
To comfort and to cheer,
Two loving daughters did complete,
His family life so dear.

A memory we will always keep,
So good, so brave, so kind,
Our greatest sympathy now goes,
To those he's left behind.

Three Royal Queens now do mourn,
The passing of our King,
A page in Britain's history,
Their presence now must bring.

As we salute our new girl Queen,
With honour and with pride,
We pray that God will guide her,
In her Dominions far and wide.

Mrs. M. Law,
Longside, By Peterhead.

REFUGEE

If we could love as fiercely as we live,
And, instead of taking, generously give
To others much less fortunate than we,
Who, by the greed of others live in poverty.

For each of us by Gods creative hand,
Was given breath to live throughout the land,
As brothers and sisters one and all,
To help the stumbling when they fall.

But how many of us pass them by,
And close our ears to their plaintive cry,
For we are complacent, secure and smug,
And ignore their misery with an indifferent shrug.

How easily fate could have twisted our life,
And placed us in a land of strife,
What then! what would *our* feelings be,
If *we* were but a refugee.

So let us pray that there may be,
Love and peace and tranquillity,
Living humbly as we should,
Then this world, Gods gift, could be really good.

Greta Lawrence,
North Shields, Tyne and Wear.

KNOCKER UP

Figures of time on shutter chalked,
Telling of time and bedtime baulked,
Knocker thumping on the door,
Rousing tired bodies to their chores.

Overworked Mums their rest disturbed,
Slicing the bread still unperturbed,
Worrying only that bait should be,
Enough to last till daylight see.

Little dreaming on leaving school,
How rough the work, how strict the rule,
Determined our father's step to follow,
Ignoring advice, no care for the morrow.

Often I've mourned the day I went,
Into the depths of dust and sweat,
Baitbag on arm, its swinging weight,
Adding incumberance to sleepy gait.

What use to mourn what might have been,
I've had my share of this lifes cream,
One must be thankful for what we've got,
Security and comfort that others have not.

Could that knocker return and see,
Bruises sustained on others like me,
I'm sure he'd alter his vocation,
And use his efforts for our salvation.

Men labour 'neath the green earths crust,
Conforming to life upon them thrust,
And yet still striving to eliminate,
Others from a similar fate.

Now the knockers day is o'er,
Mothers still fret and pace the floor,
Hoping their brood will come and rest,
In the comfort of the old nest.

Henry L. Laws,
Wooler.

REALITY

Reality – how poor a goal thou art!
How little thou resemblest Fancy's art,
Which paints thee with the brush of unleashed thought,
And with glowing colour hast so falsely sought,
To cloak thine ugliness with glamour which,
Intoxicates the mind, provoking rich,
Pulsing longings in the once dormant breast,
That, having once glimpsed Heaven, knows no rest;
But soars aloft, in mental search without,
A guide, and partially engulfed in doubt;
But yet persists in groping, aimless flight,
Through subconscious channels and through the night,
Of dreamland fantasy – to seek a clue,
To make these old enchanted dreams come true!

Miss Frances Lawton,
Warrington, Cheshire.

IN MEMORY OF A LOST OPPORTUNITY

When my tears fall with anothers grief, then I cry for you
In the days of my sorrow I did not cry
Now with hot dry eye, I record every falling leaf, every jilted lover
Undercover they identify with my too deep loss of you

For our unlived Springs my mind wings but without motion
For our silenced songs my heart sings but without sound
For our oneness my soul clings but without communion

Living now in my uncertainty
Though I do not see you in that timelessness
It does not matter
As I have no words to express our separatedness

Sleep then too dear memories in the arms of my resentment
I will mourn with every falling tear, torn from every lonely soul
Until our day of atonement

When the lamp of my passion should have flared tear bright
The stifled flame blacked the grass and dimmed the light

Barry Layzell,
Heston, Middlesex.

FACING OUT TO SEA

A Grand Hotel displaying palms
Affords a view of shambled handbill,
The sizzle of waves on precious sand
Where children once played
With buckets
And hay making spades.

Beach hut in sandhill,
Crumbling villas with swimming suits
On washing lines tucked behind,
Boarding houses with bed bugs
Like a memory of time
Long since passed
When brass bands broke up the dust
Carriages still thronged the front
And moods held their own gala.

Handkerchiefs being waved
In a seaside railway station,
Grey slags of cloud
Returning scudding spume
To drive the last dip bathers home.
A drilling of cold feet
On wet boards along the pier
Decrying all evidence
That anyone ever came and sat here
Or trampled sand in summer,
Evcept perhaps in defeated numbers
Amongst cadging gulls.

Patients of remembrance umbrellas up
Writing postcards as to how they were fairing
Beneath sea scented palm or Union Jack despairing.

Mr. John Lazenby,
Lewes, Sussex.

GREY PUDDOCK

Grey puddock padding
Around in the heat
Flipping your web feet
Across a marathon clearing,
Will you find the pond
To which you are steering?

210

You will be hopping mad
And just a trifle sad
If some unkind Kingfisher
Decides to have frog's legs
As hors d'oeuvre for dinner.

Lace up your leather jacket
And don't you make a racket
Croaking in your throat
Like a fog-horn on a boat
For you give the game away
Asking to be taken as prey.

William Lindsay,
Morden, Surrey.

THE MILL

Helter skelter doon the hill
Cam' the bairns tae Jammie's mill
There they watched the watter churn
Ower the wheel and intae the burn.
The peedie bairns gid in the mill
And luckd aroond, wi whit a thrill.
The grinding stones gid roond and roond
Mercy me – for whit a soond!
Clickety clacket gid the shacket
Mighty me – for whit a racket!
Then click clack doon the chute
The mael comes rumblan and poors oot
Intae the bag, that's filled wi' speed
And is wheeled aweye be Jammy Reid.
Anither bag pit intae fill
For that's the routine o' the mill.
The peedie bairns gid oot o' the mill
And clambered quickly up the hill
Tae tell their folks they'd seen the corn
Ground tae mak' porridge for the morn.

Clare Linklater,
Inverurie, Aberdeenshire.

Written in Orkney Dialect.

Glossary:

Peedie – little		Mael	– meal
Gid	– went	Be	– by
Luckd	– looked	Racket	– noise

THE SEA

The sea is a purring cat,
Sly, grey and fat.
But if it is fierce, it would pounce,
As if catching its prey,
With clashing jaws it would come.

And when the wind roars,
It would pound higher and higher.
When days are calm,
It would creep up slowly, slowly, slowly,
And go to sleep.

When it is cold,
It would crawl into caves for warmth.
And when it is happy,
It would roll, roll, roll,
All day long on the beach.

Miss Susan McKechnie Logan,
Larkhall, Lanarkshire.

A DREAM OR REALITY?

Halloween! all children asleep,
For tonight's the night all witches do peep,
Young Darrin from his pleasant dream he's torn;
Not quite aware where he's being drawn.

His father told him a tale or two,
About witches and warlocks and what they do,
From the house he walks as if in sleep,
Across fields, by waters where the willow weeps.

His journey now begins its end,
He reaches the coven, he sees his friend,
A disused churchyard? just the place!
But! the bodies buried here belong to His Grace.

The night is good, the moon is high,
Could Darrin's parents guess? they could not try,
The sacrificial rite has just begun,
Hymns? in words of latin are now being sung.

The members work themselves into a pitch,
They dance, express themselves, they wear not a stitch,
An animal is cut, blood is spilled,
Another soul lives on, the body is killed.

"Everlasting Life" His Majesty declared
"We'll worship you forever" – they all answered,
"My offers are good" he'll try to entice,
But be careful my friends, before you start playing dice!!

Irene Longwell,
Glasgow.

WHAT WOULD "RABBIE" DO?

If Rabbie could come back today,
I wonder what he'd think,
If instead of Tammy Shanter, he met Humperdinck.
If instead of Soutar Johnny and Jock O' Hazeldean,
He spent a night oot boozin wi Elton John and Hughie Green.
What would he do perchance to meet,
Elsie Tanner from "The Street",
If he had still stayed in Dumfries,
Would he have "Coffey" with Denise.
If a night he spent with Marty Kane,
Would he wish for it all to happen again.
If he were asked to Lassodie House,
Would he make love to "Cairney's" spouse.
If with Lulu he lingered a while,
Would he compare her beauty wi Mary O' Argyll.
If he wrote a song for Shirley Bassey,
Would she toast him from a silver tassie.
Those are his secrets of which we don't know,
Cos' Rabbie died so long ago.
But we respect the past with great regard,
And salute the man we call the "Bard".

Miss Margaret Lowe,
Dunfermline, Fife.

AN UNTITLED POEM BY LYNN LYDLE

Majestic spires reaching for the sky
From our cathedrals grand,
A symbol of the freedom we hold dear
In this our island home,
For we have gained the freedom
Of this ancient land
To worship God,
By sacrifice through many of her sons.

Now once again we lift our hearts in praise to God,
Dear monarch greatly loved,
The offspring of our freedom truly won,
Long may she reign, for in this crown
Sometimes uneasy worn,
Still shines the freedom each her subjects share.
Let us then in her year of Jubilee,
Pray God, preserve and guide
This symbol of our freedom held so dear.

Lynn Lydle,
Annfield Plain, Durham.

THE SEA

The sea was veiled in mist
And seagulls screaming
Above forlorn rocks their stories told,
Of myriads of fish and wrecks and sunsets,
Of storms at sea and fishermen so bold.

The waves upon the rocks were gently breaking
The tide was ebbing
From the haze drenched shore,
Oh waters never still since the creation
Ride on, ride on, ride on for evermore.

Miss Kathleen H. MacArthur,
Jordanhill, Glasgow.

RETURN TO THE SEA

Tinselled ribbons of crystal,
Agleam in the sun,
Cascading to pool,
Where deep waters run.

Rushing torrent of foam,
Leaping and twisting,
Round grey, granite boulders,
Defying, resisting.

Wide river flows on,
Majestic and proud,
Past tree-lined banks,
And fields, newly-ploughed

Salt tang in the air,
Wholesome and free,
Brown waters reach out,
To merge with the sea.

Bold surge of the ocean,
Sweeps on without falter,
Pounds on far-distant beach,
In foaming welter of water.

Tinselled ribbons of crystal,
Agleam in the sun,
Rushing back to the sea,
Where deep waters run.

Mr. Hew L. McCallum,
Girvan, Ayrshire.

THE LEPERS CRY

Look on me Lord and pity me,
Hear my sigh
From impropriety
Take me to your garden
Take from me this burden,
With which I've been saddled
And feel bedraggled,
In ghastly condition I dwell
With sores I could not foretell

215

That hurt my looks that looked so well
It almost seems like a living hell,
Will the day quickly dawn
When again I shall feel better
And be lifted to newness from out of the gutter,
Meanwhile I'll save and look out of the rut
Perhaps I'm a sinner you have not forgot,
And you will take me from this den
And in purity guide me to heaven,
Where we shall rest in beauty best
Nothing forever shall ever molest;
Nevertheless from a state of distress,
I'll continue to pray
For my Lord and his day.

Irene W. McClean,
Bournemouth.

LOOK INTO MY EYES, THEY PLEAD

Well past my three score and ten, I've wandered down lifes way,
And now I'm coming to the end, as in this bed I stay:
And, oh, I am glad that this is so, I am weary, tired, and sore:
But you refuse to let me go, why must I suffer more?
Life has no more to offer me, nor I to give to life,
I am finished with this living, with its cares and with its strife.
But still you try to keep me here, you struggle day and night,
Do you never look at me, and pity me my plight?
Your Penicillin cannot give me back my health, my youth:
Your skills, your medicines can do no more: in truth
I have no wish to linger here, hour after hour in pain,
Why do you keep me from my rest, what do you have to gain?
Another day that I might live, holding death at bay?
Why can't you simply turn your back, and let me slip away.
Were I young, or in my prime; or had I work to do
Ah, then I'd fight, hold on to life, give gratitude to you.
But life has passed, my work is done, I have earned my just reward:
So let me go, that I in peace, may now "Rest with the Lord".

Mrs. Phyllis M. McCormack,
Montrose, Angus.

216

GRANDPARENT IN SUMMER

We'll sit beside the boating pond
And we'll listen to the band,
And you'll poke the funny tadpoles
As they wriggle in your hand.
We'll watch the busy jet planes
As they scribble on the sky,
We'll laugh and feed the ducklings
As they go bumping by.

We'll hide from the sunshine,
In the greeny shade of trees,
We'll wonder at the butterflies
As they dance along the breeze.
And we'll laugh at the ladybirds
Crawling up your arm,
But we'll put them carefully down again
In case they come to harm.

And when the thunder rolls above
And grumbles through the night,
I'll be your guardian angel,
I'll be your armoured knight.
And when the web of morning
Spins gold across the land
Your fears will be forgotten,
I'll be there to hold your hand.

And when the morning sun
Chases stars across the skies,
He'll chase them down a rainbow
And hide them in your eyes.

Mr. Walter McCorrisken,
Renfrew.

ARRAN

Island seen since childhood
Recumbent upon the ocean
Time and tide have swept over thee
For endless years so long
Around thee the Firth of Clyde
And Kilbrennan in motion
Dear to our heart and view
In history and song.

Low lying to the south
And peaks north, loom to the sky
Goat Fell towers over thee
With tall serrated form
Encircled by salt water
With peaks upstanding high
O'er thee storm clouds gather
With approaching storm.

Dominant are thy peaks
Pointing towards the sky
Sometimes smothered by the mist
Or shadows that decline
Kintyre lapping its lullaby
And the seagulls crying
Around Drumadoons knoll
In the bright sunshine.

Azure in summer time
But in winter with sombre hue
Thy lands and field fertile
With abundancy of rock
Warmed by the rising sun
And kissed by sparkling dew
With head unbowed you stand
Against time and shock.

Island of childhood memories
Floating on a watery stria
Not inanimate, and fixed to earth
Sparsley inhabited by men
Filling them with inspiration
The beauty of the everlasting hills
How sad to leave those scenes
And vanish from their ken.

Carpets of purple heather
Thatched thick on thy slopes
Sheep and deer grazing
And from aloft we view Kintyre
And Jura's paps far distant
And below the fields with crops
The setting sun in the evening
With crimson glow like fire.

Departing day, good night
As the darkness gathers around
And unbidden shadows fall

218

As they depart into oblivion unseen
The sheep and kine lie down
And quietness reigns over an Island
And no man can tell us
Where the day has been.

John T. McCrindle,
Maidens, Ayrshire.

DEDICATION

Destined for high office, then beckoned overnight,
  in the morning of your day.
A princess born, cradled in the arms of April,
  when new hopes rise from Earth's pulsating
  breast that lay.
Nature endowed you, the love of delicate yellow primrose,
  and spring-meadow's fresh, new green,
Delight, beholding blossom unfolding on a tree,
  shining pearl-like, caught in a crystal sunlight beam.
To you, more beautiful than all the Crown Jewels ever worn,
  amid the timeless joy of birdsong, on the breath
  of a new morn.
The wonder of woodland, quiet walking on heather-clad hill,
  Gold of a breath-taking sunset, such priceless jewels
  of the heart, with awe to overspill.
The charm of a handshake warmly given, that makes
  the waiting so worthwhile,
For the curtsying child with a posy, your most
  reassuring smile.
That trusting look exchanged, when a Queen
  pats her favourite horse,
And the voice that wags the tails –
  of fireside corgis of course!
A loving and understanding Mother, and also our caring Queen
  for twenty-five years, Dedication, thus it has ever been –
Since the vows you made in the Abbey,
  heard by millions of listening ears,
Are shining still today, to prove, through the smiles
  and also the tears,
Endearing us for all time to you –
  Elizabeth our beloved Queen.
Blessings be yours anew.

Silver Jubilee 1977.

Miss Mary N. McDermott,
Newcastle-Upon-Tyne.

ARNHEM

A holiday in Holland
The loveliest time of the year
Arnhem in the springtime
A few days to linger here.

To see the British War Graves
Was on our itinery
We drove out there, no speaking
Paying homage, silently.

Rows of small white crosses
Marked where each hero lay
A name, a rank, a number
A regiment and age, they'd say.

So very young those boys were
Some barely out of their teens
Never again to see their loved ones
Never to fulfil their dreams.

But, amidst the powerful sadness
That pervaded all the air
I seemed to feel around me
Youth, triumphing everywhere.

Young voices gaily saying
"Do not stand and weep
We've not gone forever
It's just a little sleep."

Cut down in their young lives
Grieving there, you say
But we're still here beside you
Though ahead a little way.

Tell our loved ones that of us
We've never gone away
That we're happy here in Arnhem
Till we meet again some day.

Mae McEwan,
Troon, Ayrshire.

THE EXILE

Oh, give me England
And a Cotswold slope
A cottage made of stone
And country folk.

A leafy lane where lies
The world serene
Bright sunlight dancing on
A silver stream.

Oh, give me time to pause
And contemplate
To hope for just one glance
From fickle fate.

. . . And give me back again
The sun drenched hills
A garden with a gate
And daffodils.

A slender sacred spire that
Stands nearby
A gentle wind that
Whispers with a sigh.

Oh, give me air that I can
Breathe like wine
A little grey stone Inn
Where we may dine.

Tall candles tremble, flicker
Dance and shine
. . . Where is the lovely dream
That once was mine.

Mrs. Dorothy McGarry,
Whitchurch, Hants.

SEASON OF LOVE

Autumn is oncoming in Lochaber
  — And always I love thee.
It is the time of the heather
And the lower hills are rich in purple
  — And ever I love thee.

The bracken is turning a beautiful brown
Contrasting with the evergreens.
    – How could I love thee more?
The rowan trees are rich with red
Of the berries hanging in profusion.
    – What is love without thee?
The thistles stand dead by the roadside
Their purple heads given way to silver grey
    – Don't turn away my love.
The tiny leaves of the silver birch
Have changed to yellow gold.
    – Lovest thou me?

Catherine A. MacGill,
Eaglesham, Strathclyde.

THE WISH

Walking near two old pitmen
It seems like yesterday
I overheard their conversation
As one to the other did say

If you could be granted a special wish
Something you wanted most
Come on Geordie tell me now
For I know you will not boast

Why man whats the good of having a wish
On this earth it won't be given
Unless it happens when I'm dead
And if I go to heaven

Just give me a pub
Where I can sit
With a bonny coal fire burning
A drop of the hard stuff
Just enough
To set my throat a yearning

Then I'd wash it down
With half a pint
Of the beer that's Newcastles test
I'd take a draw on my old clay pipe
Among the folks I loved the best.

Mary A. A. McGowan,
Blyth, Northumberland.

SENSES OF LUING

I can see: the crisp green bracken growing on the hillside,
The grey ragged edges of the rocks as I walk along the beach,
The dark muddy brown as I look deep down into the waters of the
   quarries,
But best of all is when I walk over the hills to see the ferry,
Going across the lovely waters of Luing.

I can hear: the seagulls skirling above my head,
The noise of the boats engines as they go out to sea,
The cars as they go on and off the ferry,
I can also hear the little grey pebbles crushing together as people walk
   on them.

I can smell: the cows and horses dirt as I walk over the hills,
The smell of fish at the pier,
There is a smell of salt in the air,
I can smell the wind as it swirls around the island.

I can touch: the smoothness of the grey pebbles as I walk along the
   beach,
The roughness of the different colours of heather as I walk along the
   hillside.

I can taste: the freshness of the lobsters as I walk near the pier,
The taste of salt melts in my mouth.

I can see: I can hear: I can smell: I can touch:
I can taste: the Island of Luing.

Fiona McGregor
Pollok, Glasgow.

HOME

Her byways I've wandered Scotia's beauties to see,
Round the peak of "Schiehallion" down to bonnie Dundee,
From the mist on the Coolins and by sweet Rothesay Bay,
With the moon on Loch Lomond at the close of the day.

I have flown to far countries, I have sailed o'er the foam,
Trod the sands of Morocco, seen the Fountains in Rome,
But tho' many fair treasures in the world I did see,
Yet the beauties of Scotland fairer still are to me.

Like the sparkle of moonbeams on a Lochan by night,
The sunrise o'er hilltops by the dawns early light,
The snow in the Corries, where they reach for the sky,
And the mantle of purple when the autumn draws nigh.

I will sing you her praises as I go on my way,
The grandeur of highlands the green banks of the Tay,
And as on through the lowlands and the borders I roam,
How I thrill to the magic of this land I call home.

Home, home, home is for me,
Where the dear Scottish mountains and her valleys I see,
Where birch and the rowan,
On the breezes blow free,
And gold of the bracken all spell homeland to me.

Margaret McIntosh,
Edinburgh.

THE WORST TIME OF OUR LIVES

It was good, really good,
While it lasted . . .,
At first life was hard,
Difficult to follow.
Full of anti-climaxes,
Never seemed worth the effort.
Eventually we triumphed,
Succeeded where they had failed and
Mounted the regal throne of fame.
We lived in a dazzling dream,
Kidding ourselves ecstatically,
Telling ourselves how good it was.
We relied on a second life,
A fantasy world
Full of injections and pills
Just to give us a smile.
That was one step in the wrong direction
Amongst a multitude of others . . .
Drifting was our downfall.
We drifted slowly apart,
Slowly down from our pedestals.
Few of us survived the strain.
The survivors were unlucky,
They faced the press,
Tried to express
What busted us.
How hard it must have been,
To have to act again.

Shirley McGuire,
Ralston, Paisley,
Renfrewshire.

THE DEATH OF A HERD

Oft' do I start up in the dark, and the sweat creeps ower my brow,
For in the silence of the nicht, I'd swear I hear the blue coo lowe,
Then as I shack my muddled heid, and sleep forsakes my een,
Fine div I ken, it's jist a dream my byres are teem.

My beasties were my pride and joy, I prized them sair,
Reared them fae lang legged baby calves, we every care,
They didna boast a pedigree, but bonnier beasts ye couldna see,
'Bout ony fairm toon, for miles a' roon.

The dread scourge struck, I couldna' think t'was true,
When the waited verdict came, without a doot, ay fit and moo,
Much wid I g'een to stay the slayer's hand, it couldna' be,
For ithers' sake, and to clear the land, they had to dee.

They named a compensation price, which I didna' hear,
For the price to me in heart ache was full dear,
There's some that said, the siller made amends, or even mair,
Oh foolish eens, oh foolish eens, sic ignorance, maks me greet.

Noo, there's a great broon pit, a'hin the dyke where they a' sleep,
My kye, my stirkies, and my gentle grey faced sheep,
Where in a month I'd dared to dream their frisky lambs,
Would leap, I dreamed o'wer seen.

Ay, my byres are teem, and a' my parks are bare,
There's an eery silence, roon the fairm toon, that's ill to thole,
Yet I must hide my grief, for it ill becomes a man to weep we hear,
But in the friendly dark, wi none to see, I do not stay the silent tear.

Mrs. Isobel M. McIntosh,
Ellon, Aberdeenshire.

A LONDON TRILOGY

February

The cry of seagulls vibrates against the taut,
frozen membrane of my ear. The industrial pink
light of morning is visible beyond pouring factory
smoke and, crossing the wrought iron bridge, I
wonder at the separate rhythms of tide and city
dweller, at flossy mist of morning cloud pierced
by harsh stabs of neon lighting and at the
intermittent wild utterances of birds above the
constant throbbing drone of automated man.

London in the early morning of a week day is a
swift hurrying of silent figures in a still,
dormant world as if once again the worries of rush
hour travel and office hours break into a life still
breathing with quiet independent activity. Waking
to the stirring of this City each morning brings
an awareness of the pressures we create by our
ruthless organisation and demands for routine action
to keep the wheels of man-made life revolving. In
our desperate efforts to abide by our self-imposed
discipline, we fail to notice that at Putney the
tide is on the ebb having lipped in by the full moon,
arranging its contour of slatted boxes, drift-wood,
spars and tell-tale debris against walls which control
its spread. And, as the City's pulse shrinks by day,
it seems to leave abandoned on the tarry shingle,
hosts of foreign souls which whirl and wheel about
with shrill soprano cries forlorn against the rumbling
bass accompaniment of rush hour traffic.

June

Summer promises a glorious show of poppy buds and
passion this year. Laburnum has almost suffocated
the space where it droops its soft, abundant lemon bunches.
The lawn has grown too high for grace and comfort and the
sickled scythes complain loudly as they sheer to bristles
slender lengths of waving grasses. Rumbling beyond,
a temporary obliteration of the carefully issued sounds
we make, the tube trains pass; many people passing through
our conversation, mowing through a meadowland of thought.
This grass will not be good for reaping when so much
uninvited traffic passes through.

226

October

People talking everywhere.

Sitting in a High Street cafe,
Riding buses,
Standing queues,
Hear those leaves of gossip dropping
All around . . .
And I cannot see a way of stopping
The dropping of the leaves as litter
Like an everlasting flitter
From the mind.
Please help us not to scatter
But to gather
Together
The feathers of our fluffy minds.

Solveig M. McIntosh,
London.

SCAVENGERS OF THE SEA

See them swoop with wings outstretched
Gliding fast and free
Searching for food, to feed the young
Scavengers of the sea.

With Glistening feathers sprayed with salt
They come in twos and threes
With sharp yellow beaks grabbing fish
Scavengers of the sea.

They ride fast and free on the crest of the waves
Searching, diving endlessly
From where they come, we do not know
Scavengers of the Sea.

Picking at crusts so carelessly thrown
By trippers down for the day
Searching the rubbish along the shore
Scavengers of the Sea.

The beach is deserted, the waves pound the shore
But still there appears to be
A beating of waves as the shore is patrolled
By the Scavengers of the Sea.

Charles MacIntyre,
Bellshill, Lanarkshire.

PRO-UNION

Now a man on his own he is naught – just alone,
And is lacking a part of his life;
Though he outwardly may be carefree and gay
He still needs the balm of a wife.
A wife, after all, since the biblical fall
Of Eve, is still his main need,
And though she be shrew, or be false, or be true,
She can be a comfort indeed.
Though the man may decree there is just solely he,
And he on his own is complete
He will later regret that he never did get
A wife, if only to beat!
Now the wife is the one who is never outdone,
And is right even when she is wrong,
But we masculines know that it's much better so,
'Cause she always will win by a tongue.
Now I'm sure you'll admit, when it comes to the bit,
And with this you must all agree,
That if we're short sighted, and are not united,
There just will not be you or me!

Alasdair MacIomhair,
Brora, Sutherland.

THOUGHTS

I would like to say what is in my mind
Like the time on the clock,
I would like to unwind.

Though I know you are deep beneath the dew
Are the thoughts that I think the same as you
Do you hear all the feet as they pass you by
Do you see the sad looks with no tears in their eye
With some flowers for you they are there then gone
With no words to say how they carry on
Yet they may be thinking the same as you
But then, the things that are done
They can't undo.

Lizzie J. MacKay
Forres, Morayshire.

228

POLLY'S LAST

O Foal a kent yer mither well
She wis a horse a'd never sell
She cam tae me wi'thoot a shoe
The year a mind wis fifty two.

She always hud gentle way
An' greetit me aye wi' a neigh
A bonnie colour brightest bay
Fur her ma faither he did pay.

We travelled wide the countryside
Oorsel's fur company
And of'en in the mornin' tide
We paddled in the sea.

But, then yet Mum she did go lame
And never went quite soond again
That's why a hud her pit in foal
Yae ca' pit horses on the dole.

A' her foals she mithered well
Some of coorse ave hud tae sell
Lots o' stories they can tell
Except fur wan, who tolled the bell.

Seven foals, then twins wer' born
But they wer' gone by early morn
She picked up well regained her strength
When Spring cam roond she hud her tenth.

They've a' done well when pit on show
Never in the bottom row
A famous son who likes tae run
Flew ower the jumps an' races won
So foal when you wer' born that night
In the field held up a light
Nae time at a yae stood upright
An tae yer Mum a welcome sight.

Wis no like her tae lie sae long
But at the time saw nothin' wrong
Sometimes she never ate her feed
No makin' milk that wis yer need.

The vet wis called, He rubbed his chin
"Yae ken, yer mare, she's gittin' thin
The foal as well is ower slim"
Yer Ma. sae quick quickly she did fail
Yae drank yer milk then, oot a pail
A saw the glint went oot her e'e
We didnae ken that she wid d'e
The vet did come an' dae his best
Guid her a jag tae mak her rest
She knickered richt up tae the last
Did slowly drift intae the past.

Hazel McKendrick,
Markinch, Fife.

REMINISCENCE

It is the beginning of the end,
This broken body will not mend.
When I was eight,
My back was straight.
My steps were light and brisk,
I could walk without risk.
That I would fall at every turn,
Others help I could spurn.
Crossing roads held no fear,
For these eyes were blue and clear.
But now they are dull and hazy,
People say I am lazy.
Because I am not clean,
They have never seen.
How hard I've tried,
And having failed. cried.
Tears of bitter anguish,
My only prayer and wish.
That they would cease to scold,
My only fault is, that I am old.

Richard McKeown,
Thorngumbald, Nr. Hull.

AN HOUR OF YOUR TIME

Can you spare an hour of your time
To welcome bluebells in their carpet so fine?
In the Spring of the year where the wild flowers grow,
Let's hurry, let's hurry, woods beckon and bluebells are nodding hello.

Can you spare an hour of your time
To welcome birds in their plummage so fine?
In the Spring of the year where the wild birds sing,
Let's hurry, let's hurry, woods beckon and birds are on wing.

Can you spare an hour of your time
To welcome waves glinting in sunshine so warm?
In the Spring of the year where the wild seas depart,
Let's hurry, let's hurry, sands beckon, waves dance with such heart.

Can you spare an hour of your time
To welcome Spring in glorious raiment so fine?
In the Spring of the year every meadow, wood and shore
Re-echoes, please hurry, do hurry to see our offerings once more.

Hilda S. McKerron,
Barrow-in-Furness.

AUTUMN

Autumn is an artist with palette riot-loose,
He flames the evening sunset in a myriad of hues;
Orange bronze and lustre, he tints the falling leaf,
Full range from blush to golden, he guilds the harvest sheaf.

On hill and moor with loving brush, he tops the heather-bell full lush,
The passing clouds soft tinted blue, reflect in loch of deeper hue
And whitewashed crofts against the light, assume a Florentine delight
Of ruby glass and sapphire stone, in radiant evening light.

Roses, blood-red glad the eye, and pink-tipped seagulls heavenward fly,
While silver herring ochre flecked, in purple harbour lie.
Familiar scenes of toil and care released from dull-eyed duty,
The heart of man by Autumn's brush beholds eternal beauty.

Now empty tube and palette bare, Autumn stops to stand and stare
At landscape, master hand revealed, as neither Spring or Summer dare
Full soon devoid his Regal might, he bows, avowing Nature's right;
The torch of life to Winter's hand, he passes on at God's command.

Mrs. Nessie McKinlay,
Glasgow.

KELT OR KILT?

The coose Merch wind brocht rain an' sleet
The fishers a' were cauld an' weet
Bit fifty rods were on the watter
Brosie lads wi' lots o' patter

A' at eince a roar rang oot
"I've hooked a fish there is nae doot"

A scrunty chiel stood in the pool
His rod wis bent bit he wis cool
While fifty lads wi' bated breath
Waited for the salmon's death

It didna loup nor show its snoot
It wis sullen, sulky brute
Aneath a boulder it wis snug
An' gart the mannie pul' an' rug

The wind hid drapped bit nae the chatter
For fifty tongues went yakerty-yatter
There wisna a chiel bit kent fit tae dee
For abody there wis expert ye see

Bit fan at last the fish was teen
The experts sa' it wisna clean
An' sae the gadgie seen wis telt
The fish he'd landed was a kelt

Bit the Birkie widna agree
An' blawed he'd hae it for his tea
So fifty fishers lost their heid
An' telt the chiel they wished him deid

Bit syne anither fish wis seen
So fifty chiels stopped feelin' mean
An waded deep intae the watter
For feels wi' kelts were gie sma matter

They'd hardly got their lines richt oot
Fan the mannie hooked anither troot
Pride an' panic crossed his face
As oot he stepped anither pace

An' oer his oxters went the gump
A dreepin', slimy, soggy lump
An' fifty times that chiel wis telt
Tae change his troosers for his kelt

Charles Thomson McLachlan.
Aberdeen.

NOTE FOR NON FISHERS
    A kelt is a salmon which has just spawned and is consequently in a weakened condition. Anglers should return all kelts to the water so that they can regain their strength.

THE FAIRGROUND

I love to see the fairground,
With its lights so bright,
I love to see the fairground,
When it's lit up at night.

I see the scary big wheel,
I also see the swings,
Oh what fun it is there,
What fun the fairground brings.

The hotdog stall is busy,
The crowds all crowd about,
Everyone likes the fairground,
And that's without a doubt.

The smells are rather welcoming,
To you and to me,
The waltzers they go round about,
Just like a bumble bee.

But now the fairgrounds closing,
There's litter everywhere,
But we'll be back tomorrow,
Don't you worry we'll be there.

Heather McLaughlin,
Kilwinning, Ayrshire.

233

THE CHRISTMAS TREE

With apples, oranges, sweets and stars,
Fairy lights twinkling like Mars,
Lametta glinting in the winter sun
To the children such fun.

Their eyes light up with delight
As they look apon this wondrous sight,
They gather around on Christmas Eve
Lovely gifts to receive.

Off to Church they will go
Gaily laughing, through the snow,
A carol or two they will sing
"Glory to a new born King."

The Christmas tree stands so bright
An emblem of that wonderful night,
When trumpets sound, angels sing
To herald the reign of Christ The King.

Mrs. Mary Irvine McLaughlin,
Cambuslang, Glasgow.

HIGHLAND MEMORIES

My view from a hill
Overlooking the sea
The wonder and thrill
Bringing peace to me.

I think of Uist so often
A place of heaven on earth
My eyes and heart aye soften
Recalling days full of mirth.

The children with me always
For loving and caring was me
Laughing, chattering every day
Round "Suinish" down to the sea.

Auntie cooking and baking
Times for her usually hard
How she keeps on smiling
A truly remarkable card.

A new generation growing
So close to our way of life
Loving kindness they are sowing
Far away from the city strife.

Mrs. Mary MacLellan,
Rutherglen, Glasgow.

ATONEMENT

She hides behind a rock
And watches through tired tearful eyes
The factor and his men
Evicting the souls from their styes.

Her hands clenched in prayer
Does not avert the scene of shame,
Where in the winter glen
The hovels are all set aflame.

When all is quietly still
She views lonely desolation,
And asks herself, oh why
Her husband condones the action.

He hides behind the rule
Of servility to ones peer.
But his reason simply
Is the one of cowardly fear.

His guilt weighs heavily
Upon her heart of bereavement,
So she decides upon
Sacrifice as his atonement.

At night the manse burns down
With the minister's final sleep,
And his flock mourns him not,
For it is but a flock of sheep.

James R. MacLeod,
Kylesku, Sutherland.

LAMENT

Where is the Scotland of the past,
When all her sons stood firm and fast,
The heritage we gained in trust,
Has long since gone through greed and lust.
Our Fathers bled this land to keep,
Yet from its shores we seek to creep,
The bureaucratic hand engraved
Once more a nation now enslaved.
In fear and love we held our god,
Now cast aside with passing nod,
In pride we held a wordly place,
Where now stands this Scottish race.
In war we stood above the rest,
Now we rate but second best
In many ways our worlds advanced,
The quality of life enhanced.
New found wealth the power to spend,
Yet much is left to comprehend,
The age of science holds its sway,
But linked with ails, disease, decay.
Hardship poverty and derelict grime,
New Laws enforced to cope with crime,
What vision in this new decade,
When aims and ideals seem mislaid.
Social status strife unrest,
Let old traditions meet the test,
O' for the power some guiding light,
To indicate whats wrong and right,
In place of selfish gain to thirst,
Better still their country first,
Sound the clarion call again,
Scotland with our might and main,
Let the lion rampant fly,
As of old lets do or die.

James McMillan,
Aberdeen.

THE GHOST

I rode along the road that night
No sign of people or of light.
I feared a ghost was following me
That came from behind a shady tree.

236

The ghost was charging at all speed
But so was my young chestnut steed.
I wondered how long the chase would last
For my little brown horse was tiring fast.
At last I saw a friendly light
But still the ghost was in my sight.
One final urge, but all is lost
My faltering mount had paid the cost.
The awful thoughts, the great despair
The ghostly thing now touched my hair.
Suddenly I woke with piercing scream
Then realized it was just a dream.

Malcolm J. McMillan,
Aberdeen.

REFLECTIONS OAN A BICENTENNIAL

Twa hunner years ago the noo
The Americans up an' did a coup,
An' sae tae Britain cam the crunch,
Lood the cry "Nae Vote" "Nae Munch!"

At Boston jings they hid a pairty,
By o' accoonts, it wis jist a stairty!
Intae the sea they threw the tea,
Which didnae comfort George The Three!!

At last in the city made by Penn
Declaration deeds wur signed, an' then
Wae joy they rang the Liberty bell,
An' sent darn taxes doon tae . . . Well?

But time great healer in this life,
His pit an' end tae o' the strife
Noo haun in haun as brithers should
Thigither we wark fur mankind's guid.

Annie J. McNab,
Glasgow.

EVENSONG

Silver
birch
slender
as
grace
of a
girl
against
summer
blue

can break
the heart
in stillness
as easily

as you.

Mr. Robert McWhirter,
Dumfries.

THE GLENS

My mind is so full, as I sit at my desk,
Of days spent in Angus's glens:
There's Isla and Prosen and Clova and Esk —
And each with its river and bens.

Oh Isla, sweet Isla, your river flows fast
From Monega Hill to the Tay
'Twas there on your banks that I ate my repast
'Ere walking up-river one day.

The autumn was with us so down came the sheep
From bens to the valley below;
So safe in the care of the shepherd who'll keep
Watch over them through winter's snow.

The wind blew down cold from the mountains so high,
Which were touched very lightly with snow —
But the sun shone quite brightly from out the blue sky
And we walked with our faces aglow.

We next went to Prosen – 'twas wide at the start –
The road wound up hill and then down;
The autumnal colours brought warmth to the heart –
From yellow to deep russet brown.

We walked by the river – 'twas late afternoon –
No sound broke the stillness that day –
The mountains looked eerie – the twilight came soon –
From blue the sky now turned to grey.

With Prosen behind us to Clova we come –
It starts around Cortachy way –
The beautiful castle, the ancestral home
Of the head of the Clan Ogilvie.

South Esk is the river which flows through the glen
From the Grampians down to Montrose,
Through Braedownie and Clova to Brechin and then
Eastward and seaward it goes.

'Tis a picturesque glen, and we lingered awhile
To enjoy the delights of that day,
The weather was fine – we walked many a mile
Seeing no-one at all by the way.

No humans were there, but the fleet-footed deer
On the mountains did merrily rove,
Stags gathering hinds with their call loud and clear
Which echoed and echoed above.

To Edzell we go now and on to Glen Esk –
'Twas a day with its showers and sun;
The rainbows we sighted were quite picturesque
Ere our day of exploring was done.

At the head of the Glen lies little Loch Lee
And Invermark Castle's there too,
But a path leading northward beckoned to me
As I looked at the breathtaking view.

Along here, 'tis said, Queen Victoria came
On a day many long years ago,
She drank at a well – now it's marked with her name –
That all who pass by there may know.

Our days in these glens were full of delights
Their memories stay with us yet;
The long winding rivers, the mountainous heights
Are things we will never forget.

Marjorie Maddock,
Chatburn, Lancashire.

THE DISASTEROUS BAKER
(*Dedicated to Cousin Gavin*)

Once upon a time,
A long and almost never ending rhyme,
Was written in the British Isles,
About a baker who used to bake nothing but pies.

But although he was a baker,
He never quite could make . . . er!
Bread, biscuits, pies and sweet treats,
And everything you would most like to eat.

If you wanted something too,
I'd tell you what you'd best do,
Book three solid weeks in advance,
For the baker would appear to be in a trance.

If you asked him early,
Everything would go hurley-burley and topsie-turvey,
Even though the baker was an excellent maker of pies,
You would always get the custard ones on the corners of your eyes.

If you were so misfortunate, on your clothes,
And even in between your toes,
But no one knows why the baker was such an accident-prone one,
For even when baking a bun; he'd blow the oven up.

On Monday the baker tried making bread,
But at the state of his bread no-one got fed,
So on Tuesday the baker baked biscuits,
But the people wouldn't risk it;
To take a little nibble,
At his strawberry and raspberry ripples.
On Wednesday the baker had a rest,
He thought he would try his best
Through the remainder of the week.
On Thursday he got up before dawn,
The earliest he'd ever done in the morn',
He was determined if it took he all day,
Whatever come what may.

He'd make them custard tarts beautiful and gay,
For presentation or possibly consumption the very next day
So he presented them in an ordinary array,
But his tarts were not so gay.

The Consumer Protection Society,
Came to see the baker and gave him priority,
He told him a week in advance,
That the leader, the sun would give him a chance.

But it was too late; he had to depart,
His bakery blew up and sprang all apart,
And he joined the great bakery, among the clouds,
Where he baked a thousand loafs and his leader was proud.

Michael Maguire,
Bradford, West Yorkshire.

RETURN JOURNEY

As sure as dawns keep coming,
As the flux 'tween night and day,
There's bound to be an Eden of a kind,
And there's sure to be a garden,
Where solitude will flourish,
And man can come to rest his weary mind.

For it's weariness of working,
With the strains of modern living,
The speeding up of plutocratic greed;
The cajoling of the minions,
As with carrot and the mule,
With monetary gain their only creed.

Please God, calm the avaricious pulse,
Restore mans sanity,
Take us back to Adam, be so kind;
Let us taste unselfish freedom,
In the garden known as Eden,
I'm sure the solitude we seek, we'll find.

Mr. Leslie P. Male,
Herne Bay, Kent.

PRINCE CHARLES IN WESTMINSTER ABBEY
CORONATION OF HER MAJESTY QUEEN ELIZABETH II 2ND JUNE 1953.

A small boy watched his mother crowned,
With mystic wonder in his eyes,
Love, pride, and joy shone there renowned,
Sweet innocence, and bright surprise,
The reverence on that childish face
Shone with a holy heavenly light,
The Lord Himself was in that place,
His spirit granting blessing bright.

A small boy watched his mother crowned,
His father paying homage rare,
Love, pride and joy shone there renowned,
A gentle hand upraised to share,
A Royal Sovereign deeply moved,
Receiving grace, and sweet accord,
She knew how dearly she was loved,
And praised, and thanked her gracious Lord.

A small boy watched his mother crowned,
And listened to the music clear,
Love, pride, and joy shone there renowned,
To see the ones he loved so dear,
The choir the joyful anthems sang,
And Grandma held his tiny hand,
The bells with melody they rang,
And chimed their joy o'er all the land.

A small boy watched his mother crowned,
Prince Charles so sweet and stately stood,
Love, pride, and joy shone there renowned,
He knew he must be very good,
And all the people waiting, there,
They cried, "God bless our gracious Queen"
God blessed Elizabeth so fair,
God blessed our lovely, gracious, Queen.

Nellie Malpass,
Walsall.

A STRANGE FEELING

Back to a house where once I thought of you,
More than half a year –
Since when they've been so many phases,
Such a range of changes.
I can view that girl who once sat here,
I can inspect Time's pages:
There were discoveries of people,
Whole new worlds,
But through these a discovery of her self,
It was a slow and solid progress
So that now with such finds on board,
It's strange to review times before
I can almost pity that girl –
She was so earnest in her dreams,
She has long ago had to relinquish realistic theme
Looking back on the sheer strive,
She wonders whether it was not a dream,
but a nightmare, on which she thrived.

Macia De Renzy-Martin,
London, W.14.

THE GARDEN OF PARADISE

Once there was a garden called Eden,
A paradise – so we are told
Where the hand of God,
Turned everything into the colour of gold.
The flowers which grew abundantly
Were fragrant with His love
Even to the rainbow shining brightly right above,
But in this lovely land,
Man was not content,
He went to war with everything he didn't
    understand.

God sent to this garden a wonderful man,
Who told us all about this heavenly plan,
He tried to assure us that all would be well
As long as love in our hearts did dwell,
We listened to this and seemed eager to learn the
    gentle words which he spoke so well,
So much he offered,
So much to receive

If only we'd listened and tried to believe,
But alas, our cunning and selfish desire
Led us astray, and we went our own way,
We battled and killed the love that was offered
And in our rejection lost all as we suffered.
That garden of paradise could still be found,
If we cleared the weeds we could see the ground
That which with riches did once abound
Could still be ours if we looked around,
Seeing the beauty everywhere
Making use of the good which is always there,
Clearing the weeds and the ground
Laying bare, offering to God our first design
By sowing the seeds of love divine.

Mrs. Thora Louise Mason,
Glasgow.

GOODWILL

Why do we all wait for Christmas
To wish "Goodwill toward man"?
To pocket our pride in the autumn
Is as good a time if we can
To visit the sick and the poorly
For a task they need to have done
Would please them far more than your praying
Where you, not they, would have won.
The world is so full of envy
All over pounds silver and pence
Let's call to our neighbouring countries
Shake hands with them over the fence
Churches are bowing and praying
Governments are loading the gun
Why cannot we all get together
To live with a smile and some fun.
Don't let us wait until Christmas
To pocket our pride and be brave
You can't give a man a good handshake
If he's dead, asleep in his grave.

Martin Paul Maund,
London.

AT TWENTY-ONE LIFE'S BUT A DREAM

At twenty-one life's but a dream
We're eager, young, and yet we seem
Uncertain, wondering how to tread
Untasted years that lie ahead.

Our childhood days seem far away
Yet do we ever really stray
From teachings that we learned at home
However far away we roam.

As on the highway steps you trace
Look carefully into each face
They are but masks in life's great drama
And you will find you'll need an armour.

You'll learn to judge with open mind
Like jewellery – the trashy kind
But most of all you'll learn to know
The heart that has an inner glow.

New friends you'll make and some will stay
With you all along the way
You'll learn to give and learn to take
Them as they are for friendship's sake.

No other blessing can compare
For friendship's made for all to share
But greatest of all lessons learned
A worthwhile friendship must be earned.

Mrs. Maisie May,
Mansfield Nottinghamshire.

TWENTY-FIVE YEARS

Goodness how the time does fly,
Have twenty-five years really passed by,
When I was but a child at school,
And our dear Queen began her rule.

Arrangements soon were under way,
Planning for Coronation Day,
Flags in streets were hoisted high,
"God save the Queen", was our loud cry.

And in our school we held a play,
Commemorating that historic day,
A party in our street was fun,
With souvenir mugs for everyone.

But soon festivities were 'ore,
And life went on just as before,
Into adults we children grew,
Hoping our dreams would all come true.

And since that day we've seen some change,
Some good, some bad, some rather strange,
Singers now no longer croon,
And man has walked upon the moon.

Now motorcars fill all our roads,
There's wagons with enormous loads,
And right across our countryside,
Motorways stretch far and wide.

Now she who's reigned so happily,
Has reached her Silver Jubilee,
A Queen who never seems to grow old,
Pray may her Silver turn to Gold.

Mrs. Dorothy Mellish,
Jarrow, Tyne and Wear.

DEDICATION TO A SON

Our son is a boy with joys untold,
Blue eyes and fair hair and so bold,
He smiles and laughs,
And plays with ducks in his bath,
Daniel Edward is his name,
Who thinks that everything is a game,
Such love and joy he brings us both,
We are a family now and always will be,
Sometimes he will cause much heartache and pain,
But we will love him just the same.

D. Mercer,
Sheffield, Yorks.

WINTER VIEW

Arran's bright majestic snow
Shining in the pale red glow
Grey waves of the firth beneath
On its shore the soft winds breath
Seagulls winging in grey skies
Echoing their plaintive cries
Arran's crags their watch will keep
Reminding us of passions deep
Sometimes they hint of melancholy
Sometimes they speak of music holy
Sometimes the sound of hawks may swell
The tales of history to tell
When birds sing in the sun's first say
Rocks whisper of eternity.

Mary Millar,
Saltcoats, Ayrshire.

EDINBURGH CASTLE

The Tattoo is at the Castle,
I hear the Pipers playing,
There's the Sailors in blue, and,
The Soldiers, in their grand array,
Showing a great display.
Edinburgh's pride is the Castle,
That is wonderful to see,
When you walk up the Strand,
And you hear the band,
You are proud of Bonnie Scotland,
When you are glancing round the land.
When you are walking through the gardens,
That is beautiful to see,
With the floral clock,
And the Castle on the rock,
They are wonderful to see,
Wonderful to see.

Mrs. Margaret Minto,
Edinburgh.

247

ISLE OF SKYE

Isle of Skye
Isle of Skye,
Magic that will never die.
Cuillins proud, now black now grey,
Changing, altering all the day.
Chasing shadows, rainy mist,
In summer heat, pale amethyst.
While along the rocky shore,
Foaming angry breakers roar.
While clouds of spray,
Leap in the air,
But when it's calm and all is fair.
The white sands shine like angels wings,
And sunshine deep contentment brings.
Sparkling in the quivering light,
Heathery hillsides purple bright.
Scent of bog myrtle, scent of hay,
Pervading the long summer day.
And the friendly homely croft,
Is snug beneath the clouds aloft.
And Quirang fortress keeps guard o'er,
The place where eagles love to soar.
Isle of Skye
Isle of Skye,
Magic that will never die.

Mollie Miller,
Maldon, Essex.

SILHOUETTES

Dark shadows of swans gliding motionless along the river
Silhouettes of old damp houses
Slowly rotting to the ground
Heaps of rubbish dumped in dark alleyways
With stray cats and dogs rummaging in the dustbins
And fighting over bones
And a dogs distant bark coming from the end of the street
Cats singing in the twilight of the moon
While fireflies glow in the dark.

Susan Milner (Aged 9),
Plumstead.

THOUGHTS OF A COUNTRY GIRL

When I look thro' my window
At the peaceful countryside
I envy not the people
Who in the city bide.

They toil in noisy factories
In offices and mills
But I would gladly share with them
The silence of the hills.

For I have the freedom of the dales
Its ways are dear to me
Its meadows, woods and laughing streams,
The sky's my canopy.

Here in God's own country
Let me live and die
Near to Nature's living heart
Under the open sky.

Margaret A. Mitchell,
Kirkby Stephen, Cumbria.

WEDDING DAY

Wedding bell
Joyful bell
Happy bell
Over tree and dell
Down and fell.
All they tell,
Not to sell –
But wishing well
To boy and girl.

R. J. Mitchell,
Rugby, Warwickshire.

HILLS OF HOME
Written in New Zealand before returning to Scotland.

Spring is fresh, and buds are new –
Season when life begins anew;
Follows summer, and fulfils
Promise of spring; now see the hills
As autumn comes, in all their splendour
Robed royal purple in September.

Blooms the heather, rich and wild
Free and windblown. As a child
I gathered riches beyond all ken
In waning gold of autumnal fern.
On, up the hillside, cheeks aglow
Sandy bay and loch below;
Absorbing (though yet unaware)
Love of homeland for evermore.

Years roll by. Too soon one finds
Childhood paths are left behind.
Lochearn, Strathyre, north to Glencoe
Along all roads I had to go,
One golden day upon another
The whole of Scotland to discover!

Past wayside burn, and Perthshire bens
Jewel lochans and quiet glens.
And all around, where'er I'd roam
Would rise about me the hills of home.

Land of contrasts!
Of grey, gaunt crag,
Of golden eagle and royal stag.
Keen highland air, unsullied, pure,
And snow – white and glittering – on Rannoch Moor.
Of fishing village, and seagull calls
And artists painting on old harbour walls.

Red sandstone abbey, and (turn back the clock –
Fishing smacks rounding the Inchcape Rock)
Seas crashing on rocks in a flurry of spray
And caves, long forgotten, in Flaers Bay –
(Young explorers always find such places)
And spindrift, wet upon our faces.

Yet, the Western seaboard's another door;
Of seal-strewn skerries by cockle shore.

With mountain grandeur of Kinlochewe
(And palm-trees flourishing at Poolewe;
Nature's diversions the Gulf Stream brought)
And the Isles of the West, that Time forgot.

Staffa's gigantic basalt columns
Of Fingal's Cave; majestic, solemn.
Barra, Isla, Jura, Skye
'Neath hebridean summer sky
Hardy crofts where peat smoke curled –
Surely this is another world!

Dark Lochnagar, brooding, austere –
Yet, rich pastoral county of Angus is near.
Industrial Glasgow! Of working and learning
Yet of this "no mean city" would I be yearning,
But for Mallaig's sands, and dark Loch Hourn
This is the land where I was born.

But, broader still have horizons been,
New lands and vistas have filled the scene.
England's flat and docile plains,
Old world villages, winding lanes,
Cars pay homage to tarmac of grey,
Wide grey sealed path – the Motorway!
Across the channel, by the Siene
I'd bide awhile – then back again.
But, restless, my spirit was eager to go
'Cross the waste of seas to this land I know.

This wild lovely country, by nature endowed
Maori "Land of the Long White Cloud"
The hills here are grand, and their peaks are higher
But I see Ben Vorlich girdled in fire
As the westering sun sets over the hill
And the gloaming is hushed, and Strathyre is still.
Forestry hills populated by deer,
Happy hunting grounds of yesteryear . . .

Here, there's sun and there's wind, and in drought there's more sun
While the grass becomes dry and shrivelled and dun
And though glacier-fed rivers flow through the parched land
The sheep, with no fodder, motionless stand.
I look all around me, and nought do I see
For the hills of the Clyde they are hidden from me.
Man changes the cities, they can't be the same.
But, watching and waiting, the hills still remain.

251

Here, the sun is warm upon my face,
But my thoughts return to another place
Where, enfolded softly in highland mist
Gently beckon the hills in the gathering dusk;
Dear hills of home. In sun or rain,
Grant that I may behold you again.

Helen M. Moffat,
Arbroath, Angus.

THE BUD UPON THE TREE

High upon a hill-top looking down I see
A quaint little town that is very dear to me.
Here I spent my childhood, grew up with secret dreams
Of far away places all part of my schemes.

But when I grew older it was here I met my love
Not in any place I had been dreaming of.
Just around the corner not far away from me
Love was waiting to burst forth like the bud upon a tree.

Then one happy springtime after showers, cloud and sun
We two were married and so became as one.
In love a tree was planted and a new bud was born
Oh we were so happy to have a tree without a thorn.

With humble admiration we watched it as it grew
Fondling it with tenderness as loving parents do.
In thankfulness to-gether we saw our bud in bloom,
Now when days are dark it brightens up my gloom.

For part of me has left the tree but the root is firm and strong.
And the bud that grew keeps returning to the branch where it belongs.
Now on a bright horizon signs of new life I see,
Silhouettes of offsprings from the bud upon our tree.

Chris. S. Moncrieff,
Newburgh, Fife.

PLASTIC FOOD

Twentieth Century folk,
Your food is no more than a joke,
The cheese tastes like soap,
For bread there's no hope,
And the bacons as salt as the sea.

The masses are fed that's most true,
The vitamised fodder they chew,
With fortified marge and cereals large,
There not hungry or thirsty, just blue.

For good food is a pleasure,
When taken at leisure,
Its taste should give more than its content,
But content we must be,
Every he and sweet she,
For taste is for folk of good measure.

For those who have "thyme"
(Oh pardon the rhyme),
Or those priviledged few,
Who can find a venue,
That's foreign and strange,
And can offer a range,
Of Foods from a menu cxtensive,
Not to mention expensive.

Mrs. B. C. Morgan,
Scunthorpe, South Humberside.

THE SEA

The sea is always changing,
It is never quite the same,
No one can ever fathom it,
No one can make it tame.

When it is wild and rough,
And is roaring up the beach,
You wonder will it ever stop?
How far up will it reach?

Then for no apparent cause,
It will woo you with its charm,
From being a breathtaking roaring thing,
It is quite flat and calm.

It comes and goes and never fails,
Day in day out all year,
Always there by day or night,
Yet never seems to wear.

It has so many secrets,
Asleep there on its bed,
It is a thing to understand,
Something to always dread.

For Children in the summer,
It is happiness and joy,
They splash and bathe and paddle,
To them it is a toy.

The fishermen all love the sea,
It also grants their wish,
To let them open wide their arms,
Tell tales of great big fish.

To some it just means sorrow,
The brave men that were drowned,
Who gave their lives up with their ships,
Their memories renowned.

With joy or sorrow, fear or dread,
The sea is always there,
So treat it with the utmost respect,
And always be aware.

Linda Anne Morgan,
Ilkley, Yorkshire.

IONA

Island of Scotland, an isle of the West,
Where the sky meets the water blue,
When sunset comes, and all things rest,
I'll remember you.

In evenings when skies are tinged glorious red
Or when grass is a-sparkle with dew,
My thoughts through the mists of the seas will be led
And I'll remember you.

Here the last sun-worshippers, bowed before the sun,
Here Columbia and his monks, toiled till day was done,
Here the tide rolls softly in, tide of eternity,
Breaking upon the coasts of time, the voices of wind and sea.
Yonder wheel the sea-birds, there the grazing sheep,
And in the sparkling water there, the seals, like children, leap.
Those who search for the Fount of Youth, it's here, up on Dun-I
Linger at the enchanted hour, of dawn, and memory.

Just to the South of Machair, the boulders trap the sea,
Escaping through a blow-hole, the water spouts up – free,
Against the thyme-set cliff tops, the thin spray quivers free
Below swims Mar-Tarbh, dreaded creature of the sea.
From Lochan Mor, to Spouting cave, Dun-I to craggy steep
The joy of life vibrates – and yet – so many heroes sleep.
Martyr's Bay where the monks were slain, and barges or ships of old,
Brought famous dead from many a land, to sleep in graves untold.

Twenty-one stones on the ridge of Kings, nineteen on ridge of chiefs,
Six hundred monks killed at Martyr's Bay, who died for their beliefs.
Columba, Saint and Christian, he lived and died right here,
Died saying "Oh children do preserve, peace and love sincere."
The flame that lit Pagan Europe, was the lamp that was lit on this isle,
Here learning and faith found a tranquil home, while wars raged all
    the while.
From age to age, the lonely hearts, burdened with care and fear,
Have come to this isle from all over the world, and have lost their
    burdens here.

So this is the Isle of Iona,
In this dark world a light,
Fountain and fortress of Faith and Peace
Where past and present unite.
And when I am weary and ill at ease,
When nothing seems right good or true,
My thoughts through the mists of the seas will be led,
And I'll remember you.

Mrs. Patricia A. Morris,
Gullane, East Lothian.

THE HAND OF GOD

I see the hand of God in everything,
I see it in the merry birds that sing,
I see it in the variegated flowers,
I see it – yes, in all the passing hours.

I see the hand of God in all its might,
When dawn does break and sheds its rosy light,
When lambs do frisk and gambol merrily,
And children play and laugh so heartily.

When whispering winds do sigh so eerily
Reminding one of phantoms fearfully,
And lightning strikes with blue and silver light,
Yes, then I think of God in all His might.

I see the hand of God when falls the night,
The pointed stars that shine so very bright,
The moon – a ghostly galleon in the sky,
These are the things God's given us for aye.

I see the hand of God in everything,
The sun, the moon, the stars, the birds that sing,
Dear God, I pray that I will always see
Your hand in everything you do for me.

Vanessa Grace Morrison,
Greenock, Renfrewshire.

LOVING, LOSING

Forgive me please
My hurting, hollow soul
Who cared too much, too fast,
Then lost,
You deserve much better than I.

My hurt is public
My pretend is gone
I am naked, exposed,
A fool to all
Cold to friends once dear.

"Time will heal" they always say
"How long" I ask
And "Why must I be the one to pay"
I now resolve to care no more
The risks too high
Rewards too small.

Yet in these words
I slowly see, my tattered soul forgive me
My reckless time
My price to pay
I ask for peace
Take my pain away.

Mrs. Peggy Morrison,
Uddingston, Lanarkshire.

POSTMAN'S KNOCK

My goodness we are missing the cheeriest sound
Of postman Leslie doing his round.
He whistled a tune as he went on his way
And cheered us up for the rest of the day.

He would pop in to deliver letters and bills
And enquire if everyone was free from ills,
And even if he had nothing to take for Old Joe,
He would pop in anyway, just to say Hello.

To do a favour he was never to ask
He took it on as another task,
Allowances, pensions and Postal orders too
Or groceries from the shop as he passed through.

He had many a load as he travelled the miles
Down muddy lanes and over stiles,
But he still found time for a laugh and joke
Among his friends – us country folk.

He had quite a wide area, and to cover the like
He travelled around on a good old bike.
No matter the weather, rain, hail or snow
A cup of coffee and away he'd go.

When not on the post he would be seen
In his garden – He is very keen
I thought this lad was worth a mention
Because now he goes to draw his pension

Our letters now are delivered by van
We never see the face of the man
Because he hasn't got into the knack
Of calling in – just for the crack.

When I look out into our yard and see
That chap sitting in his van of luxury
I think our Leslie deserves a medal
For all those miles that he did pedal.

Mary Mounsey,
Penrith, Cumbria.

MEMORIES

I sit alone in my ain wee hoose,
So very quiet I don't even hear a moose,
Och I am no longer in my dear auld den,
This is a pensioner's new bungalow ye ken.

Nae cheery, cracklin' bonny fire burning,
Nae toaster in front wi' bread needing turning,
Or girdle wi' bannocks abune the flame,
A bonnie lass watching, my wife the same.

Ilka July frae my ain large garden,
Midlothian potatoes my graip upturnin',
Early pilot peas a delight to shell,
A young cockerel, the auld oven cooked so well.

So proudly my Dear dished up sic treasure,
We all ate up withoot stint or measure,
A dumpling boiled six 'oors or there,
No man on earth could wish for mair.

Saturday evening was oor bath nicht,
The auld zinc bath came intae sicht,
Young Robin was first, he went a-dancing,
An early age to start romancing.

He's a grandpa' noo, this year seventy-five,
I thank the Lord I am still alive.
Nae mair dąe I sit at the Sacrament Table,
For music and noise, I am just not able.

I am still gey fleet, I have mony a walk,
I can drive my car, a friend with me I tak',
Sometimes to the sea, sometimes to the hills,
I feel nearer to God – He cures all my ills.

The murmuring waves, the golden sands,
The far out ships from foreign lands,
Then home I come, a wee bit trauchled,
I doff my coat, put on my auld bauchles.

The kettle on, some tea I do make,
Sometimes old snapshots oot I take,
Nearly four years since I lost my Dear,
Memories unbidden unfold year by year.

Such happy days we both have had,
I try so hard not to be so sad,
Grandsons, grand-daughters I now can see,
A bonnie great grandson to rest on my knee.

Many visits I get, I love them everyone,
I count my blessings, some old folk have none,
They make me look on the bright side again,
Will I see them grow to be women and men.

I must write down their sweeties to get,
I'll away to Glenwood before I forget,
East Lomond before me, the hill I do love,
Upwards I look, is there a God up above?
When I lie down to sleep tonight,
I'll count my blessings, Dear Lord – goodnight!

William M. Mudie,
Glenrothes.

DEVOLUTIONARY DOGGEREL

Doesn't it make your head swim round,
When you think of the fluctuating £?
Whether it be sterling or whether it be green,
It wobbles up and down as on a see-saw machine
Why has once proud Britain got into such a mess?

By reckless overspending and borrowing to excess
Talk of strict econ'my must be something more than froth
The Chancellor *must* cut his coat according to the cloth!
Every single one of us who calls this country home,
Whether born in Britain or far across the foam,
White or black, or half and half, yellow or red or brown,
Must stand together, shoulder to shoulder, all barriers broken down,
In spite of Powell, we'll save our £ before it drops to zero,
(Would Enoch fiddle while it fell, emulating Nero?)
As for Devolution, which rhymes with pollution,
(Some folk think that both words mean the same!)
This is no time to spend millions on Assemblies
It would not be "playing the game"
Bureaucracy just now is proving too expensive
It must not be allowed to grow even more extensive
Could the issue not stand till we're back on our feet
And able to grapple without undue heat?
Englishman, Irishman, Welshman and Scot
Let bygones be bygones as we know we ought
For united we stand; divided we fall
And "UNION IS STRENGTH" is true above all.

Jean Munro,
Ardrossan.

DAFFODIL TIME

Isn't it nice to be out in the country,
Yes, it is nice to be out in the country,
The daffodils are nodding their heads,
Nodding their heads, nodding their heads.

Saying are'nt we pretty today,
Yes, Oh yes, we are very pretty today,
A blaze of yellow by the road,
Here and there on every road.

A blaze of yellow in the grass,
Makes you look as you pass,
The scene is so different now,
They are so pretty as they bow.

Nodding their heads as if to say,
We'll make you welcome if you stay,
Moving gently on the hill,
Come and see us if you will.

Mr. Patrick Munro,
Mintlaw, Aberdeenshire.

EPITAPH FOR THE BUILDERS OF A CATHEDRAL

We are immortalised in stone: the brains
That this conceived are dust; the hands that
Fashioned it are also dust,
And we are dust and in our graves we lie.
Yet we live on in this, and while it lasts
Then so shall we. Dust did this build and out
Of nothingness it rose; to nothingness
We've gone, and yet it shall remain for always.
And so from brief mortality this comes,
And we, mere mortals, are immortals made.

Ben Murray,
Upper Norwood, London.

BLACK MAN, WHITE MAN

Black is black and white is white
Never the twain must meet.
Close not the door, but give them right
to worship at His feet.

Jesus said come ye to me
He knew no colour bar.
And hundreds flocked to see
upon his brow the scar.

Who are you to bar the door
of Church and any place
Because his skin is not the colour
of the chosen race.

When at your house death has called
and you are laid in state,
Black or white and side by side
your souls pass thro' the gate.

And ye who turn the man away
would expect to find salvation
Obey the teaching of the Lord
and throw out segregation.

And ye who turn around and say
he is just a "God dam Nigger"
Be very sure there will come the day
Poor white trash he will snigger.

Ian Murray,
St. Cyrus, Nr. Montrose.

THE LITTLE MAN

I only am a little man,
My possessions are but few,
And yet of thoughts and memories,
Well, millions could I strew,
Of this my own beloved land.

This island is yours and mine,
Britain is its name,
England, Ireland, Scotland, Wales,
Please God unite us once again.

Together we could show the world,
In voice, in word, in deeds,
That Britain once again can be,
Unto ourselves be true.

So let us pray Dear Lord again,
That peace and love shall reign,
United we shall surely stand,
As in the days of yore,
Great Britain evermore.

Mrs. Hilda Newall,
Bolton, Lancashire.

MEMORY LANE

When I sit alone at night,
Down memories lane I stroll,
I think of olden days gone by,
And happy times I've known.

As a child I would hurry home,
Our parents were loving and kind,
My sisters and brothers were really nice,
And a happy family we made.

T'was a lovely little village where we lived,
With cornfields all around,
A lovely old church, and a village school,
And a dene where we often played.

Our parents would take us to the dene,
Whenever they cut the corn,
Their laughter rang out as they sat in the sun,
Whilst we kids paddled in the stream.

In winter I often sat at the window,
And watched my friends at play,
This time of year I was often ill,
So could not join in the fun.

One night I'll always remember,
As I sat on my mother's knee,
If I was going to die this night,
I was where I wanted to be.

Her tears fell upon my face,
I whispered, "Mother do not cry",
She nursed me until morning came,
This memory of love, forever will remain.

Time is swiftly rolling by,
And I am growing old,
I like to sit in my favourite chair,
And dream of long ago.

I close my mind, to the world outside,
And I stroll down memory lane,
So, with a smile upon my face,
I relive my life again.

Mrs. W. M. Niblo,
Arborfield Cross, Nr. Reading,
Berkshire.

BUILDING YOUR LIFE

The passings of life's time,
Is like mortar and lime,
Build to the fashion of your dreams,
And the bricks are the years in between.

It's up to you how it stays,
You are the tradesman of your ways,
Mix your mortar with great care,
Don't have it crack up with Dispair.

A foundation deep and strong,
Will hold up against all wrongs,
A fortress from the trails of life,
Protection for your children and wife.

For you have built this house, it's you,
Stand erect, your whole life through,
Treat the timbers, and preserve,
The happiness and health, you deserve.

William Nichol,
Northolt, Middlesex.

MEMORIES

As I gazed through the window from the lonely croft,
Standing high on the heather clad hill,
I thought of the many times and oft,
I'd stood just there and drank my fill.
Of the beautiful Sound of Sleat.

And down to the shore I'd go each day,
To watch the sea in variant mood,
From tranquil blue to a surly grey,
And there transfixed with awe I stood,
By the beautiful Sound of Sleat.

At night as I lay in my bed at ease,
Lulled to sleep by the sea on the shore,
In the lonely croft midst the tall fir trees,
I felt, of life, I could ask no more,
Than to stay near the Sound of Sleat.

And when the time must come to part,
From this most wondrous Isle,
It is with sad and forlorn heart,
I board the ferry boat for Kyle,
And wave farewell to Skye and Sleat.

Caroline M. Nicolson,
Tillicoultry, Clackmannanshire.

THE SPILT OIL

Oil in a puddle,
Makes patterns so gay,
It looks like a muddle,
Some people say

The colours are quite bright,
As they twirl with the rain,
It's such a pretty sight,
As they flow down the drain.

The colours change again,
As they flow quickly by,
Driven by the rain,
Falling out of the sky.

First it looks plain,
Then turns blue and green,
Now look again,
New colours are seen.

These colours stand out,
As the oil flows away,
And still there's no doubt,
It brightened the day.

Denise Nixon,
Derby, England.

IF I HAD A MILLION POUNDS

If I had a million pounds,
This is what I'd do,
I'd buy a midget submarine,
Or a boxing kangaroo.

I'd use the midget submarine,
To voyage under the sea,
To search for long lost treasure,
Or sea anemone.

I'd use the boxing kangaroo,
To fight along with coppers,
For when they made their get-away,
They'd always catch the robbers.

But why would I want all of this,
I am happy where I am,
My little house upon the hill,
And my tatty laundry van.

I'd only give it all away,
To deserving charities,
As money can't buy everything,
Except for novelties.

Amanda Jane Norman (Aged 11),
Gillingham, Kent.

IMPASSE

I will try to write a poem
About you;
Not about us – our love,
You-and-I amalgam;
But only you.

I will write a poem;
Not about your eyes, your lips,
Your breasts,
The cushion of your thighs,
The honeyheat
Of your seduction;
But the half-smile
Shrouding mental echoes
Of sudden doubts
Swift-brushed away.

I will snare – in words –
Yearnings wild and violent,
Yet quiet as rushing pulses
In the soul's penumbra
Where your ego meets the id.

I will suffer the invisible thorns
Of hurt silences,
Of inner surging ecstacies,
Of secret agony;
I will see birth
With your vision.

266

I will enter like a surgeon's camera-probe
Your very being,
And read the sentence
Scratched inside your skull
About senility and death.
I shall bathe in the blood
Of your maternity
And breathe the essence
Of your sex.

I will write
A poem –
About you –
And whisper it –
Slowly – alone –
In an empty, vast Cathedral;
I will –
I will –
I will.

David E. S. Nutt,
Horfield, Bristol.

TEENAGE MEANDERINGS

Search the spirit,
Question mind,
Strip the conscience,
Try to find,
What lifes all about.

Whether my views to shout out loud,
Not heeding those of my friend,
Or with brain alert, a listener be,
To consider, where issue should end.

Should I firmly demand all my rights,
And take everything I can get,
Or, give all I can to my neighbour and friend,
Without any remorse or regret.

Shall I be a leader? have my own way,
Tell other folk what to do,
Or, shall I be carefree? accepting my lot,
Hopefully, struggling through.

What about loving? Should I be free,
To give and express what I feel,
Or should I reserve my passions until,
With a man at the alter I kneel.

Whether to worship in orthodox way,
Without, any question or doubt,
Or to find my own image of Father in Heaven,
To guide me within and without.

Searched the spirit,
Questioned mind,
Stripped the conscience,
Yet to find
What lifes all about.

One thing only do I see,
I must find out just who is me?

Audrey M. Oldroyd,
Mirfield, West Yorkshire.

ENCOUNTER WITH A MIDGE

From out another world she came,
On sure, determined wings, and fleet.
In silent ease, her target marked,
With fond anticipation sweet.

Proboscis poised; my hand beneath;
She spirall'd down with marv'llous skill.
Then firmly fixed on steady feet,
She plunged her spear, and drank her fill.

So eagerly, tail up, head down,
This minute pow'r ferocious worked.
Oblivious of her giant host,
Not knowing there that danger lurked.

Nor knowing there that mercy dwelt,
For I could see myself as she.
Sucking the bosom of the Earth,
But hoping Fate were kind to me.

Robert S. Owen,
Rothes, Moray.

Poem based on Aldous Huxley's "BRAVE NEW WORLD"

Not to feel, not to love, not to hate,
Only live to meet ones fate.
A mere existence, a computed number,
No names, no places,
No expressions – no faces.
Abide by the rules;
Slave to the ruler.
Servant to the command,
Obey the every order,
Do our every duty,
Never face the truth.
Never experience happiness,
Or sense in sadness,
Or to see the gladness.
Taught to be a person,
Taught to do our jobs.
Not to see the sun rise or set,
Not to know that once two lips met,
And, never to taste the sweetness of freedom.

Gail Ann Oxley,
Mitcham, Surrey.

TO AN UNTIDY HUSBAND

My name is unimportant, my position is unpaid,
My days are filled with backache, tidy-upper is my trade.
I wish my home was tidy, all neat and full of gleams,
But my husband is so messy, my hopes have turned to dreams.

He leaves the bedroom cluttered; clothes lying inches deep,
The bed he leaves all wrinkled, with crumbs piled in a heap.
Oh how he likes to munch in bed, jaws going like the clappers,
Looking through those dirty books at all those "jam-stuck" flappers.

Our bathroom carpet's blue, you know, it covers all the floor,
But most of it you never see, talc meets you at the door.
The toothpaste tube lies battered, it never has a top,
The paste is stuck all round the sink, for teeth there ain't a drop.

The plug-hole's got a problem it's rarely ever free,
From soap and hairs and cotton buds and slops of stagnant tea.
I'll curb his lazy ways, you'll see, I'll catch him on the hop,
I'll haunt his shadow night and day with my dustpan and my mop.

Or a plan of action I'll adopt, I'll sicken him instead,
I'll leave the dishes for a month and read all day in bed.
With rollers jammed beneath my scarf and teeth smiling from a mug,
I'll kiss him with my face pack on then turn over with a shrug.

But . . . deep down I'm not a rotter, my plans I'll not see through,
Cos I've got this little daft streak, suppose that's what made me fancy
    you.
Well I know I'll go on bending, tidying up; my pace quite steady,
With my brush and 'pan thrust in each hand and backache at the ready.

Mrs. Diane Page,
Paisley, Renfrewshire.

DEPRESSION

Songs without words,
Sadness, with no tears,
Dreams, with no awakening.
– Why not death?

Trees with no leaves,
Night without day,
Flowers with no scent.
– The soul is dead.

Beggars without food,
A child uncared for,
The struggle to "be".
– Where is God?

In life there is death,
The soul struggles far into the night
As though in a dream.
– Bach, he is my God.

Anna Paola,
London.

LANGLAND BAY – GOWER

Morning. Summer warm and tingling.
I ducked under my shirt.
"You're brown," she said.

I sat down
Just for a moment to relish the sun,
And the piquant, cold gleam of the waves,
Creamed by a wind that was done,
Restless and calling.
"Come on," I said.
Then a man ran by.
He was shaking his head.
From his own need he cried –
"A girl has died!
Drowned!"
We stared.
She's just been found –
Dead!
The water creamed in – Calling,
Calling a warning.
"Come on," she said. "Come away."
So we left the bay.
Left, with minds just ajar,
Not open too far –
Lest the wound should gape wider
And swallow the scar.

Mr. H. G. Parfitt,
Wedmore, Somerset.

TWO SHADES OF NIGHT

Deep inky blackness all enshrouding,
A velvet cloak encompassing Earth,
A blind mans world.

A timid silhouette evolves
Branching out from unknown depths,
A bush, pale flow'ring glows.

A long limbed tree, smudged headdress of leaves,
Stretches to touch illumined stars,
The crescent moon showers her silver jewels
Upon the rippling surface of the lake, soft
As a whisper . . .

Heavy leaden sky, funereal black,
starless, lifeless, God-forsaken;
Weighted down with hammering hail
Battling to overtake earlier floods in
the dash to the sea.

Derelict tenements stand roofless, empty-eyed,
While soggy sooty rain makes river-beds of
dreary pavements, cracked and strewn with broken
brown glass.
Dark corners conceal darker deeds, abetted by
forlorn unlit lamps,
A stench of mangy cats competes with refuse
over-flowing from long-forgotten bins, and
over all lies a desperate sense of desolation.

Elizabeth Parker,
Greenock, Renfrewshire.

THE FISHERMEN

To battle on against all odds,
The fishermen must go,
In raging winds and heavy swells,
The dark sea is their foe,
They cast their nets into the deep,
For loaded nets they pray,
So they can run before the wind,
And shelter in the bay.

Upon the rugged windswept shores,
The wives and mothers stand,
A fear has come upon them,
Their mens' lives are in God's hands
They raise their voices up in prayer,
And dry each others tears,
And strength flows through their frozen veins,
To wash away their fears.

Men take their lives into their hands,
Each time they go to sea,
And brave the elements, to catch, fine fish
For you, and, me,
They're hardy, and God fearing men,
The sea is in their veins,
The seagulls cry, is their lament,
A haunting, harsh, refrain.

Mrs. Margaret Paterson,
Hamilton, Lanarkshire.

FAIR LAND OF SCOTIA

Fair Land of Scotia,
Dark gem of the sea,
Thy heath covered mountains,
Are calling to me.

The wild Moor of Rannoch,
Where bounds the red deer,
Proud snowcapped Schiehallion,
And bonnie Glenshee.

Land o' Bruce and Wallace,
Of the bold young Chevalier,
Culloden's Moor, and Bannockburn,
Land o' memories dear.

The grey peaks of Arran,
The banks o' the Clyde,
Majestic Ben Lomond,
I'd fain walk beside.

The land o' warriors bold and free,
Brave men who've fought on land and sea,
Heroes who've shed their blood for thee,
The land that we hold dear.

Arise ye sons of Scotia,
The day of freedom dawns,
Draw nigh unto thy Destiny,
The Gods, the Fates ride on.

Catherine I. Paton,
Glasgow.

THE SNUFFLE

Have you ever had a snuffle?
Ugh! it's a rotten thing to have,
When one simply aches all over,
And one's really feeling bad,
I'm snuffling up, and blowing down,
Which nearly drives me mad.

With dewdrops on my nose end,
And teardrops in my eyes,
I think oh heck! just what's the use,
However hard one tries.
My friend calls in and say's oh my!
You haven't got it to,
I've been in bed a couple of days,
I think it must be Flu,
I study when she's gone away,
Wondering have I got it to,
So I quickly 'phone the doctor,
And ask what I should do.
The poor old chap's run off his feet,
Then say's oh goodness! is it you,
Just get yourself to bed my dear,
It's certainly the Flu.

Mrs. Mary Alexundra Peacock,
Keighley, West Yorkshire.

SPRING

Spring is here the sky is blue
The trees are budding green
The birds are singing
The bees are winging
There way from bloom to bloom.

The wild flowers come out one by one
A new thrill every day
Yesterday the Speedwell blue
Now the primrose gay.

The birds are busy with their nests
Once more the sprouting grain
Creation manifests itself
O're all the land again.

Isabel Philip,
Brechin, Angus.

LOVE

Love, alas, is finite;
Love is never belittling, critical or demeaning; it is demanding.
Love is both totally disoriented and fully aware,
Love doesn't stop you liking others but it does stop there!

Love expects perfection – and is;
Love is insecure: a lot jealous and always a little suspicious.
Love is not needing words and talking twice as much!
Love is loyal and generous but not kindness, as such.

Love is a constant tenderness;
Love wants to probe, it will not – and it suffers.
Love is always, always there,
Not fair . . . not fair.

Patricia Marjorie Pierce,
Sale, Cheshire

THE MESSAGE OF DEATH

It came on throbbing pulses
Of Winter's gales –
It told of human suffering
Fearsome tales
But we saw not,
And heard not . . .
We fed on the fat of the land –
And little suffering children
How pitiful –
They stand in rows of ravished humans,
They know not why they wait . . .
But hope to find a fallen crumb,
Or scrap off someone's plate.
Death's portals open wider
To draw the children in –
If we stand and see them suffer
We fill the world with sin.
Give of your best to help them –
Take the sadness
Out of their eyes . . .
Pray to God in His Goodness –
That all may
Hear their cries.

Mrs. Nell Pinkney,
Harrogate, North Yorkshire.

Peer rabbit ye hiv nae long ti ging,
Tho ye might hae young ens up ti bring,
But I hiv te,
So keep still will I get an aim at ye,
Cany noo dina fle,
Until a get a shot at ye.

So a took a shot,
An a dout it you for the pot,
Peer rabbit maybe it wis the best way ti ging,
Nen o this suffrin gist the thing.

Ye hiv a hefty feel,
And should make a big meal,
Maybe keep some for the morn as well.

Ma wife she'll be glad,
And sae will ma wee lad,
But thinkin o ye maks ma sad.

O God dina blame me,
It's the Laird can't ye see,
He pays me little as little as can be.

Mr. Alistair Pirie,
Banchory, Aberdeenshire.

KITTIE BROON

The cattlie chiel at oor fairm toon
Fell in tow wi' a quine ca'd Kittie Broon,
She wis ketchie deem at a place near bye,
Sortit pigs an' hens an' help't milk the kye.
Gweed looks she quidna rechtly claim
An' naen wis sure fae far she came,
Bit naen the less she wis weel kent,
For chasin' loons she wis hell bent,
Naen o'er perteek fit like they look't
Muckle an' fat or rael sma' byook't.
So it cam tae naen o' much surprise
Fin it got plain tae see she wis changin' size,
Tae a' except oor cattlie chiel
Fa cam hame ae necht lookin' recht nae weel.

"Gweed sakes," sez I, "Man fit ests adee,
Ye've seen a ghost it looks tae me."
"A ghost ma fit, it's yon Kittie Broon,
She's tellin' me I've lat her doon.
'Hullo Dad' she sez 'Ken fit eev deen,
Tae the doctor's hoose the day I've been,
He says ye'll hae tae hurry quine,
Twa month fae noo will cut it fine.
So seek yer man an' sattle doon,
Ca't something ither than a Broon.'
So it's me she says that she'll be haein'
An' tae cottar is fit we'll be daein'.
Her plans a' made bit I'll nae fa' in line,
I'll up tail, an' awa' the militia jine."

Mr. David Pirie,
Kelty, Fife.

DEVOLUTION FOR SCOTLAND

Scots wha ha'e wi Wallace bled
Scots wham Bruce sae nobly led
Remember now though all are dead,
Scotland still lives on.
Renew our faith in honest pride
And grant to us what e'er betide
Our way of living to decide
With real integrity.
Let the Queen Mum our new "Head" be
For truer Scot we'll never see
Beloved by all and honoured she
For her sincerity
And then let those who would deride
Our hope and faith and honest pride
See north and south live side by side
And still "Great Britain" be.
So let us now true partners be
In shaping Britain's destiny
In dear old Scotland let us see
We're all born free.
And for the Queen her turn will come
We hope to be a new grand mum
In history to all, not some
Beloved Elizabeth II.

Dorothy Pirie,
Coatbridge, Lanarkshire.

MY EVENTIDE THOUGHTS

Now the sun is setting
On this busy life of mine,
There will be no regretting,
But for swiftly passing time.

There is so much to accomplish
Before I toe the line.

I pray the Lord will
give me.
Some extra living
time.

Dorothy Porteous,
Newcastle.

WHAT SHALL I TELL THE CHILDREN?

What shall I tell them?
How to explain?
Your Father's not coming home again?

Did I love him?
I don't really know.
You sow seeds of friendship
And watch them grow,
Into a great and glorious story
Full of love and personal glory.

I knew I loved him enough to say
I will if you will –
God heard us pray
As joined together as man and wife
We promised to share in this wonderful life.

I know I loved him –
I always will
Though the arms that held me
Are cold – and still.
I miss his laughter and easy grace
But – somehow – I can't recall his face.

My love! My love!
Where have you gone?
The days are empty;
Nights so long.
I hope in my heart you will come again
To take me away from this life of pain.

The fruits of our love
Are here with me.
Soon to grow –
Independent –
Free!

What shall I tell them?
How to explain
Their Father is not coming home again?

Jill Sheila Prasad,
Ruislip, Middlesex.

PATTERNS

Out of bed I hit my head,
Go out to see the powder,
   a spiders web
   a lacy pattern,
   frozen window,
   frozen pane.
Oh! how nice!
The little sprite had been,
He's been, he's been.
Oh! I like the pattern
   Glistening,
   Gleaming,
   Glancing,
   Sparkling.
Ice cold
   Icy,
   Frozen,
The sun's come out and melted the snow.

Miss Julie Pringle (Aged 9),
Cults, Aberdeen.

BLACKTHORN

White froth against blue sky,
The blossom dances briefly
Through a few sweet April days,
Brave herald to the Spring.

The twigs bereft of life
During Winter's stormy blast,
Are wakened by birdsong,
Clothed in fresh green
And warmed by Summer's ripening sun.

Crisp, hazy days appear.
The leafy green gives way
To golden hues and mellowness.
Leaves fall and Autumn comes.

So do we live our lives:
Are born, mature and weather many storms
And hungry for the hope of rebirth,
We symbolise the blossoming tree
In all its beauty, durability and grace.

Valerie Pringle,
Bothwell, Glasgow.

YOUR GOLDEN WEDDING

'Tis the Golden Annivers'ry
Of your Happy Wedding Day
When you vowed you'd love each other
As you went along life's way.

When the road you first did traverse
And no cares were on your brow
You were Happy and Contented
With your Man behind the plough.

But he fancied something different
And to Peebles you did go
Then you'd four Bonnie Bairnies
And your hearts with Love did glow.

280

Now that Love it still is burning
But the Bairnies they have grown
While each one in their turn
Has a Love Nest of their own.

They have gathered here this evening
For this Happy "Big Event"
And from them who can't be with you
Their "Good Wishes" they have sent.

So may you All be Happy
On this Golden Wedding Day
And may the Bride and Bridegroom
Be yet spared for many a day.

And here's my Hearty Wishes
Sent to you with All God's Speed
To "The Golden Wedding Couple"
Who live beside The Tweed.

Miss Jenny I. Rae,
Biggar, Lanarkshire.

SONG OF THE NEW SEEKERS

In deminished dawns, we no longer sing of "Silver Darlings"
We have forsaken our nets and left them lying
On sick shores!
We have a new song on our lips: A song which sets our hearts
To the steady flow of the syphon-sump
From whence the black bile of the sea is spew'd up
In our faces!
We have turned from the crofts which our forefathers tended
And, were put out of! . . . We are quit of the loss that comes
When those cold disciples of the sea deny and betray us
Like Peter and Judas did Christ!
We are concerned now with rigs and derricks
Which hoist not crans of fish; but peeling pipe-lines
That will blurp their viscous liquid to shore-harvesting!
We sound substratum . . . hope gushes up and floods our veins! . . .
We have struck oil!

Mr. Edward Borland Ramsay,
Glasgow.

NOTHING MUCH

It was only a smile, but its warmth reached out, to a lonely heart that
    day,
And how it cheered and lightened, her dark and cheerless way,
It seemed as if her lonely room, at once was filled with light,
For someone's smile had touched her heart, and made the way seem
    bright.

It was only a word that was spoken, but to one it meant so much,
For it came when life seemed empty, and she needed that homely
    touch,
A loving word, so full of hope, like rainbow, after rain,
At last, the clouds had lifted, life could begin again.

It was only a friendly letter the message so simple and clear,
But to the one who read it, it brought such joy and cheer,
For bound within the walls of home, she needed just to know,
That friends had not forsaken. but were ready their love to show.

It was only the clasp of a friendly hand, when life seemed all in vain,
It showed that someone really cared, and it helped to ease the pain,
Of bitterness, and hatred, that was burning in his heart,
And it gave him strength and courage, a new life so to start.

It only takes a little time, to see what we can do,
To ease the burdens, lighten loads, be faithful, loyal, true,
But little things are often, the ones that count so much,
The quiet word, the loving smile, and the little homely touch.

Miss Elsie Randall,
West Drayton, Middlesex.

FOR ALISON

My child is sleeping,
Her face radiating innocence
Has shed at least half
Her few and tender years.
We stand and gaze at this
Most precious part of us,
This gently breathing girl-child
Trembling on the brink of womanhood.
You squeeze my hand,
And knowing that you are
Aware of my thoughts
I feel an overwhelming gratitude
For this living symbol of our love.

Soon she will discover life
Outside her sheltered environment,
Adolescence will bring an ever increasing
Awareness of a strange and dangerous world,
Where pain and pleasure of hand in hand,
Where all is confusion until illuminated
By harsh and sometimes bitter experience.
I wish my child that I could
Be your buffer against the many hurts,
But this would only stifle you.
I must wait and feel
Your bruises with you.
My child, I wish you love.

Robert Reeves,
Milford Haven, Wales.

THE CHILDREN OF DONNACHAIDH

And so the clans were scattered
From land and sheiling torn
Their tartan was forbidden
And their culture held in scorn.

And then there was the quiet time
Long years of dark despair
When the great great family of the clan
Seemed broken beyond repair.

Then somewhere in the distant past
A pipe was heard and then
The feet in dance began to stir
And the tartan blazed again.

And all the stories of the past
With pride were now retold
Of how the clan was bound by love
Of the brave and of the bold.

And children listened and felt the blood
That stirred within their veins
And the clan that once seemed broken
Began to live again.

And now the spirit of the clan
Is felt in every clime
And heads are raised in every land
For now is the gathering time.

And here we meet in happiness
And often part in tears
For in the children of Donnachaidh
Flows the love of a thousand years.

J. W. L. Reid,
Bishop's Stortford,
Hertfordshire.

CANTERBURY

I went into the Cathedral.
Cool it was after the hot street.
Above me the soaring arches,
Behind me the splintered fragments
Of shining colour from the great window.
The dead slept in peace in the Cathedral,
Lying in their marble topped tombs,
Their faces serene, their hands folded.
But the living knew no peace, no serenity.
Chattering and jostling, pushing and pressing,
They "did" the Cathedral, eager to be on their way.
Staring, but not seeing, pursuing but not praying,
The living milled and thronged,
Laughing, pointing, gibbering.
Not one a pilgrim, not one a partaker,
Transforming beauty and majesty
Into a peepshow. And I wondered
Who were the living and who the dead?

I came out of the Cathedral
Where the sun shone on the cobbled street,
And there was no coolness in my spirit,
Only a dull ache and a hot anger,
For I had witnessed a desecration,
A raping of beauty and purity,
And I felt unclean and ashamed
As I joined the crowds of shoppers and tourists.
My heart wept for the Cathedral,
So beautiful, so majestic,
Offering strength and tranquillity,
Calm and quietness;
Yet having its gifts trampled and torn.
I shall not go again into the Cathedral.

Sheila Campbell Reid,
Colby, Isle of Man.

THE SONG OF THE SEA

The lonely cry of a gull is heard,
The answering call of a friendly bird,
The sea batters against the rocks,
Cruel and harsh it pounds and mocks.

"The ruler of this land am I,"
One can almost hear its triumphant cry,
"Even Canute was no match for me,
No mortal hand can still the sea."

"Ships and men, I toss them away,
Covering their bulk in foaming spray,
The essence of life I suck and sift,
Then carelessly toss the dregs adrift."

"But use me well, and you will find,
I can be useful to mankind,
For my bounties, they are vaster,
Than puny man's, of whom I'm master."

Mrs. Anne V. Richardson,
Carlisle, Cumbria.

ULSTER'S LAMENT

In the midst of the evil of political upheaval,
Whilst people are assassinated.
Leaders contend, at their wits' end,
To have the killers incarcerated.

Political discussions and their repercussions,
Come weekly by the score.
But fast as they make them, opponents deflate 'em,
And we're back as we were before.

United we stand, but, I don't understand,
About unity's beginning or end.
Unionists dither and Nationalists blither,
In vain search for an ideal blend.

Seven years gone and trouble's still on,
Still there's no sign of an answer.
What must we do to emerge from the brew
Of this frightful sectarian cancer.

We're tired of all schism and lack of precision,
We now look around in dismay,
For the magical touch of someone of such,
Who can find the Utopian Way.

Give a little here and take a little there,
And somewhere about the middle,
There's surely some ground where a sage can be found,
To solve Ulster's historical riddle.

Robert Ritchie,
Magherafelt, N. Ireland.

A SHETLAND CROFTERS PRAYER

Our island home is God's own country,
Let us try and keep it so,
With its hills of purple heather,
'Tis a dream to friend and foe.

Spring arrives, with all its beauty,
Bringing with it strife and toil,
But we must press on regardless
To eke a living from the soil.

With the harvest safely gathered,
With God's help we did our best,
Autumn leaves are softly falling,
We are grateful for the rest.

Winter comes, and we remember
'Tis the time our Lord was born.
Let us bow our heads in reverence,
To Him who gave us each new dawn.

Help us, Lord, to face the changes
Progress now has brought about,
Help us keep our own environment,
Peace within, and trouble out.

Keep our children safe from evil,
They who know not right from wrong,
Guide them on the path of righteousness
When they join the cities throng.

Mrs. Janet Robertson,
Scousburgh, Shetland Isles.

THE FAITHFUL ONE

Gyp the old collie her life it is waning,
Her days on the hill are now almost through,
Gathering, shedding, to heel with her master,
She follows him, ever obedient and true.
Guarding the house in the cool of the evening,
Watching the lamb does not stray from the ewe,
Driving the cattle home to the milking,
It's all in the days work old Gyp has to do.
Tired and weary her legs they are aching,
With age creeping on, her rest overdue,
Gladly she'll lay down her life for her master,
And go to Another to whom she'll be true.

Mrs. Margaret Robertson,
Dollar, Clackmannanshire.

IT SEEMS SAE WRANG TAE ME!

The earth's a planet broad and fair,
Wi' trees an' rivers, an' guid fresh air,
Clouds sae blue, and birds that flee,
But pollution now fills sky an' sea.

Earlier, when life wis truly led,
When plants an' beasts each other fed,
An' man his tasks, he didnae shirk . . .
A wonderful system . . . fuelled wi' work.

Man used tae live in sweet content,
Close tae the land, ahead he went,
But, he forsook that way o' life,
Tae suffer frae industrial strife.

Man aye thocht, the best he kent . . .
As the bowels o' the Earth he rent,
In search o' loads o' jet black coal,
An that wis whaur he lost his soul.

First 'twis coal, then iron ore,
An' heaps o' waste were a' skelt o'er
Whaur corn an' tatties, bonny grew,
. . . but nothing fresh is seen there noo.

An syne there's oil, deep in the sea,
A source o' wealth for you an' me?

... ye spill the oil ... does it matter?
Jist nae fish, upon y're platter.

We maun he power, is aye the cry,
As anither source, puir Man does spy,
It's nuclear power ... a generator,
But whit o' Man, in decades later.

For as we generate this power
We think oor plate is running o'er,
But No ... this niver will be so ...
Where is the active waste to go?

"Intelligent" ... Man wis said tae be,
But he is blind an' canna see ...
Tae send oot cars ... an' buy back food,
... does little for the Common Good.

Why send sae far, when at oor door,
There's a lot o' wealth an' food galore,
Sae spend mair siller on the land ...
... an' we'll hae loads o' cash in hand!

Mr. Sid Robertson,
Cumbernauld, Glasgow.

TO MAY

Darling! That night you looked your
    most entrancing,
In that dim bower where first we
    told our love;
The lovelights bright, that in your
    eyes were dancing,
Outshone the ancient stars that beam
    above.

The scent of roses, wafted on a
    zephyr,
Mingled sweetly with the perfume that
    you wore;
The memory of that moment will live
    with me for ever,
Treasured in my heart till my life is
    o'er.

Mr. Leonard Robinson,
Glasgow.

LANDMARK

Rooted deeply to the river bed,
She stands there full of pride,
Towering high above the water's edge,
Watching the boats going by.

She used to stand there all alone,
That was her domain,
Another has come to share her load,
But to me it is still her reign.

If she could speak many a tale she'd tell,
The good and the bad things she's seen,
Apart from all that she is still looking well,
She is set in a beautiful scene.

All different races have taken her picture,
Children, Mums, Aunts and Grans,
Her rival stands looking immature,
They're so close they could almost hold spans.

There are other bridges of great renown,
From down South, to away up North,
But to me there's only one with a crown,
And her Palace, the old River Forth.

Mrs. W. Robinson,
Reading, Berks, England.

ENDEAVOUR

Let all our people rejoice and sing,
Let bells peal out and anthem's ring.
Proclaim to the world that we intend to conquer
The ills and troubles that have split us assunder.

There are those around who would plot our defeat.
Enemies without and those at our feet,
But we are a race of endurable mettle,
We fight the hardest when tough is the battle.

We can look back with pride at the wonderful story
That Britain has written on the pages of history
It is not enough to dwell on the past
We must work and prosper for the glory to last.

Hope was reborn that grey June day
When men predicted a new Elizabethan way
Of life to be lived, of fame to be won
To grasp the challenge, it could be done.

There is a chance for us yet, come let us unite
And surely we'll see that victory in sight.

Myra Robson,
Carlisle, Cumbria.

OUR WORLD

Our world is in England with her hills and her dales,
Our world is in music and the sweet songs of Wales.
Our world is in Scotland with the pibroch and heather,
Our world is in Ireland and her grey misty weather.

Our world is a fortress bound in by the sea,
With sea-spray and white cliffs, and sweet childish glee;
With long sandy beaches and seaweed and shells,
And long waving grasses, oak trees and bluebells.

Far over the ocean where bitter winds blow,
The eskimo lives mid iceberg and snow.
That vast icy waste is his world and domain,
His home is a fortress against wind and rain.

America rises so sturdy and proud,
Her manners are showy, her voice brash and loud.
But all who come seeking their fortune and fame,
Find a "Star-spangled world bearing liberty's name".

Across the wide oceans, in field and in glade,
Is a wonderful world that our father has made.
And if we would serve him and give love to others,
We must look beyond our world and shake hands with our brothers.

Miss Agnes Rogers,
Stockport, Cheshire.

THE ACCIDENT

The rain fell like needles,
Onto the car and,
Bounced onto the road.
The windscreen wipers swished,
Back and forth,
In steady rhythm.
I saw the red lights in front,
Get nearer; I knew,
Then I saw nothing.
Voices, people, glass, chaos,
I'm alright really,
I'm alive.
I'm tired so tired and cold,
More blankets please.
Thanks I'm O.K. now.
My eyes are closed but,
Still I see, I know
What the scene is.
Many voices, all strange,
I don't speak, I
Just can't be bothered.
Realisation now; my new coat,
My face and head
All warm and sticky.
They don't know I,
Can hear them.
Talk of scars and blame,
Sirens now, at last,
Really, don't fuss.
I'm lucky really,
And I wonder why,
I never thought to
Wear a seat belt.

Jacqueline Rogers,
Sutton Coldfield,
West Midlands.

THE SALE

The Auctioneers are moving in,
The old home has to go,
The carpets and the furniture,
The silver too must go,

291

The curtains and the pictures,
The glass and china too,
How sad to see it swept away,
In just an hour or two.
The people will come thronging in,
A bargain their intent,
They'll nod their heads,
And make their bids,
There'll be no sentiment.
Away they'll walk with treasures,
Their worth they'll never know,
And I shall hide my stinging tears,
And turn my head and go.

Jane Roskell (Aged 14),
Preston, Lancashire.

MY SCOTLAND

Scotia, dearest Scotland,
My land beside the sea,
My Homeland, dearest Homeland,
My land of people free.
History flowed oe'r her,
And left so much behind,
A culture ever growing,
So many gems to find.
Her customs and traditions,
Her buildings old and rare,
She welcomes all, though strangers,
To me, this land so fair.

This tiny land called Scotland,
So much to teach and learn;
A freedom bought by martyr's blood,
A gift, so hard to earn.
Her sons and daughters many
The world has spanned so wide
She brought to many nations,
Their chance of national pride.
So many times her enemies,
Have thought that she was done,
A thousand years, and still she's free,
No matter how they come.

292

I love this land called Scotland,
My heart is buried there,
Her rivers, lochs, and mountains,
To me, are places dear.
Remembered for a life time,
'Tis here I learned so young,
Her lessons I've accepted,
For her my work was done.
I'll always dream of Scotland,
I'll never her decry,
I've lived and loved for Scotland,
It's there, I pray, I'll die.

Thomas Ross,
Gloucester.

COLOUR BLINDNESS

An absence, so the painters say,
A void of colour, negative.
A nothingness of shade or hue or tint,
Quite blind.
No sheen on jet?
No glow on ebony?
Yet, surely,
White-hot light in coal.
And silver spray in oiliness,
And amber gleam in boiling tar
Are seen.
Fertility of peat, green breeding,
Reflected copper on the negroid brow –
God's own black magic.
Deepest night,
The balm of effort, effortless,
The murmuring silence echoing.
And death,
The sleep of blanket-bosomed peace.
Of everlasting dreamfulness,
And freedom.
Who are these artists who deny,
That black is
Positive?

D. Gwynneth Rostrup,
Bromsgrove, Worcester.

PROGRESS

I stood and looked at the new wide road –
And the smart skyscraper flats –
All this I knew was the signs of times
And progress follows along these lines –
But the voice within me had to say –
Why did the old house go this way?

I remembered the little house and shop –
And the room where I was born –
All this I knew was of the past
And slums and back-streets cannot last –
But I heard a voice within me cry –
My childhood haunts have had to die.

So I turned my back on the new wide road
And the smart skyscraper flats –
And this I knew was wrong of me
And progress always has to be –
But I heard a dear voice from the past –
Saying houses fall but memories last.

Dorothy Ruby Sanders,
Coundon, Coventry.

SOMETHING VICTORIAN

Something
Is haunting me today. Strange thoughts
Intrude, and I am wondering
All day long.

Someone is following me today,
As I step from room to room.
When I stop to listen, I hear
The rustle of her long skirts touching the ground,
And yet . . . no-one is there.

Some small song reaches me;
A tune, played to fill an idle moment
Whilst sitting at a harpsicord; like a laugh,
Interrupting the silence of some sew-er.

And whilst I sit here, I hear a sigh,
And it touches my heart so much, so much.

My hands tremble,
And my head reels with questions,
And the main one is:–
Why does this happen
Whenever I enter a Victorian house?

Who is the lady who follows me
Through the summers?
And why is her hand so very cold
when she reaches out
To touch me?

Christine Sanderson,
Accrington, Lancs.

PREVIEW

A strange man born before his time
Came to the court of Good Queen Bess.
Odd Fish! his clothing though sublime
Was far too scant for formal dress.

Where was his doublt, cambric ruff
And padded breeches vast and wide?
As if these tortures weren't enough
A scented leather cloak beside.

He wore black patent-leather shoes,
A creaseless suit of gaberdine
And round his neck a nylon noose
Framed by a shirt of terylene.

"I've brought along some things," said he
Before the courtly populace.
"Behold! The Twentieth Century
Reposes in this zipped up case."

There's ball-point pens, so cast aside
Those foolish goose-quill pens today
Or for the more discerning scribe
A fountain pen to glide its way.

A ray to pierce the darkest gloom
Is locked within this pocket torch
Revealing candle for your room
Sans soot, sans smell, sans flame to scorch.

Here's nylons for my lady's knee,
Foundation garments for to tame

The wayward bulge so sad to see
Upon a lovely sylph-like frame.

And non-iron shirts, drip-dry as well
Will steal another hour for you.
A windless watch, the time to tell
So bid yon sundial swift adieu.

Here's razors for to shave and leave
A skin far smoother than before;
Harsh pumice-stone cannot achieve
Such speed upon a hirsute jaw.

If you would dazzle with your smile
Here's dentifrice for teeth and gums
And lipstick that will quite beguile
Whom, within your radiance comes.

There's tinned meat that will last a year
And fish and beans and fruit and rice
All in their cans provide a fare
That's free from danger, cheap of price.

This camera will capture now
A new-born child and keep it young
And when full-grown with furrowed brow
His image will to youth have clung.

"Well spoken Sir," the Queen replied.
"We are well pleased with all we see
And progress must not be denied
To subjects of this century.

And when these marvels run their span
We'll need replacements to be sure
For once they've tasted, maid and man,
They'll come again for more and more."

"Ah! there's the rub" the young man cried,
"For there's just one of each, you see,
Just one of each, is zipped inside,
Enough for all your Company.

So Madam, use them sparingly
Because 'twill be some time before
We reach the twentieth century
With all the things it has in store."

Leonard Saunders,
Corby, Northants.

SCOTLAND'S GLORY

I know the road that I would take,
To find such beauty not a fake,
Loch Lomond sparkling like a gem,
Ben Lomond tow'ring at her hem.

From Inverness I'd take the road,
Where nature has herself bestowed,
The rugged splendour of a dream,
Kyle of Lochalsh reigns there supreme.

And out of nowhere but the sky,
Suspended seems the Isle of Skye,
Enchanted island beckoning,
To hold your heart beneath her wing.

Then on in one gigantic sweep,
Ben Nevis makes your pulses leap,
Your gaze is held in wonderment,
A crown that needs no betterment.

On such a road her glory lies,
For Scotland's beauty none denies,
Wherever life directs my way,
Her grandeur in my thoughts will stay.

Maiden Scott,
Edinburgh.

MEMORIES

When day is done and night is nigh
The sun slips slowly from the sky
I sit and think of days long past
And to my memories I cling fast.
I think of him whose gone from me
How long and drear the years from me
We had good days and sometimes bad
But we were really never sad
We took the smooth also the rough
To be together was enough
But one has got to be the first
To break the happy chain
But he will live within my heart
Until we meet again.

Mary Scott,
Edinburgh.

THE ENTERTAINER

The pianist is seated on the stage at last,
The audience all have waited for ten minutes
Which seems to them an age.
Patiently they have sat there with bated breath.
He starts the piece with speed and his skill is evident.
He does not seem aware
Of all the pairs of eyes, which almost fill the hall,
And watch now as he plays.
They stare, dumbfounded,
As he accomplishes feats which seem to them an impossible task.
Now with equal expertise he repeats the exposition.
The audience ask themselves,
Why this pianist has no fears of playing
So hard a piece with such speed.
All the audience agree, he appears to have no fears
And does not even read the music.
Now the piece is nearly o'er for the first time.
At the end there are cries
For the pianist to do an encore,
And again this sonata fills the skies.

Willis Scott,
Glasgow.

THEREBY HANGS A TALE

I never used to own a dog – and now I foster two!
They came to me as puppies and won my heart, it's true.
Exactly why I feel this way is difficult to say –
I really think I must be mad, in some strange, doggy way!

The breed? They're two Salukis – should you care to know,
Hounds, both lean and beautiful – eyes with an amber glow.
But when it comes to naughtiness, they're really at their best,
They'd maybe win a "best of breed" – but no obedience test!

They've chewed up all my furniture and even window-sills.
They've walked me miles o'er roads and fields, o'er bogs, and burns,
    and hills.
They've even smashed a treasured vase, and as if that's not complete –
I can never find my slippers to shod my weary feet!

But still, they've got their good points – I know they love me, too,
I can see it in their welcome – and, yes, that stolen shoe.

And when it's dark, and I'm alone, and snuggled up in bed,
I know it's not hygienic, but I can always touch that head!

Oh, yes, they may mischievous be and cause me many sighs,
But they only need to look at me with those appealing eyes.
Or crouching down, in playful pose, tail wagging in the air;
Head to one side – I'm hooked, I'm lost – I love this stupid pair.

So, with their help, I fill my day with sighs, and laughs, and care,
With two such friends, I can't complain – I happily will share,
My home, my life, their walks – and even, now and then, my bed!
With these, my two protectors, some guardian angel bred.

Margaret Graham Semple,
Latchingdon, Essex.

UNTITLED POEM BY MINA SELBIE

Exasperation, nae inspiration,
Especially for the Bard
Oor winter has been long and dreich,
Aye, been gie hard.

Unemployment, no much enjoyment,
And dole queues long,
Soon the unemployed will be,
A million strong.

Taxation, high inflation,
And prospects drear,
I wish the powers that be,
Wid gie's some cheer.

Determination, administration,
Scotland must ha'e,
Rights, and freedom, then will bring,
Prosperity.

Mrs. Mina Selbie,
St. Monans, Fife.

GLENCOE

In the valley of Glencoe
Where clear and crystal waters flow
Overhead no golden eagles fly
And voices in the wind do sigh.

Whilst in the hills the fox is sleeping
Yet, in the vale, the vale of weeping
Ghostly sentinels
Their vigil keeping.

At night the valley's dark and drear
Where mortal man would tread with fear
And, at the dawn, the sky is red
It's hue reflects the immortal dead.

Albert Shaw,
Glasgow.

WOMAN

Complexity
Perplexity
Anorexia
Obesity
Unpredictable
Irrational
Uncontrollable
Even masochistic . . .

Yet Desirable
Lovable
And quite irreplaceable.

Mr. Tony Sheldon,
Salford.

MY WEE AUTOMATIC CAR

It tak's me oot tae Arden Hoose, tae the over 60 club,
It tak's me tae the Rural, an' it tak's me tae the Guild,
It's a little yellow Mini, an' it is my pride an' joy,
"Mum's dodgem" say the faimily, an' treat it as a toy.

I gaed tae try my drivin' test, he had me near tae tears,
"Fit kin' o' box is this?" he says "It hisna ony gears."
But I wad be lost withoot it, though I'm nae that aften oot,
An' there's aye some bits and pieces lockit safely in the boot.

Now parking has its problems and I hate the noisy crash,
My brakes failed at a duck pond – you should have heard the splash.
At rinnin' doon the male sex I'm really very bright,
They find naething mair confusing than me daein' something right!

To the hills I go in summer, to admire trees in the fall,
To a pantomine at Elgin, an' whiles tae Rafford hall.
An' if I miss my dinner, at the wheel I tak' a bite,
But it's proved gey tough I tell ye, though I chew wi' a' my might.

To see the Loch Ness Monster I've even ta'en a run,
But the elusive Nessie is seldom oot for fun.
An' though I tried tae tempt her wi' the best o' Moray beef,
The craiture jist ignored me, pretendin' she wis deef.

I called at Findhorn Motors, I wis using too much juice,
An' Sid discovered that my choke wis bein' wrongly used.
'Cos richt oot I had pulled it (every minute there's one born),
An' it wis awfu' handy tae hang my handbag on.

"It's been actin' up again," I said, an' pointed tae the fender,
"Oh, yes" he said, an' smiled at me, wi' looks saw true an' tender.
But he sauntered ower tae Mel an' I could hear (as through a flannel),
"If she went tae the desert, she'd acquire a dented camel."

Now Lot's wife's story you have heard – a very sorry plight,
The same thing happened unto me on my way here tonight.
Remember she turned into salt because she dared look back,
Well! I turned into a telegraph pole – but I survived the whack.

Now, I'm gaun ower tae France this year (They drive upon the right),
So I thocht I wid practice, but I got an awfu' fright,
For comin' fae the toon ae nicht (I wis on the right, ye see),
The sirens blared an' lo' a thoosan' bobbies efter me!

"Name an' address?" the sergeant asked, an' I at once replied,
"My name is Greta Garbo an' from Hollywood" I lied.
"Oh sign your autograph" said he, *This* line I'm not pursuin',
I signed an' off! Before he saw the name was Ruby Shewan.

Mrs. Ruby Shewan,
Forres, Morayshire,

AN UNTITLED POEM BY ROBERT SIDDLE

As I walk down a narrow street of my home town,
I see yellow police notices where the prams usually stand,
And black cars where the children used to play,
And the thunder clouds are blacker than on any normal day,
And the tears fall faster than at any normal funeral,
And the crowds are bigger than on any normal day,
And the street is quiter than for any normal funeral,
And the silent cortege is longer than on any normal day,
And all this for a box just three feet long.

Robert Siddle,
Bingley, West York.

ST. KILDA

Far out St. Kilda twists and turns
A spinner in Atlantic burns.
The gales that tear the heather now
Feel neither side of colt or cow;
Wind in its whirl of spindrift salt
Has not a tree to call it halt;
Wind in its turmoil seeks the lums,
Devoid of reeks devoid of mums.
The weather long since tore out God
From ancient church and hallowed sod.

Stone age hairy ones and friars
Made this landfall, and lit their fires;
Danes and Vikings travelled through
Raiding sheep for mutton stew.
Each his score made on this earth,
Burning peat on his stone hearth –
The mice are friendly but not the wren,
The sheep grew wilder than the men.

But wilder still the petrel nests
In stone heaps on the windy crests.

No girls now look to a lover stone;
The cragsmen have long left the cliffs alone,
It mattered not that old drearies said
That they were all far too young to wed.
But the loves of crag and cliff live on
In the long islands and beyond.
They spin and weave in modern mills
And suffer all the fashionable ills
The stone heap cleits now look to sheep
Which find them dry in death or sleep.

Gannets, still, lift and plummet clean
Through the green seas where the fish are seen.
Fulmars with the long waves glide
As they come and go on the eternal tide.
The burlesque puffins, in colours share
With seriousness chicks and summer air.
The black back gull and bonnie fly
To kill the young and hurtle by.
Sad is death on a summer day
Regardless of how life is taken away.

Locked in misted rain each stack
Seen through the distance answers black.
The eddies round these distant places
Jummel to foam edges in white traces.
Always deep water troubles the land
Abrasive ever with suspended sand.
By bay of shingle and rock and bones
And storm beach with its might of stones
With air dead cold in stone dry cleits
Surrounded, the forsaken village somewhile sleeps.

Mr. Thomas Skelton,
Larne, Co. Antrim.

LONELINESS

She sits in her chair, the fire has gone out.
Her limbs are so stiff, she can't move about.
Her husband is dead, she misses him so.
Her children are gone, they don't want to know.

The room has grown cold, she must go to bed.
Ah, now she remembers, she hasn't been fed.
The day has been long, no neighbour looked in.
It is too much trouble to open a tin.

She struggles to rise from the depths of her chair.
She crawls into bed, so glad to be there.
O Lord, spare a thought for the lonely tonight.
They have lived and they've loved and fought a good fight.

Catherine Skillin,
Auchinleck, Ayrshire.

TRAPPED

One day free,
Next day –
Trapped!
Caught – never to run wild,
Never to feel the wind in his flowing mane,
But to stand,
With the energy and life he once contained, draining away,
Life draws to an end, in this slowly dragging world of
    men, whips and hunger
And death is not sad or feared
It is an escape – he is free.

Susan May Skinner,
Tullibody, Clackmannanshire.

BLACK DIAMONDS

Brave are the men who go down to the bowels of the earth,
To the vegetation of centuries past where all is dark and still,
Below, there is no day, only night, no sound, only silence,
Except for ghostly echoes heard in the deep black grave,
Creakings and groanings as of the earth itself.
Daily, men scrape and dig and breathe the dust that can kill,
Coal, the valuable source of energy is withdrawn,
To enable man to live more comfortably on earth – But –
At what cost? the deprivation of natures sounds,
Life giving sunlight, and pure air.
What compensation can there be to miss daily,
The song of the birds, rustle of leaves, hum of the bees,

Sounds of the rivers, waves of the seas,
The blue of the sky, the greens of the Spring,
Sweet flowers of Summer, golds of the Autumn,
And the white snow flakes of Winter.
Tis said, one day, man will utilise the rays of the sun,
To replace the power of black diamonds,
Then, man need not go down to the bowels of the earth,
He can walk upright and enjoy life to the glory of God.

Mrs. Margaret Slight,
Pathhead, Midlothian.

AN UNTITLED POEM BY JACK SLIMM

I found on climbing up the misty mountain side,
A quiet world, busy within sweet silence.
The mountain flowers smiled with knowing mien,
At tree tops seen above the misty sheen.

Racing clouds dwelt on craggy crown,
All was foreign to a mortal frown.
Wordly troubles emptied at a splendid rush,
Chased swiftly by sweet song of minute thrush.

This place is never lost yet seldom found,
Down misty mountain on the lower ground.
The minor plans of man are here unwrapped,
Yet solitary, as mountain tip, you are aloof, unbound.

I must return to recapture treasured peace,
Rising to the heights of purer thought.
Where no erring bat is ever caught,
By cruel web of spiders trap, be-jewelled by Dawns refreshing dew.

Gazing down upon the smaller depths of heaven,
The Golden Eagle swoops uncaring for tomorrow.
Today pulsates for her waiting brood,
This fragment of the lofty treasured picture,
Completed for the hungry Spirits mood.

Seeking the end of Eternity,
Beyond this tall horizon never reached.
Refreshment found! footsteps turn recounting downward trend,
Without a word the Spirit has found a friend.

John Ernest Lewis Slimm,
South Tawton, Devon.

SUMMERLAND (TIR-NAN-OG)

In Summerland, the day is long,
'Tis there, the weak become the strong.
The children grow up to their prime,
The old remain young – all the time.

In meadows, parks and gardens, too,
Grow shrubs and flowers of every hue.
The wimpling burn runs crystal clear,
By it, are those we love so dear.

For those we mourn, have come to stay,
With those we lost, for many a day.
No sadness, gloom or sombre colours,
No mourning for the sake of others.

'Tis selfish in our grief we are,
To want them back, who've gone so far –
Into the realm of endless day,
We must go forward come what may.

Our spirit here in mortal clay,
Is ever with us night and day.
And though nightly it doth roam,
The silver cord will bring it home –
To the body pent – No bournes of sed
Can keep it back – for it is free
To wander North, South, East or West,
And to that fair land we love the best.

Until in its long exploration,
O'er country, town, and every nation.
We know not when 'twill be severed the cord,
Then our spirit 'twill soar to join the Lord.
Where, up in Heaven, on different planes,
Our friends and forebears, free from pains.
Will welcome us for many a day,
We'll live on, there for ever and aye.

Mrs. Marjorie J. I. Paterson Sloan,
Castlehill, Ayr.

THE FOURTH DIMENSION

What lies beyond this earthly bond?
We see but sky and sea and ground.
But what of things beyond our ken
That are not known to mere men.

Can it be as we are told
That a Heaven exists to receive our souls.
Or is there a hell for our retention
To hold us in a fourth dimension?

Does there exist around mankind
A parallel to which we are blind.
Is it a world of ghouls and ghosts
Awaiting as macabre hosts.

Is it a world for our repentance
How many will escape the sentence.
Of being condemned to only see and hear
Those whom we love and hold so dear.

As I lie now on my death bed
These thoughts are present in my head.
Will my end be in God's redemption
Or will I enter the Fourth Dimension?

Malcolm T. Smillie,
Dunoon, Argyll.

I NEVER UNDERSTOOD HER

I never understood girls in general
That does not mean I don't like them
After all, they're man's lifelong companion
But that girl had me beaten;
When she was with her friends she used to giggle,
But alone she swaggered, putting on airs
Boys were bad, rude, in her book,
Which proved she didn't know
A thing.
But her confidence, that was good,
You could but only admire
As she supervised the laying of the table
Confident she was in charge.

I used to shrink from her when I was young,
But now I'm older I never do, but stay
And be made to clear up
At times I'd like to turn and shout
And really put her in her place
But she would just ignore it
Or make some comment to which
You couldn't answer back
I'd never shout anyway, because
You're meant to be nice to your sister.

Alan Lenox-Smith,
Welwyn, Hertfordshire.

A SMILE

A smile can stem the flow of tears,
A smile can heal a rift of years.

From a child it can melt a mother's heart,
Towards a friendship it can be a start.

Who has not seen in a crowded room,
A smile relieve the tension and gloom?

The memory of it can ease the pain,
Of parting with one we may not see again.

Do you know who really makes life worthwhile?
The person with the biggest smile!

Mrs. Doreen Smith,
Red Wharf Bay, Anglesey.

MY BEAUTIFUL ISLAND

As evening folds around me, I close my eyes in sleep
And dream of my beautiful island, land of my sweetest sleep,
Magical island of dreamland, beautiful island of sleep
Peace – Peace on my island, joy on my island of sleep.

I stroll with you in the leafy glade beside the sparkling stream
And butterflies dance above the flowers, and smiling sunbeams gleam,
Magical island of dreamland, beautiful isle of sleep
Peace – Peace on my island, joy on my island of sleep.

When all is fair in my dreamland, why must I say "Farewell"
Why must I now awaken in this sad world to dwell,
Magical island of dreamland, beautiful island of sleep
Peace – Peace on my island, joy on my isle of sleep.

Someday I'll stay on my island, then no more shall I weep
When home at last on my island, home on my isle of sleep,
Magical island of dreamland, beautiful isle of sleep
Peace – Peace on my island, joy on my isle of sleep.

Hazel F. Smith,
Aviemore.

WOODLAND MAGIC

In a wood many miles away,
Did a man on his fiddle play,
Soft and gentle, sweet and low,
Caressed the instrument with his bow.

Unnoticed by this talented man,
Engrossed in music he,
Did not see the fairies,
Standing behind a tree.
Faster played the quaint old man,
The fairies pirouetted round,
Little creatures down below,
Came hurring from the ground.
All agog and happy now,
Birds joined in from every bough.

Shrill notes, harsh notes,
Sweet notes to,
From every bird of different hue.
The bees and wasps,
Joined in as well,
Oh! How the joyous sound did swell.
All combined as best they could,
This makeshift orchestra of the wood.

Fox and rabbit danced side by side,
Snakes they did the palais glide,
They performed this ballet of grace,
Quite unknown to the human race.

'Trees they waved their branches high,
Bluebells rang out clear,
Even fragile butterflies,
Joined in all this cheer.

Now stretched out from end to end,
All the colours seemed to blend,
As if some giant hand bewitched,
With upmost patience carefully stitched.
A fair isle pattern all aglow,
Unsurpassed by any rainbow,
And as the music on it played,
So the pattern gently swayed.
Keeping time to every beat,
Alas this performance could not repeat.

Robert Smith,
Leeds, Yorkshire.

THE YOUNG WIDOW

She looked forlorn
How could I know
The joy within her heart
For safely lay
Inside her womb
The child they'd planned to start

A senseless death
In Belfast town
Had robbed her of her man
And all the world
Just shakes its head
While statesmen have no plan

Let's pray she'll teach
That little child
About the Prince of Peace
Who taught us love
To give and take
Then hope shall never cease.

Lancelot Snape,
Morton, Wirral.

THE COST OF LIVING

We will soon be runnin' barefit,
Amang the frost, and snaw,
Tho' buits are sic a fearfu' price,
They'll nae haud oot a' ta.

The worsit that we're gettin' noo,
Ye maun admit it's dear,
I weave their hose, as weel's I can,
But yet they winna wear.

The draper's van, the chemist's van,
The soutar and the pigger,
They come roond ilka ither week,
Although my pay's nae bigger.

We've chances ilka day we rise,
Tae spend a pickle siller,
They wad tempt ye wi' their nylons,
Tho' ye had'na payed the miller.

If corn rises, ony mair,
We'll hae tae scll oor hens,
What we'll dae, withoot an egg,
Guidness only kens.

For we maun hae, oor bite and sup,
As weel's oor buits and claes,
I've never been sae trauchled,
In a' my born days.

Some time I'm sae forfochen,
It's like warslin' in a bog,
An noo they say, they want tae raise,
The Licence on my dog.

Margaret Jean Spence,
Duns, Berwickshire.

AN UNTITLED POEM BY VERONICA STANWAY

The clock continues its tuneful peal,
The minutes pass, the time to seal.
The moment that was now,
Has already been lived,
No chance to have a better deal.

No regrets for time ill spent
The actions speak, despite what's meant
What good is sorrow?
Or placing blame?
For each has choice of minutes sent.

What!!
Are you going to keep your seat,
Taking for granted the stroke's repeat?
It's best to be ready,
As tomorrow is past
Is no one prepared the new day to meet?

(Soon there will be no more time)

Veronica Stanway,
Milton Keynes.

DEBRIS OF WAR

PAST: Hark to the drums that sound afar,
Brace up to the bugle call and caw.
Scurry men scurry as you shout, "Hurrah!"
Too long you say was the wait for war.

See! Already your women darn up the shroud,
Tearless and accepting the toll of war.
Then to mourn by graves, where trees stand bowed,
Their sap near gone as they wait for more.

PRESENT: Political compromise if no one's winning,
Yet in Vietnam and Ireland it's lives we're losing.
Isn't "nuclear deterrent", a dream we're living?

FUTURE: I see only the shadow of a child,
Circled by a lost identity of charcoaled heaps.
In blood where the child squats, a finger traces . . .
"I am the child still-born
From my mothers' scorched womb.
I am all that is left to breathe the void,
To exist as the, 'spirit of creation destroyed'
I AM, THE DEBRIS OF WAR."

Maureen A. Stevens,
Dalguise, Nr. Dunkeld,
Perthshire.

WRONG CONCLUSIONS

How wrong we can be at forming conclusions,
How our minds can wander on
Making mountains out of molehills,
Making geese out of swan.
There's two sides to everything,
Two ways of looking on
Our mind can play havoc,
If we let it wander on.
It's easy to take for granted,
What we think others do
Unless we look at both sides,
Question and answer too.
How can we keep these minds of ours,
From getting embittered views
For until we give and take,
The friends who matter most
We're sure to lose.
Let's turn over the page we've blotted
And not bother to sign our name,
There's always another chance for us
As long as we play the game.

Mrs. Jennie Stevenson,
Stoke-On-Trent.

UNIVERSAL

The Universe within my ken
Stretches a bit past Seaton Den
Circling the coast with freezing green
Lake of long tides of slow incoming
Sprinkled with seagulls' squeals and mutters
Day into night, night to day.
And I must reckon those bordering woods
Hover on brink of all that is,
And if I were fool enough to venture
Past them the land is dark for strangers,
Not for those whose rising sun
Circumscribes time in sickle skies.
For as I was born to know, expanses
Settle and sink in grand finale

Journeying miles beyond the prom
Where cliffs slide easy to the east
And needles of sound surround the west,
Where all's made clear in furling fern
And ants that earthward helterskelter
Spiralling stem, dodging spike
Hold truth in trust cocoon-like.

James Stewart,
Arbroath, Angus.

THE POPPY

Beneath a sky of thunder cloud,
Black as locusts above fertile land,
The flower of peace, the poppy plant,
Sits in the cupped hands of time.

It was in the mourning dawn of a new day,
Damp dew fell with the rain of hate,
Teasing fears that struggle like fish,
To a breaking strain in their last breath.

That progressive eternal tide of soldier time,
Stepped forward a seed to plant,
That fed upon manure of decaying remains,
Bloomed red in the soil of spilt blood.

So the reign of hate that was as the eye of a mole,
Succumbed and upheld its stubborn tongue,
Then wrapping itself in its own agonies of death,
Looked to that face of love.

Night the cold being yawned,
And spread its fingers as tar to a surface,
So, said the body to the soul,
Shall we, shall we ever meet again?

It was in the still morning of a new day,
Atop a fresh mound of earth,
That a grey battered helmet lay,
Near where the seed for peace grew.

Robert Sumner,
Rugeley, Staffordshire.

AN UNTITLED POEM BY D. SUNDERLAND

Oh foolish humans must you fight and kill and die
In pain and anguish beneath a gloomy sky
Made gloomy by deeds of violence and actions ill
Without a single thought of pity and goodwill
You wound and maim emotions lashed by hate
Undaunted by deadly penalties defying fate
Guns and bombs become the tools each passing day
Life was not given to be taken and cast away
A sudden bang and bodies fall and many moan
A woman just widowed a child left all alone
It is not meet that we live this life in gloom
Weighed down by expectations of impending doom
Good feeling stifled by this constant blight
Making of day this black and seeming endless night
Came then the dawn with things that might have been
And sunbeams lighting up this sad and doleful scene
Shining full upon us and guiding us to plan
And aim at giving love to fellow man
Melting the ice of hate with a sustaining glow
The milk of human kindness then may flow
With love and good feeling and aid to those in need
And end the hate and envy and take heed
That all the steps we take shall lead to peace
With life and living taking an extended lease
Let enemies of old join hands and shout
That co-existence is what life is all about
Then unity and amity can be a joyful way of living
When we end the taking away and begin the giving
All nations could make this global happiness a goal
People not living as divided but as a whole
No young and innocent lives nipped the bud
And each can say in voice sublime I shed no blood

D. Sunderland,
Glasgow.

DEVOLUTION

Our Queen was born as thunder rolled,
Destined to wear a crown of gold.
Born to a Scottish lass, born to a throne.
Born to sit on the Stone of Scone.

Jubilee year is a time care,
A time to give, a time to share
Give back the Stone to our Scottish friends
Set it rest in St. Giles before the year ends.

Let our own Queen Mother from Castle May
Present the Stone on Jubilee Day
What pride as a Scot she never will lack,
Think of her joy in giving it back!

A. Mary Sunter,
Brooklands, Cheshire.

TOBERMORY

We watched the ships sail round by Tobermory;
The sea so blue with ripples in the sun.
We sat together hand in hand like lovers
As though our lives had only just begun.

We watched the ships sail round by Tobermory;
The sun began to lower in the sky.
You smiled and said, "I think we should be going"
We strolled away together you and I.

I watched the ships sail round by Tobermory;
The day seems long, young lovers pass on by
You smile and say, "I think you should be going"
I wend my weary way; the seagulls cry.

Mary Barclay Sutherland,
Thornliebank, Glasgow.

A KIND OF SILENCE

The noise is there, beating, throbbing, living,
A thing apart, surrounding and drowning.
How can I stand aside, yet within me is a peace.
The people shout, jostle, push, busy in their ways.
What do they need, what is it they seek?
I want no share in all their bustle and their haste.
The peace that I have here, it's calmness deep,
No scurry or hurry can remove its roots.
At night the cars still hum, people shout and sing.
How pleased I am to feel its gentleness within.
Its source must come from something high and bright
Removed so far from this world and yet so near.
In all my life I feel its presence there,
A kind of silence no one else can share.

Mrs. Margaret Swaffield,
Telford, Salop.

FALL-OUT

I woke up one morning,
I knew something was wrong.
Not a song – not a song.

I looked out of my window,
What did I see?
Not a tree – not a tree.

Houses that were, yesterday,
Rubble heaps are today,
All gone – all gone.

Ghostly faces stared at me,
Never had a chance to fight.
What a plight – what a plight.

Atomic dust filled the air,
Darkness, where the sun shone.
Desolation – desolation.

Poetic licence bids me tell,
The scene of havoc all about.
Fall-out fall-out.

Bridget Tavani,
Luton, Bedfordshire.

THE FALLOW DEER

The light from our room shone in his eyes,
Rounded, large and mesmerised . . .
For moments long he stood.
There was dignity and loneliness,
Graceful charm and friendliness,
Were we his brotherhood?
He'd wintered in the wooded glen,
Alone, and only now and then,
By chance in view.
But Spring returning to the earth,
Stirred latent depths, links with his birth –
He sought his herd anew.
He looked for company with sheep,
And gambolled round with frisky leap,
And friendly air.

This scared the poor slow witted dams,
Who then, too early, cast their lambs,
And ran for care.
A shot or two, reluctant fired,
To tell though loved, 'twas not desired,
He dwelt so near.
Did nothing to abate his game –
He greatly added to his fame,
He ate our newest weeping willow,
And this – the worst of ravages –
He then ate Hugh's fresh cabbages.
But we shall never quite forget,
The sight of him, head spatulate,
Not pointed like the red,
And bigger than the roe: He stood,
Against a fading eastern sky,
Upon our lawn,
A lonely fawn . . .
Then with a wicked twisty doff,
Of sporraned tail, he trotted off.

Mrs. Margaret Irene Bell Tawse,
Alford, Aberdeenshire.

COLOURS

My friends all in the city dwelt
Like prisoners in a cell they felt
And dull they were as browns and greys
And colder than the Autumn days.

And so I sought a life of greens
And blues and shaded in-betweens,
I found them in the summer rain
And in the golden fields of grain.

I found pale yellows, pastel shades,
Soft butterflies and everglades,
I saw a purple-tinted dawn,
A hopeful amber-coloured morn –

And still and still I cannot blend
A colour that will match with FRIEND.

Mr. Albert Taylor,
Denton, Nr. Manchester.

PUBLISH, AND BE DAMNED

Five forests fell for this edition
Five minutes flat to ferret out the facts
Peruse the features, flicker past the pin-ups
Five seconds to forget the lot.
Five long decades to furnish
Enough new timber to refurbish
Fleet Street's foolishness
For one more footling issue.

John Taylor
Kilmarnock, Ayrshire.

H.M.S. EDINBURGH
(*Scapa Flow to Murmansk and Back! and Back!*)

They wrote a book about her and they called it "Ulysses",
But the *frozen hell* of Arctic seas knew no such Ship *as this*!
For those who ran the gauntlet of the ravenous "Wolf Packs",
Must surely put the records straight *in face of* "Alright Jacks".

From the Highlands and the Islands – Glasgow and Liverpool,
Sailed the bravest of the brave, to Russia – with fuel!
To keep alight that "Precious Flame" and scorch the Nazi boot,
Ere darkness veiled the world and *hope became caput*!

I write of this more easily now, for time has dulled the pain,
And that brave ship "The Edinburgh" will never sail again,
But knowing how old salts will talk of ships and foreign seas
Don't ever, for "The Edinburgh" *misquote* Ulysses!

Donald Morrison Thomas, D.S.M.,
Alexandria, Dunbartonshire.

THE SIMPLE LIFE

To hear the sound of seagulls cry
And Atlantic breakers roar,
Above my head a bright blue sky,
Beneath my feet a golden shore!
Oh why, oh why must people rush
And close their eyes and ears!
If only they would stop their fuss
And rest a while o'er here.

A rainbow rests upon the hill
Where little lambs are sleeping,
The night is calm and deep and still
And moonlight is a-creeping
Tomorrow is another day,
We know not what it brings,
But as we close our eyes today,
Thank God for simple things.

The boats tied in the harbour
Have many a tale to tell,
Of men with courage and ardour
Who brave the heavy swell,
To bring home fish and lobsters,
And tales of Joy and Woe
To loved ones who await them
With faces all aglow.

Around the cosy peat-fire flame,
The wise old grand-dad tells his tale
As tiny tots with eyes a-glow,
Listen to tales of long ago –
Of big ships sailing on high seas
And pirates' treasure beneath the waves!
Soon their tiny heads are sleeping,
Dreaming dreams that are worth keeping.

They say our pace of Life is slow,
But we have time to Live and Learn
What city people do not know,
The crafts of nature we will spurn
From tiny shells and pebbles too,
Fine lamps and jewels we make,
So please respect our way of Life,
And our example take!

Miss Catriona Thomson,
Bowmore, Isle of Islay.

THE ALPHABET

Many words, we have today
To describe, our meaning, in what we say
The English language, is gigantic
Descriptive, duplicate, words, to drive us frantic
We could start, from, A to Z
Words and words, till we see red.

Every generation, shall introduce
New expressions, they shall produce
Like the one, "You are a square"
And, so, the old, up they flair
To our, abhorrence, we do hear
"Drop-dead", they shout, and make it clear.

Then we realise, that words, are cheap
Not beneficial, for us to reap
Upliftment, from, no joy
Of abominable words, which do annoy
Then we know, we are misled
To be commanded, "To drop dead".

With such, a vast vocabulary, to use
Beautiful words, we need not abuse
To define the Alphabet, we shall try
Finding, more gracious words, we won't deny
We won't endeavour, to make a pun
As this is written, for a bit of fun
So let us start, with the letter "A"
Defining words, to our dismay.

"A" starting, a true beginning, is "Almighty"
Restraining us, from, being flighty.
"B" is next, meaning "Beautiful"
Enticing us, to be, more beautiful.
"C" does bring, the word, of "Charity"
Unfolding, to others, love in variety.
"D" is for, anything, "Delicious"
Obliterating, anything malicious.
"E" illuminates, the word, of "Effulgence"
Never too bright, for religious indulgence.
"F" creates, a feeling of "Futurity"
Helping anyone, toward purity.
"G" could mean this "Generation"
For future years, a new administration.
"H" can sound Oh! So "Heavenly"
Creating Man, manly, and Woman, so womanly.
"I" could stand to be "Independent"
To show, the world, something, resplendent.
"J" is solid, for "Justification"
To hold, the rank, of commendation.
"K" could bring us, much more "Knowledge"
To parlez in French, on our sea voyage.
"L" we could use for us to "Liberate"
Introducing a happier state.

321

"M" we claim, for "Ministration"
When we give, admiration.
"N" positions, "Negotiation"
To bring a state, of prostration.
"O" can make us, "Obliterate"
Taking away, an unhappy state.
"P" is for a word of "Permission"
Following with, a state of remission.
"Q" must surely, give us "Quality"
Subtracting from, the word of quantity.
"R" we introduce, with "Reverence"
A nicer meaning, than the word of relevance.
"S" most likely, is for "Spirituality"
Portraying to all, individuality.
"T" for "Truth", for us to find
Something concrete, in our mind.
"U" is for, something "Unique"
Open to all, for all, to seek.
"V" is very, very "Virtuous"
Making a person non-conspicuous.
"W" holds, words of "Wisdom"
Originating, in the Heavenly Kingdom.
"X" I write, for "X-Ray"
Letter "X" extinct, in a way.
"Y" is given, to us, to "Yield"
Especially, in a wider field.
"Z" can really, give us "Zest"
Important in life, to do our best.

Words, we could have written, more "ecclesiastical"
Which we shall leave, to the Academical
Always, remembering, to be quite humble
While still remembering, not to grumble.

For we are reminded, that we shall reap
What we saw, and shall not leap
Into words, above our head
Which can't be pronounced, or can be read.

Now we recognise, a word or two
Always adding, Something New
So we can say, "Thanks for the treat
To have a language, which sounds so sweet."

Mrs. Elizabeth Thomson,
East Kilbride, By Glasgow.

NESSY

Dear Nessy sleeping in the deep,
While vigil on the banks we keep.
Through all the winters and the summers,
The loch draws curious newcomers.
Scientists and Naturalists and Peter Scott and Co.,
Have finally convinced the world to give the Loch a go.
The Anglo-Scottish meetings to sort the mystery out,
Have helped the gathering of the clans to rub out any doubt.
All the apparatus the Scientists adore,
Cables, flexes, wires and things that trip you on the shore.
The Scots so very canny now start to think again,
And for the sake of Nessy do not so much complain.
How lovely when the monster finally appears,
With everybody cheering and believing eyes and ears.
I love that dear old Nessy and long may she remain,
In Scotland's Loch of mystery and fascinating fame.

Dinah Thorpe,
Canterbury, Kent.

CONSUMMATION

Fire flickered
Flame
Uniting
Brightening
Fullness
At last

Consummation
Consuming
Reviving
Enlivening
Warmth
So vast

Let it roar
And restore
Blaze
And amaze
Love
Unsurpassed

Alastair Tindall,
Kilsyth, Glasgow.

I REALLY AM

Oh! I'm glad I'm not a Man (I really am)
What a bother it must be,
Everyday to get whisker free.
OH! I'm glad I'm not a Man!!
They have all the bills to pay,
Put up with people who come to stay,
Let's the Missus have her say,
And never answers back!!
OH! I'm glad I'm not a Man (I really am)
Up first every morning to make a cup of tea,
And if he's in a good mood, he'll bring one to thee.
Each day of the week he commutes on train,
Misses the bus, and it's pouring with rain.
OH! I'm glad I'm not a Man!!
When he gets home, wife's in a state!
Where have you been? you're very late.
Take off your shoes, hang up your coat,
It's our anniversary and you forgot.
OH! I'm glad I'm not a Man (I really am)
A fuse has blown and the dogs got out,
The fence has fallen on the brussel sprout,
The car won't start and the tele's on blink!
Now do the washing up, you'll find it in the sink!!
OH! I'm glad I'm not a man (I really am).

Mrs. N. Tomlin,
Leigh-On-Sea, Essex.

TELE

Every night we sit and watch
With expectation what's on the box
It's such a waste of time you see
But without it where would we be.

The cartoons are a great delight
The children sing and dance each night
To see the antics of the cat and mouse
Chasing each other through the house.

We like to watch a "weepie" too
But they are getting to be so few
Films without endings are the thing
You don't know the end from the begin.

Gardening we watch with delight
To see those flowers so coloured bright
Green fingers is a gift from God
Everything so neat like peas in a pod.

Holidays we watch so tight
Imagine a different place each night
To see once more the gorgeous sight
Blue skies and sunshine look so right.

We like to watch a quiz or two
We're not very bright, but try to do
The children's ones we like the best
They don't put our brains to test.

We hardly watch the sport at all
Eleven men playing with one ball
Give them one each and make them happy
When one scores give him a "Clappy".

We laugh at some of the ads
Of people's likes and fads
Of washing powders that work wonders
And washes out all spilt blunders.

What would we do without you
You lovely work of art
You took a lot of years to make
Me and you we'll never part.

Mrs. Kathleen Tough,
Insch, Aberdeenshire.

MATCH OF THE DAY

Match of the day
And there you are
Well content
Well away
But if you did but glance
A little to your right
Your loved one stands with carving knife
Just about to strike.

Match of the day
And there you are
Everything to hand
Even something on a tray

325

Happy as a clam you are
Well away.

Smith brought down from far behind
And Jones has failed his kick
But if you did but glance
Just above your ear
Your loved one stands with carving knife
About to plunge it clear.

The pipes have burst
The freezers off
She tried to have her say
But the news must wait
For the midnight hour
And the end of match today.

Mrs. Katherine Trimmer,
Stillington, York, Yorkshire.

CONTRASTS

In the towns and in the cities,
It's a busy busy life.
Plenty grumbling, plenty worry,
Constant struggle, constant strife.
People rushing here and there,
No matter why, no matter where.
No time to rest or stand about,
And hear the other people shout.
No time to think, no time for prayer,
But hurry here and hurry there.
And shut the door and never care,
About the other people there.

But in the country life is slow,
With time to think and time to know.
With time to reap and time to sow,
To plant a seed and watch it grow.
To see the birds upon the wing,
To stop and listen when they sing.
To hear the wind sigh through the trees,
And hear the rustle of the leaves.
No, I don't want a city life,
With all that hurrying and strife.
Just give me one small country plot,
I'll be content with what I've got.

Mrs. Katharine Turnbull,
Jedburgh, Roxburghshire.

LOVE SONNET

A poet said the sweets of love are mixed with tears:
First primroses are found beneath the Winter snow.
The laughter is not deep enough to cancel fears
That starve the plant ere it to fullest bloom will grow.
And yet what joy there is in each great love extends
The heart until it feels it's reached its farthest bound
And can no more; and so the pain when that love ends,
The measure is of joy that fell to frozen ground.
And we are also told: except the seed shall die,
There can no harvest be. Have faith to let love die,
That it may rise again with richer, stronger fruit,
And let the hope of love in cold regret take root.
Love is not love till it is lost and found again,
And great as is the love, so great will be the pain.

Althea Isabel Tyndale,
Great Shelford, Cambs.

MODERN WORLD

God made the earth, the sky, the sea,
The air we breathe that is so free
But man does mar these precious things,
The mountain range, the birds that sing,
The fish that swim beneath the sea,
The animals which are born free.

Man builds the planes that fly the sky,
To drop destruction from on high,
He builds the ships that sail the seas,
To kill the things that do not please,
His narrow soul; he makes a hell where
Heaven was, regardless of the cost to God,
The animals he stalks and kills, have every
Right to live as he, as in the eyes
of God, they're free.

Man is the devil's advocate,
Men, women, children, he'll destroy,
His soul is lost, oh, hear him cry,
Out of the wilderness save I,
Out of destruction, and of greed,
Can we just plant a hope, a seed;
To live in peace forever more.

327

For out upon life's open shore,
The driftwood that goes passing by,
May once have been just you or I.

Mrs. Mary Tyson,
Grange-over-Sands, Cumbria.

THE BIRDS

Through the thin warm air they glide,
Bodies held on arched wings.
Around the spiral curve they rise,
On hidden pathways to the skies.

Ascending circles to the clouds,
A coil of pearls hung in the air,
Supported by an unseen hand,
They rest on high above the land.

Atop the climb they briefly rest.
Then swiftly down the sloping path
They speed at leisure,
To begin once more their simple pleasure.

Mr. Richard Walkington,
Warrington, Cheshire.

EL ALAMEIN

The year was nineteen forty two, October twenty third,
El Alamein the fixed venue, where the great assault occurred.

The troops poured in and tension grew, towards the appointed time,
Infantry, guns, and armour too, lay thick behind the line.

The sweating gunners lent their weight, unloading extra ammo,
By now the hour was getting late, now soon the epic drama.

Monty's army stood prepared, from many a distant land,
The fellowship which now we shared, stretched far across the sand.

The final order came at last, fulfilling our desire,
A sudden, massive, mighty blast, followed the order "Fire!"

The sky became a blaze of light, the air around was shattered.
The desert saw a mighty fight, and soon with blood was spattered,
Five hundred rounds of every gun, was fired there that night,
And murdered many a mother's son, before the morning light.

The "Jocks" went in with bayonets fixed, behind a creeping barrage,
The pipers played, but not for kicks, my God, what awful carnage.

For every yard of desert sand, that we could count as claimed,
We must have lost a hundred grand, good lads, not counting maimed.

Terror struck the hearts of all, as through the night they wrestled,
Alas, full many took the fall, who now in graves lie settled.

The dawn revealed a battlefield, of sand with dead far strewn,
The darkness which had been our shield, had gone, revealing ruin.

Eight days the battle raged and long, with cries of pain and woe,
And bleak and weary days dragged on, while yet we fought the foe.

El Alamein your claim to fame, must surely be renowned,
I hope that never more you'll claim, that first night's awful sound.

Mr. George L. Wallace,
Glasgow.

SPRING

Slowly the days lengthen,
Frost's icy teeth bite the soil less deep;
One by one, creatures of forest and field
Stir and wake from their sleep.

The ground snow's glistening coat has shed,
Welcoming gratefully the sun's renewed warmth,
And drinks of refreshing rain
Which gently softens the frozen soil.

While newly-wakened animals forage above,
Deep in the re-nourished earth
Plants push their tender shoots
Upwards to meet the light.

New arian visitors arrive
From lands far away,
Their colours and their songs
Enhancing each day.

All round, new life is a-stirring;
All is reborn after Winter's chill death
As Spring's gay tapestry,
Before us unfurls.

Ernest Walters,
Crawley, West Sussex.

LEGACY

"Confide ye aye in Providence
for Providence is kind,"
My mother used to say to me
And oft comes to my mind.

"Be gentle to the old," she said,
"Their race is nearly run,
Look with tenderness on them,
Helping them feel Life's sun."

"Care for the young and understand
they may have much to bear,
They know not what may lie ahead;
Life's full of anxious care."

Her words I now can hear so clear,
"Oh children, Do not fight;
Love and laugh and aye play fair
And all things will come right!"

Most freely give, for you have much
and you must always share,
So many folk were greatly blessed
By her most loving care.

Oh "Courage Brother" was a hymn
that was her guiding rod,
Her example sweet placed my feet
firm on the path to God.

"Have faith and you'll win through," she said,
and often proved this true,
She left me greater wealth than gold
So now I share with you.

Catherine MacKenzie Walton,
Kettering, Northamptonshire.

330

SUNSET

Another day has slipped away,
So quick that even I,
Failed to see the beauty,
That was up there in the sky.

First it's sunrise, then it's noon,
Dinner, then it's tea,
Sunset next, and what a sight,
For all the World to see.

How quickly fly the days of man,
Too soon the sunsets come,
But we should sit and watch awhile,
When all the work is done.

Tis then we'll find the reason,
For living, you and I,
And thank the Lord for giving,
That beauty in the sky.

So try and fill your days with love,
With faith and hope and Prayer,
And when the sunset comes again,
It's glory you will share.

Helen Watson,
Darnley, Glasgow.

THE POSTIE

It's just the postie who comes down the street,
Passing the time of day when we meet,
Whistling a tune or humming a song,
His bag seems lighter as he jogs along,
Two letters, an air mail for Mrs. Brown,
And also a view of London Town.
A holiday brochure for number four,
They've never been abroad before,
The things he sees going round the street,
Some houses are so trim and neat,
And even the knocker seems to welcome you,
It keeps his day from being blue.
A cheery "hello" and "thank you so much"
Helps to give that rosy touch,
The laughter of children, the sound of the rain,

331

Beating on the window pane,
And when home at last even soaking feet,
A Postie's job is hard to beat,
So bless them all every one,
They do a good job! Well done.

Mrs. Janet Watson,
Kennoway, Fife.

BELGIUM REVISITED 1974

I've just returned from Belgian soil
After doing a tour
Of the battlefields on which I fought
For many an anxious hour.

'Twas during the '14–'18 war,
I did my fighting spell
And the awful sights I witnessed there
It does not bear to tell.

We toured around the different towns
And places where I'd been
The towns and villages all built up nice
And not a ruin seen.

We also visited some cemeteries
They were all so nicely kept
Many graves of lads I knew
I felt so sad I wept.

But for the Grace of God
I might have been just one
Of the many soldiers buried there
But my time had not come.

I also saw the ridge where I
So very nearly had it
A bullet thro' the gun I carried
And another thro' my helmet.

Another thro' my dixy can
Which hung upon my pack
But there! it was not meant to be
That I should ne'er come back.

Robert William Watt,
Aldeburgh, Suffolk.

REACH OUT

Reach out your hand and you may grasp,
Another waiting your's to clasp.
Fear not your feeling's to reveal
Speak clearly of the thing's you feel.
Waste not a moment, life is fleeting
Make the most of every meeting.
And be sure before you part
To speak the feeling's of the heart.

Tell those you care for, that you care.
Love was intended thus to share.
Not to hide, like miser's treasure
But to be given, in full measure.
In life there is so much to gain
That one must risk a little pain
True caring by its own confessing
Bring's to each life a tender blessing.

So hurry, there's no time to wait
Neither linger or pontificate
Let love then be the only guide
There's no halting, time or tide
Declare the need one for the other
Lost time we never can recover.
If brave enough, then we may find
Failure was only in the mind.

Robert Reed-Waugh,
Leeds, Yorkshire.

CRIPPLED

Not to be able to walk anymore,
Not to be able to run
Not to be able to join in the sports,
That you always thought were such fun.

I didn't know the mental anguish it could bring,
Till an accident happened to me
I was only crippled for awhile,
But gradually I got better you see.

I sympathise so with the people I meet
Who are crippled and will always be,

I wonder what they all had to forfeit
To be the fine people I see.

Most of them jolly one or two sad
Most of them helpful and bright,
I wish them all the best in this world
With fortune and good luck in their sight.

Mrs. E. S. Webster,
Irvine.

GOD'S WILL

Once the Earth lay silent, everything was still,
No grass, no trees, no animals, only God's will.
He willed it to start moving, spinning round the Sun,
The dark, the light, the day, the night, Time had begun.

The Earth slowed down, its gases cooled, a swamp-like surface formed,
As land appeared, the swamps decreased and from them creatures
crawled.
The creatures grew, they multiplied, God chose them each in turn,
He watched them live, He watched them die, so that he might learn.

At last it was the time of Man, when Earth was near its end,
Of all God's creatures, great and small, He was the last to send.
God watched him very closely, every day and every hour,
He gave him all his wisdom but Man also wanted Power.
Power to fight, Power to win, Power to rule the Earth,
Power to rule the Universe, crush those who would not serve.

God saw what was happening, his eyes were not impressed,
Of all the creatures he had chose, was this the best?
Man's rule on Earth would be the last, His time was near the end,
The pain, the greed, the suffering, God's love could never mend.

God's heart was filled with pity, his anger turned to shame,
He'd willed the Earth's creation and used it as a game.
God turned his back and looked elsewhere, the Earth's revolving
ceased,
The Sun's warm rays grew cold and died and once more there was
peace.

Mrs. Estelle Louise Wedge,
Wolverhampton, West Midlands.

THE CLANS

Noo here's a cup tae cheer my dear,
An' here's tae thee sae fairly,
Oor fathers gave their blood an' tears,
Can we dae less for Charlie.

An' wha shall wish us weel my dear,
An' wha shall curse us sairly,
For each shall hae his cross tae bear,
Wha draws his brand for Charlie.

The eagles wheel doon by the shore,
Their bairns are yellin sairly,
The bluff dragoons lie wi' the shorn,
While silent herons watch greyly.

O're hill an' dale oor step was keen,
Wi' meny a Lord an' Lairdy,
By Flodden field we blessed the green,
Where Scotland fell sae bravely.

By Derby toon we sheathed oor brand,
Lochiel did mirch us fairly,
Like wheelin shoals by Solways sand,
Wha change their course sae freely.

On Falkirks green we met the cream,
O' Hawleys german lairdy,
Like frichted dows the hawk has seen,
We flay'd their hides sae sairly.

By grey Cullodens rollin moor,
We met them fair an' squarely,
The Highland Clans will stand for sure,
For Scotland an' Prince Charlie.

The falcon wheels in the risin sun,
The Duke shall hae us early,
Noo lonely winds sigh o're oor sons,
Wha held the tide for Charlie.

The shinin clans nae mair ye'l see,
Their cairns are grey an' dreary,
The rest are o're the rollin sea,
Sold by the german lairdy.

George C. Weir,
Peebles, Peeblesshire.

. . . THE LEAST I COULD DO

Three times today
I fell among thieves.
Three times today
I lay beside the road
And saw myself
Pass by on the other side.
I did not stop –
Nor did I see Samaritans.
I gave no coins
For the tunes two cripples played.
I gave no love
To a woman's lonely tears.
I gave nothing
To my own crying conscious –
It seemed the least I could do.

Brian H. Wells,
Portsmouth, Hants.

STORM

The thunder rolled on cliff and shore,
The wind moaned louder, more and more,
The rain in torrents, it did fall,
The lightning flashed and frightened all.
A ship at sea pranced up and down.
The Captain of this ship did frown.
"Hurry – lower down that sail,"
The Captain shouted o'er the gale.
"All hands to deck, before we wreck,
And pray we're saved from a watery grave."

The rain wouldn't tire, and the wind grew higher –
And the lightning hit some village spire.
They tried to fight, throughout the night,
To put out the fire of that village spire.
But the fire – it spread
'Til the town was red;
From the flames of the fire of the village spire.

Still out at sea that ship, it pranced;
As the waves around it fiendishly danced –
Trying to lure it to its doom,

336

In the night of that awful dark and gloom.
The ship ploughed on through trough and crest –
'Til a cry was heard from the old Crow's Nest,
"Rocks! – I see them straight ahead."
And the ship towards them faster sped.
And up on high – as though in the sky –
A bright red glow lit these rocks below!

The Captain shouted, "Turn her round –
Quick, before we run aground!"
But turn, the ship just would not do:
So nearer and nearer those huge rocks flew
Suddenly, there was a ghastly sound,
As that doomed ship did run aground,
The mast it split in more than five
And fell on those yet still alive.
The icy fingers of those coal-black waves,
Seized a man who madly raves.
Some others die on the jagged rocks
And the waves stand by, as this death it mocks.

The Storm, it raged on longer still –
O'er the shell of a ship and a fiery hill.
That hill gave off a bright red glow,
Lightning the rocks not far below;
Caused by the flames of that mighty fire –
The night of the end of the village spire.
The night that a village through fire did die;
The night that a ship below did lie;
The night that for some was certain doom;
The night of that awful dark and gloom.

Nancy Welsh,
Markinch, Fife.

THE STREET

The street at dawn emerges from sleep
blinking in the first cold light of day.
The warm enveloping silence of night
is broken by bottles deposited on doorsteps.
People trudge to early shift at Lilac, Dee and Dawn
as newsboys push their papers through still and awkward letter-boxes.
Children soon to friends across the way will gaily shout,
bicycles their bells will ring and cars for office leave.

At this unearthly hour, though, the street still belongs
to those who cross the frontier between night and day.
Knowingly, reluctantly, blearily and heavily
they are in possession of the street at dawn.

The street at noon is bright and brash;
fish, chip and pie smells now fill the air.
Mothers from playschool with children hurry home,
morning's washing to complete and dinner to prepare.
Jimmy Young on Radio One competes with infant cries
as traffic in the background blends with playground games.
Sentinel at her post for little ones homeward going,
familiar figure in all weathers, Lollipop Lady stands.
Crossing too with measured tread – second time today –
the postman with his few remaining letters to deliver.
Gardens, now that autumn's here, have that look of in-between;
decaying leaves the gutters fill, awaiting soon the roadman's brush –
next to take possession of the street at noon.

The street at dusk is warm and friendly.
Sights and sounds and smells of home
give welcome to returning worker,
office, bank and factory now left behind.
Overhead glow of phosphorescent street-lamp
coincides with household glow of table-lamp and small bright screen.
Children now are called from the world they have created,
called by anxious mothers to leave their pavement games behind;
"Bath-time, bed-time, get-ready-for-the-baby-sitter-time" –
the street is changing character with the approach of night-time.

The street at night is dark and eerie.
The piercing whine of cats reaches to the skies
as proudly barking dogs their lordship of the empty street proclaim.
Television aeriels their ghostly shapes across the sky
spread from shining rooftops as the moon appears behind a cloud.
A lonely car murmurs past the silent semis –
"Where can they be going at the dead of night?"
Yet even at this time the world is moving –
smell of baking bread, reminder of tomorrow's life.
Something is astir in the street at night.

Donald Whitehead,
Oldham.

HAPPINESS

Happiness is such a transient thing,
Our guest today, tomorrow on the wing.
Soaring like lark-song in a summer sky,
Lost in the distant blue without goodbye.

And oh that we might stay that soaring flight,
That we might capture that small bird so bright.
That we might hold it in our hollowed hand,
Rejoice to find a song at our command.

But God in all his wisdom did fore-see,
That happiness could never captive be.
The heaven's blue is in his plummage fair,
His piping tune the angels taught him there.

Then make for him no cage or prison bar,
But let him fly and soar to realms afar.
Nor seek to win with honeyed word,
This wondrous migratory bird.

But sing with him the tune he knows,
Until your heart with rapture glows.
And when he deigns to grace your bower,
Remember all your days this hour.

Remember, when the darkness gathers,
The brilliance of his shining feathers.
And hear again, 'midst your distress,
The singing bluebird, happiness.

Mrs. Ivy Whitfield,
Swalwell, Newcastle-Upon-Tyne.

PERFECTION

Star, enchantress, what is she
who generates the fervent fire
within the artist's soul?
The goddess in the garish green
who stimulates endeavour,
and magnetizes man
towards his magnum opus.
She who haunts
the hypochondriac,

menaces the meticulous,
and drives
the dauntless to his Everest.
Yet, in her transparent tulle,
who can she delude?
Surely sage, or fuddled fool
must see her cloud of camouflage
has flaws
of fallibility.
An illusion she has been,
task mistress,
myth, goddess, queen,
and though she floats
beyond all parallel
without rejection,
none but mere mirage is she.
this thing – PERFECTION.

Mrs. Iris Whittaker,
Edinburgh.

FOOTSTEPS

Footsteps tapping down a quiet street,
Footsteps dragging an uneven beat,
Skipping, scurrying,
Tripping, hurrying,
Footsteps always going by, going by.

Footsteps always passing by my door,
Never stopping as they did before,
Running, leaping,
Stealthily creeping,
Footsteps always going by, going by.

Waiting, always waiting for the step that doesn't come,
Hearing only heartbeats counterpointing to the drum.

Of footsteps thudding in the dead of night,
Footsteps padding in the early light,
Leaping, bounding,
Crazily pounding,
Footsteps always going by, going by, going by.

Kathleen Mary Wicks,
Bexhill-On-Sea, Sussex.

THE SCARECROW

Alone he stands in an open field,
Martyr to the farmer's cause,
With arms outstretched in ceaseless prayer,
He pleads to the all unheeding skies:
While the cruel hands of far-borne winds tear,
At his ragged frame and in noisy torment,
Mock the shabby head bent in shame.
So still he stands, the faithful guardian,
Watching with empty eyes his charge,
The dark clean earth,
Furrowed straight as the crow homeward flies.

But one day soon, with duty nobly done,
His tattered clothes and wooden bones,
The scarecrow will be gone,
And two small boys with wonder in their eyes,
Will look and perhaps be rather sad,
For their friend of many a country day,
Has vanished forever, like a birthday passed,
As the setting sun with glory stored,
Westward turns and softly steals away.

Evelyn Ruby Wilkes,
Northfield, Birmingham.

HIM AND ME

My father was a mild man.
Kind, so kind and gentle,
The most considerate person on earth.

He was poor in health and wealth.
Sick in body and soul.
Alert in brain – not brawn.

I lived fifteen years of calm.
Peace and solitude rested on 35
Contentment such contentment.

Even so young and alone,
I was satisfied to suckle
To his soft yielding frame.

341

He clothed me, suffered me
To come to him. Never shunned,
Welcoming always welcoming.

In sickness, never health,
He was patient, seldom cross.
Loving forever loving.

For years he was dying,
But never hinted it to me.
I lived close to death.

I felt it, tasted it.
Didn't want it – never.
Now I grasp at it.

Now I shall live forever,
The life he would have lived.
If, he'd been me.

I shall enjoy every breath,
That to him was pergatory.
I wish he could have been me.

We would have wrecked the world.
Giving life to all
Living every second.

I should have been all he wanted.
But I'm trying now – I'm trying.
I live for today.

His tormented body lies in calm.
His turmoiled head rests.
He died for today.

I, shall live for every day.
Every day he died, I survive.
And survive I intend to do.

Some day when we meet again,
I hope he says to me
"You lived my life well, son."

I shall say "Thank you,
You gave it to me.
And by Christ I took it."

Albert Barrie Williams,
Todmorden, Lanc. 1.

UNITY
(*To Fort William friends exiled in the City of Glasgow*)

The rocky fields and forestry out-patterned lie
Up the far hillsides, until in distant union
They and the mountains meet, leaving the eye
To picture to itself the rolling distances
That lie beyond. Up on the nearer hills
Hotel and house and cot in steady sequence climb,
And gardens and roads and many a path
Bespread themselves, and would attain the greater heights,
Losing their distinctness within the wide horizons
Of the further hills. Down in the glen
The Silvery gleam of water speaks the message
Of the swiftly moving river. Now blue, now green,
Then grey, or maybe tinted with a riot of colours.
The delicate tracery of the trees cast shadows on her.
She windeth through the glen past crofts and cottages,
And through the town, until she also fades
Into the far horizons of the loch.

Long miles away dockyards lie along the river front,
Until they join with factory and grimy street.
In the distance, on low hills, the houses race
Up and down again, on to further street and hill.
There is a glint of Clyde, in greens and greys,
Until it too is lost in further wharf and dock.
But quiet! There is a touch of gold on Kelvin's bank.
Deep in the city an almond tree casts her shade
Upon a rain-filled pod. Distantly the river turns to silver,
And mountain winds come stealing down the darkish streets,
City and tiny town are joined together in wondrous unity.

Nora McKendrick Williams,
Roy Bridge, Inverness-shire.

I WONDER

Easter is the time for flowers,
Fluffy chicks and sunny showers,
Do you ever think, I wonder,
About him in the Great Blue Yonder.

First there was Gethsemane,
Then there was the cross,

Do you ever think, I wonder,
Just how much was lost.

As you roll your Easter Eggs
And down the hill they go
Do you ever think "I wonder"
Or can you say "I know".

Norma Grace Williamson,
Edinburgh.

THE TREE

It stands alone
On the bank of a small stream,
The snowflakes coming to rest
On its thin branches.
With fences on both sides,
It is trapped.
No way to grow or stretch,
No way to show its real beauty.
Standing at the end of a street
In a modern housing estate,
In all its splendour
It goes unnoticed.

Diane Wilson,
Greenhills, East Kilbride.

H.M. QUEEN ELIZABETH

Keystone of our Queenly Realm,
Hand on tiller, commanding healm.
Elizabeth with her princely mate,
Safely sail the ship of State.
Thru still and stormy sea,
Calm and sure Her Majesty;
All her subjects are her crew,
Loyal, faithful ever true;
A joyful, happy, Jubilee,
The wish of trusty YOU and ME.

John Wilson,
Fort William,
Inverness-shire.

344

TO THE FOX

O' fox you are a bonny beast
Yet your nature be so sly
As you slink across the heather
The whap shreiks his warning cry.
At the crest of the hill, it's there you stop,
And slyly view the scene,
For a lamb or chicken, it could be fate
In those hills you creep between.
Through the bracken, down the glen
And up the bank beyond
Once more the whap shreiks his cry,
The mallard flees from pond.
With a twitch of nose, and eyes like steel,
You head into the breeze
Wood pigeons thrash their wing in flight
The crow cry echoes through the trees.
Through the hedge beside the burn
You gaily sway your brush,
There's a twitter from the chaffinch
And a warble from the thrush.
By the burn side you quench your thirst
To help you on your way,
But still survival in your mind
You wander up the brae.
Across the hill, up to the dyke
And quietly sit beside the gap,
With thoughts of wisdom, should you cross
Or could it be a trap.
After second thoughts, you cross the road
The rabbits, they take fright
It seems it's not your lucky day
Yet your desperate for a bite.
It is by now you reach the coast
Where lies a gull, its life is past,
It's with this humble morsel,
That you will break your fast.
You scent it now and great caution take,
It's your breakfast, yes it's true,
And tightly held between your teeth
You disappear from view.
To where man must think, before he treads
In the safety of those rugged rocks,
So sly, yet nature takes its course again
For you are indeed, a bonny beast the fox.

Joseph Wilson,
Eyemouth, Berwickshire.

AUCTIONEER

Daylight is candles,
Curtains are dark,
Milk's from a bottle,
Country's the park,
Pigeons are wildlife,
Main course jam bread,
Welcoming life,
Please be fed,
Born in a cradle,
Born in a slum,
Coming unvited,
Roll of the drum,
All enter same door,
All die as well,
One bell the death toll,
Two wedding bell,
Waiting on rich folk,
Calling the maid,
Money for hoarding,
Bills to be paid,
Spare me a coin Sir,
Out of my way,
Lackeys or Lordies,
Old and grey,
Where is the meaning,
Sickness and health,
Who tells the fortunes,
Be poor or with wealth,
Who says you'll suffer,
Who says you'll die,
What is up there,
Is it just the sky,
Daylight is candles,
Curtains for dark,
Places for hiking,
Twice round the park,
Sun is a round thing,
Yellow and hot,
Who'll make the bid,
Going this lot.

Max Wilson,
Bootle, Merseyside.

MANCHILD CONCEIVED IN LOVE
(the second piece of work was written concerning the birth of my son . . .)

A momentary passing of time, a fusion of man and wife,
A hormone change, my fertile being withheld increasing life.
A seemingly endless passage of time, I nourished you from within,
My manchild I grew, to accommodate you, until motherhood slashed
   my skin.
A sudden stir I felt within, your touch a strange vibration,
My child will be no parasite to this our crowded nation.
On humid night, so destitute, I rode the tide of pain,
Vowing and cursing never to endure that lonely hell ride again.
Systematic floods of agony, my being you tried to bisect,
I reduced to a jibbering maniac, all void of intellect.
I thought, Oh God! I can't turn back, and I surely can't journey ahead,
Even in a narcotic state I was thinking I'll soon be dead.
My redeemers encircled and gazed down with scorn,
With screams "Come on push!" my dear baby was born.
Diminishing pain, I wept with joy, I sobbed "My boy, my son,"
As I snuggled him close, the warmth of my love, only compared to the
   sun.
Now a year has passed since that chapter, carved in the book of my
   life,
I have settled into the dreary routine of being a vegetable wife.
But when I feel I'm drowning in the sea of endless chores,
And try to escape through an exit, but I can't find the keys of the doors.
I stroke your golden hair, and feast in the warmth of your eyes,
And as you hug my legs, my son, one day you'll realise.
I love you so, and just for you I'd sacrifice my life,
But I'm only a mother who has to stand by as alone you will have to
   strive.
Never show fear, stand tall, be kind, and when a man you become,
I will hold my head high, and be proud to say this man is RICHARD,
   my SON.

Mrs. Julie Wiltshire,
Patchway, Bristol.

THE SPECIAL CHILD

Some people "jeer" but we forgive,
They cannot know the hurt we hide,
'Tis hard for them to understand,
The child whose born of feeble mind.

347

Some really do not want to know,
Their world's serene and whole,
Others stop to sympathise,
"Their courtesy – surely finds a role."

But over all there's those who see,
Childrens hearts who long to share,
The joys of life – be they but few,
The love of those who really care.

A life of purity on earth,
An angel near along that road,
A heavely home "no barriers now,"
"All's equal in the sight of God."

Mrs. Sophia D. Winchester,
Keith, Banffshire.

AN UNTITLED POEM BY VERA WOODHOUSE

I once was a tree in a country I loved,
I looked down from skies that were blue,
To fields round about where God's beauty I saw,
With his goodness in each drop of dew.

But man cut me down, they had need of my wood,
They saw not the hurt as I fell,
They just saw a tree that was tall and so strong,
And so gave me this story to tell.

I was stripped of all beauty and made very plain,
And then as a cross I was ready,
Whoever the criminal I had to bear,
I knew I should have to stand steady.

And this was the work that they chose me to do,
Just standing between earth and the sky,
Holding some poor tortured wreck of a man,
And his only relief is to die.

But this is no malefactor this gentle man,
His eyes dimmed with anguish and pain,
He bears all their jeers as he falls 'neath my weight,
Then he rises regardless of strain.

348

Oh! why can't they feel his great love reaching out?
It just throbs from his head to his toes,
And why don't they look in his beautiful eyes?
He could never treat men as his foes.

As nails tear his flesh he says never a word,
Then he prays to his father above,
Forgiveness for them as they crucify him;
Was there ever such wonderful love?

Two others are hanging on each side of him,
They've sinned and are paying the price,
One mocks him, the other is seeking to plead,
For a place there, in his paradise.

The wonderful one sees this sinner repent,
And so takes the guilt and the pain,
From a thief, who sees in a moment divine,
God's glory shine forth through the shame.

Now even the heavens cry out in distress,
So they blot out the sun from the sky,
And darkness descends over all of the land,
As he gives himself up to die.

The earth cries its protest, it shudders and breaks,
The veil of the Temple is torn,
As the ransome is paid, by his precious blood,
'Twas for this, that the Saviour was born.

So now it's all over, and my work is done,
Was ever a task so divine,
To be there holding close this wonderful one,
Whose great love with his glory did shine.

And though it's the end of the story for me,
For man it has, only begun,
It tells how God's son took the sins of the world,
When he wrestled with Satan and won.

Mrs. Vera Woodhouse,
Hill House, Huddersfield.

WEATHER OR NOT TO TALK

Morning, George. Looks like rain.
Yes. They said there would be.
How's girl-friend, George? Oh, not too bad
My wife's asked guests to tea.

Hi there, Fred: Sun's come out.
Aye. I felt it warming through.
Fancy seeing match tonight?
I've chores for friends to do.

Wind's got up. It's proper rough.
I'm glad we're still on't floor.
Well, sup up lad, the blower's gone
We're catching half-past four.

They didn't forecast snow, then Fred.
Trust bus to make us wait:
Get out quick. Your stop's arrived
See you: Don't be late:

Morning, George. The snow's all gone.
Their fans . . . Burnt down our stand.
Wife's disappeared with cousin, Paul.
This sun: It's really grand.

> *Jeffrey Wootton,*
> *Cinderhill, Nottingham.*

A LEITH DOO'S MEMOIRS

It a' began some years ago,
When Leith wis mair refined.
When happy birds alongside me,
On dainty morsels dined.

Ah see it yet; the auld Kirkgate,
Where we wid perch for hours.
Unconscious like the crowds below,
O' planners and their powers.

In fact, Ah never realised,
How much we're like tae man.
Until ma breadcrumbs disappeared,
Wi' each removal van.

Bulldozers came, Ah hud tae flit,
Before the brutal end.
When a' ma favourite howffs and haunts,
Were sacrificed tae trend.

Through desolation and decay,
Ah fluttered on and on.
The heaps o' rubble seemed tae point,
The way tae Babylon.

Ah demonstrated wi' ma pals,
Tae try and draw attention.
Went fleein' efter Councillors,
Tae query their intention.

"The flats," Ah cooed, "are for the 'gulls,
Ah cannae live up there."
They paid nae heed, down came ma perch,
For Doos they didnae care.

Wis Ah Hindu, and born a Coo,
Folk wid respect me mair.
But Ah'm a Scot that should be shot,
Or so ma ain declare.

And though loyalty tae ma ain country,
Implored me for tae bide.
The law for birds, the same as men,
Made common sense ma guide.

So then, forsaken, and alone,
Ah turned South, and flew.
Where Ah wis welcome; put in charge,
O' every London Doo.

David N. Wright,
Leith, Edinburgh.

TOAST TAE THE LADIES

At makin speeches Im nae haun,
But ach I'll dee the best I can,
Tae toast the ladies is my aim,
I keep a topper too at hame.
I ken ye a' agree wi me,!
"Withoot a wife!" faur wid we be?

She sits at hame, nicht efter nicht,
Shes on her own fae mornin licht.
Tho whiles they mith bemoan their fate,
Fin noo and then we turn up late;
Noo winner then, she starts a'greetin.
"Yer' denner's cauld," "nae fit for eatin.!"

Wc try their patience, thats a fac.!
We hinna afa muckle tac.,
But losh, I'm speakin for masel,
Nae doot for maist men here as well.,
Although we dinna shout their praises,
We love them as we did lang syne
Fin we said "Dear! will you be mine?"

The guidin lights o' a' oor lives
They're here the nicht, oor "Lovin wives"!
But, fit aboot the single quines?
"I've drafted oot these twa, three lines!
Of coorse we think they're really swell,
Some day nae doot they'll wed as well;
But meantime – its a treat tae see,
Their wee short skirts and plenty knee.

So, be ye Dother, wife or Ma,
It is a fac, we love ye a',
So, will ye rise noo brithers a'?
And drink a toast wi me ana,
Tae a these lassies gaithered here,
The lassies that we love sae dear.

Jimmy Wright,
Aberdeen.

SHORT STORY SELECTION

Author's Name Alphabetically With Story Title

Sunset on the Dornoch Firth. The endless sky festooned with gloriously illuminated golden clouds, intercepted with patterns of blue and green, and kaleidoscope rainbow colours overlook and engulf the reflecting sea.

The gentle waves in shimmering lights rise and fall, breathing, until they come to rest on the soft moist sand. Sea gulls, terns and oyster catchers stand quiet and still, in reverence.

A long legged scraggy figure of an exiled missionary, who had made camp in the sand dunes, in a small ridged tent, to meditate in solitude stood watching the dazzling panorama.

Unable to contain his emotions, he ran through the grass, like a school boy set free for the day, down the hillocks on to the beach, and with arms outstretched praised his Creator. He pleaded for help, for the poor souls of the world.

Exhausted physically, he sank to his knees, and stayed quiet, as if awaiting an answer to his plea.

He was startled when a hand pressed his shoulder. He looked up. Beside him, huddled in an oversized raincoat, stood an old beachcomber he had once befriended.

"I have something for you, Reverend, look, it is gold, a pouchful of gold." The old man held it up for inspection, his brown eyes shone with excitement.

The bewildered minister took the bag and looked at the contents. It was gold. Pure gold.

He stood up and accosted the old man with questions. Where did he get the gold? Why give it to him? a stranger.

The tale the beachcomber told, was a simple one. He was a lonely man given to wandering. Many years he had panned, and searched for gold in the hills, and streams, at Kildonan. Now feeling age and the aches and complaints that accompany it upon himself, he had settled in a wee cottage by the sea. He was content. Gold in the hands of folks could change their personalities and way of life. He did not wish this on his conscience.

The beachcomber trusted the Reverend to use the gold wisely. The two men shook hands, and the minister, quite overcome at such a wonderful gift, went slowly back to his tent.

While the sky folded into purple, and receded into night, the kneeling figure, a humble scraggy man, gave many prayers of thanksgiving and planned for a new mission to be inaugurated with this bountiful benison.

C. F. Blackie,
Perth.

UNDER MY THATCH

These dreamers of dreams, these beholders of vision.

Young Wonnacot – prospectuses of all academic opportunity in his mac-pocket and the world wide open, he wakes, does young George Wonnacot, to the treasure at hand on Jolliboys Wharf. It is the start of his career in the new exploration culminating in the discovery of Tradeology. The daily miracle to be observed of the way men of all nations go down to the sea in ships, handling cargoes vital to all humanity.

Posy – An amourette. Betsy tells her grandchild of her girlhood on the Cornish-Devon border. Of a sovereign gift on her seventeenth birthday, when sovereigns were current in the realm.

Cameo – of three sisters in a little Wiltshire town. They cast aside anxieties and shed their cares for this weekly ritual of coffee in a cafe where blue ginger-jars are suspended. Their children (but two between them) awed by the inflow of lorry drivers fresh from the cabins of transporters that tear the town apart.

Tale of a Tale is the tale of Nanny Dyer (Broadcast early in the Reign). True in all essentials of the woman from Northwick parish who walked to Gloucester where her two brothers were to be hanged for stealing sheep. "All the town were out to see her pass, sister, Mother or whatever she was to them young fools of gallows-fodder. And a face no man could turn aside who hoped for mercy at the last."

The Meeting An open-air gathering where the young speaker is carried away. He is offering them freedom, justice and brotherhood. "He's got Russia behind him," yells a heckler. With serene finesse the young man turns on his soap-box, bringing into view for all to see a sleepy old character smoking his pipe. The crowd laughs to a man and in that instant the speaker leaps into the golden heart of their up-gathered goodwill.

All these mirrored, met, remembered in and about the years of the Reign of Elizabeth II.

Margaret Brooks-Brown,
Bristol.

SCONES FOR A QUEEN

"Would you make Scotch scones, shortbread and a chocolate cake," said the cultured voice of the elegant lady in front of me, "enough for six people will be required." "Mrs. Findlay," she continued, "Yes Madam," I replied, keeping my puzzlement to myself, as to who I was speaking to. "There will be no dinner tonight," she said as she left. That was good news anyway. It meant I would be free after lunch. It did seem strange to someone from the Highlands to be called Mrs. Findlay while still single, but I had learned this was the custom, in such households.

No sooner had the door closed behind her than I saw the imposing figure of Mr. Jones, the butler, bearing down on me. "What did the Princess want, Mrs. Findlay?" he said. Realisation dawned on me: the elegant lady had been Princess Arthur of Connaught herself. Yes, this was my first week as cook in Her Royal Highness's household, working in a beautiful modernised kitchen. Any orders from Her Royal Highness had hitherto been conveyed to me by the House Controller. So her visit to the kitchen meant an important guest was expected.

There was much speculation downstairs, especially in the butler's pantry, but all I could tell the butler was that there would be four for lunch, six for afternoon tea, and no dinner that night.

Time for speculation was limited. Lunch had to be prepared and cooked, the baking done, and the chocolate cake iced. Mr. Jones, with his usual precision, would expect me to have everything ready to hand over to him after lunch.

Soon after 3 p.m. I was ready to go out, leaving 16 year old Muriel on duty. Some three hours later, I returned to be met by a stammering excited Muriel, who gasped out. "She was here, Mrs. Findlay, she was here." It took me some time to calm Muriel, only to learn the mysterious she, was Her Majesty Queen Mary, who with her keen interest in domestic affairs, had decided to inspect the newly modernised kitchen. It was the Queen's keen eye for detail and searching questions that had so excited and flustered Muriel.

How disappointing it all was, to think that Queen Mary had inspected my kitchen, and I was not there. It was some consolation to learn, however, that she had particularly enjoyed my scones and shortbread.

In this the Silver Jubilee Year, it is a striking thought, that while Queen Mary inspected my kitchen, Her two Royal grandchildren, Elizabeth and Margaret, were being entertained elsewhere in the house.

Flora Chisholm
Aberdeen.

EMERGENCY CALL

The rain was beating down harder now, thought Sally as she shivered and pulled her coat collar closer around her neck to prevent the cold and wet from getting in. She would be more than glad to get home, she thought, as she trudged on into this wet winter night.

Then she stumbled and almost fell. She looked around sharply to see what had caused her to trip and saw what at first looked like a bundle of old clothes. As her eyes became accustomed to the light, however, she realised it was a body. She hesitated for a second or two, several thoughts clamouring, all at once, in her mind. Should she run and forget all about it: suppose whoever it was was dead? Sally shivered, more violently this time and not from the cold: in fact she was standing there quite oblivious of the rain.

Her thoughts gradually began to focus properly and she realised that she just couldn't walk away and leave the poor, pathetic bundle – her conscience just would not allow it. Slowly, with trepidation, she approached the heap on the floor and saw to her surprise that it was a youngish man. She thought at first that he was dead but as she placed her hand inside his coat, she felt a very slight movement of his chest. Whatever could she do? She looked around wildly but there wasn't anyone around; this was terrible, she couldn't walk away, but what good was she doing here? She tried to feel his pulse, when her hand came into contact with a bracelet on his wrist. If only she had a torch, she would be able to see him better.

As she glanced around again, her mind registered the light that was shining further down the road. Of course! the telephone box, why hadn't she thought of it before. Taking another hurried look at the young man Sally rushed down the street and swiftly entered the phone box; with shaking fingers she dialled 999.

The girl at the switchboard looked up expectantly as the light flashed in front of her. Pushing in the plug she intoned, "Police, Ambulance, Fire, which service do you require?" and a voice full of concern crackled over the line.

"I think its the ambulance, but it might be the Police as well," Sally said breathlessly.

The girl at the switchboard with cool proficiency asked for the location. Sally looked around the box desperately: she hadn't lived here all that long and she wasn't sure quite what the area was called, so she repeated the name of the telephone box and gave the number, also a brief resumé of the circumstances. The switchboard girl said kindly "Could you hang on there and an ambulance will be with you directly". After what seemed an age Sally heard the urgent clamour of the ambulance bell or siren filling the air. It drew up to where she was waiting outside the telephone box.

"It's just up the road a little way," she explained and the ambulance followed her directions until they reached the spot where the young man was lying.

The ambulance men quickly and expertly examined him and quickly and efficiently transferred the young man to a stretcher and into the ambulance, after first reading what it said on the bracelet they discovered on his wrist.

By this time the Police had also arrived and had established the position. After the preliminaries had been dealt with, the policeman congratulated Sally and told her she had done a good job.

"That young man will have reason to thank you," he said and then as he turned to get into the car he added,

"You see he happens to be diabetic and needs insulin treatment; the bracelet around his wrist gave us the information we needed. But for your prompt action, it might well have been too late."

As the ambulance and its raucous sound disappeared into the distance, Sally started on her way home again and although it was still raining as hard as ever, she glowed with the satisfaction of having done her best, and thanked heaven that help was within reach, through three little numbers, 999.

Cynthia Cooksey,
Birmingham.

HOME SWEET HOME

Seven-year old Beenie was playing "schools" outside the thatched cottage that was her home. Her blackboard was one of the stones – worn smooth by years of wind and rain – of which the cottage was built, her chalk a small piece of mortar prised from among the stones. She was teaching her imaginary class Hymn 288, "Now the Day is Over". She could not be sure whether her fondness for the hymn stemmed from its neat, compact appearance in the hymnary or from her ability to read, and almost understand, it unaided.

"Now the darkness gathers". She gazed up at the square chimney whence a puff of smoke made the only cloud in a flawless blue sky. "Gran's chimneys have pots," thought Beenie. Everything seemed to remind her that, today, Gran would come to collect her to spend the school holidays at her cottage. For months Beenie had looked forward with eagerness to the visit, but now that the actual day had arrived, she was filled with trepidation.

Running into the garden, she clung to the trunk of the old rowan tree, whose leaves in summer formed a perfect screen for "The Housie" which her Dad had painted green. "Buckingham Green" he called it. "Was *Her* 'Housie' that colour?" Gran's one was ivy-covered.

The little girl scrambled over the dyke to the pen where four hens, Rhodie, Exchequer (because of the colour of her feathers rather than her economic qualities) Blackie and Whitie had given up trying to eat the pancakes Mum had baked for Gran's tea, for "You could sole your boots with them," said Mum. Last year Gran had grumbled that the rhubarb jam was a little too solid and Beenie's Dad had declared, loyally, that he did not like the kind of jam you had to herd, anyway.

Crawling under the lowest wire of the fence, Beenie made her way to the meadow, where she spent the afternoon making daisy chains.

"Tea time, Beenie," called Mum. Gran had arrived and was already seated at the table. "Eat up, Rubena," she said (Gran always used her proper name). "We must catch the six o'clock bus." To Beenie, the oatcakes tasted like sawdust and a morsel of bread felt like a marble that would not roll down her gullet in spite of numerous gulps of tea. "What's the matter?" asked her mother. In a flash, the little girl realised that her malady must sound convincing. Of course, she would confide in Mum later. "My hair is sore," she blurted out. A look of alarm came into Mum's eyes, followed by the dawning of under standing. "You will need to stay at home, dear; you've had a little too much sun." were her words.

As Gran put on her coat to depart, Beenie reflected that she was really rather fond of her, especially now that the visit had been post-poned. She glanced obliquely at the elderly lady's arms and pockets. They appeared no different to most people's. She had overheard cousin Rachel say that Gran's pockets were too deep and her arms too short. Rachel, of course, was fifteen and very clever.

Then Beenie received a kiss from Gran and she, Dad and big brother set off running the few yards to the bus stop.

"Glory to the Father,
 Glory to the Son,
 And to Thee, blest Spirit,
 Whilst all ages run," sang Beenie.

"Next year," she promised. It was such a long way into the future that she could anticipate the visit with pleasure.

Barbara Cooper,
Auchterarder, Perthshire.

PEACE

I left the house and wandered slowly down the slope towards the gate which opened into the road leading to the moor so bleak and lonely. Nothing stirred as the mist descended and rolled across that wide expanse of barren land. Along the road and at the bend I left it. Not a breath of air – not a sound ensued, only my feet descending on the heath told of life on the moor. The bullrushes stood like swords of warriors on guard. Down, round the hill to the hollow, and there lay the peat moss at my feet. No lizards basking in the warm sun – today all was cold, clammy, still and silent. I began to hurry now, for the mist forming round the feathery silver birches held a ghostly and even haunting look. The milk came spilling from the can. I was obliged to cease my rushing and fall into the motion of the things around me.

The mist now covered all. The stream appeared before me – down its banks I walked, and coming to the bridge, I crossed. Skirting the bogs I carried on, till the fir wood, looming out of the mist like a many towered castle stood there robed in the fragile shrowd of mist. Past the wood – and on past the caravan which belonged to the woodman long since dead – I came once more to the road. Mist there too, but not so ghostly now that houses appeared and sounds of music coming from within. The hens picking corn and clucking cheerily, a kitten playing on the step. My journey almost ended – on, up the road I went till I reached the top and there I turned at the little green gate, all damp with evening mist – I bent my head in silent prayer to marvel that such peace could possibly exist.

Oh! that man could leave what God had made –

PEACE, PURITY AND RESTFULNESS.

Emily E. M. Craig,
Aberdeen.

LAST LOVE

We used to watch him each mid day, my friend and I. Across the narrow strip of park – in faded coat and scarf, a gnome with piebald beard and stark white shock of hair. Arriving with his rolling walk, a soft-sung tune upon his lips. In well-cared shoes, but when he smiled the lines would deepen in his face and kindness light up everything about him.

Seated under friendly pines, he carried sandwiches to eat. But he was never first to take the food – a ritual he observed, as would a priest in saying some small prayer to bless the staff of life.

He first would whistle lilting notes that echoed in the trees about him and, in time, there was a trembling of the branches as a squirrel hastened down with twitching tail, and sat up silent at his feet. And then the others came – the starlings, ring-doves, pigeons, vying for a share of all he gave. Except the robin, who would await his special treat. A crumb of cheese on palm of hand. The robin briefly sang, flew down and safely took the gift. And all the while the old man's face was lit with simple joy. Except the time the robin failed him twice, when nests were being built in early spring. But soon it had returned and then the face was beautiful to see and had the pathos of a gentle clown. So much that I was moved to tears that I should sit and see his heart worn openly upon his sleeve.

And when the summer sun was warm and others walked the park in numbers, so they shared his joy and gathered round to smile or point,

361

as if he were a small Messiah whose flock was here, about his feet, for all to see. Contentment on a shoe-string, simple as a sunset, beauty in the whitening Indian summer of that funny little man.

The children often stood about and watched and smiled the same pure smiles of happiness. Nor did they ever misbehave, but seemed to know that here was something precious, not to be destroyed. He never was the first to speak and only answered when they wished to talk. And then his words were soft and he would tell them gestured stories, all of far-off lands, until their eyes were full of wonderment. And parents, come to look for them, would stay to listen to his words.

I met him in the street one day and greeted him. He smiled his bright, blue twinkling smile and almost stopped. My friend remarked he looked so like a saint, a kindly man – Saint Francis of the Park.

We later met again. He stopped, the first of many times.

And Saint he was and is. For, even now, he goes each day to see his friends while I just sit alone and watch. For that's a private thing they share together. Then I see his rolling walk and – deep inside – see only grace and I could watch all day. Until he finishes and walks to me, to touch my shoulder, lightly kiss my brow, then quietly say, "I'm back, my last love – all the little ones are fed."

He takes the wheel-chair bar and pushes me along through scented air of pine and fresh-cut grass. I hear him hum the song that ends . . . "he loves her as he's never loved before".

A funny old, little old man, with a funny old, crippled old wife, both rich in love and happiness.

Stuart Drinkwater
Poole, Dorset.

A SALTY END TO A ROMANCE

Linda knew the other girls in the office envied her. Ever since she came to work in the office over a year ago it was obvious that the boss favoured her. Now in addition to being her boss he was also her fiance and they intended to get married in the spring which was just seven months away. When Linda informed her Mother about her engagement she had been delirious with happiness but now she was not so sure about things. Her mother did not like John Graham and had warned her daughter not to go out with the boss as she did not like him at all. Now she was reluctantly accepting him as a future son-in-law. The various comments about him had sunk into Linda's brain, however, and she stood idly in the office thinking of the times he had told her to tell someone on the phone that he was not in the office or some other such excuse so that he need not talk to the person telephoning. Linda did not like telling lies and usually had to fabricate some excuse to explain why John couldn't come to the telephone.

There were other things as well, when he supplied figures which she knew were not accurate to encourage potential new clients to his business. All in all, she knew now that she did not like his business methods one little bit and was slowly realising that she was no longer as much in love as she had been at the start.

Meditating in this manner, she thought of the steady boyfriend she had had before she came to work for John. Longingly she remembered how kind he had been and how straightforward and honest. Being in the same line of business as John, he had remarked to her that he did not think much of John's business methods. Now that it seemed to be too late, she wished she had remained Norman's girlfriend. Linda was brought back with a start to the present when the telephone rang. On lifting it, she heard a girl's voice say breathlessly "Oh darling, I have such a pleasant surprise for you", and without waiting for a reply continued "See you in half an hour John", and rang off. Linda was taken aback, knowing that John had told her he was going to interview a client that afternoon. She thought over various incidents in the past and realised he was having an affair with someone else. She thought of the cancelled meetings lately and remembered that her friend had told her that she had seen John on the beach one afternoon with a young girl. She had not believed it and had not challenged him but felt now that perhaps it had been true. She knew he was returning to the office about 4.30 p.m. for a meeting and decided to have it out with him this evening when they were going to a party.

Just before 4.30 p.m. he returned looking very fit and she decided to test him and said "You look as if you have been on the beach". "No!" he said quickly, "I have been busy with a client", and bent over to kiss her briefly. As he did so, she felt a saltiness on his lips and knew he had been swimming, obviously with his new girlfriend. She knew then that their romance was over and seeing into the future felt sure that Norman and she would soon pick up where they had left off previously. She was glad it had happened like this as she would not have liked to have got married and then found out about John's girlfriends. Thanks to the girl's phone call which put her on her guard, Linda's romance had come to a salty end.

Isabella S. Gibbs,
Bomere Heath, Shrewsbury.

THE STORM

The fishermen knew it was coming. They had seen before that strange glow in the sky. It was still mid-day and yet the air was dim as dusk. The men gathered together in the harbour, their faces still and strained as they watched the clouds turn grey on the horizon. The clouds thickened as the men hurried to secure their boats to the harbour wall. The men pushed impatiently, rudely, through groups of wide-eyed tourists gathered along the beach – passing a girl who laughed as she twirled in the quickening breeze, her yellow hair streaming behind her.

The wind freshened, scraps of paper danced down the narrow streets. The first few drops of rain spattered the ground. The women of the village hurried home to fasten shutters and secure gates. They carried their washing indoors, fighting the teasing wind which dragged the wet garments from their hands.

The waves were lashing the harbour walls now. They reared high, higher, then hissed frustration as they fell. Gaining momentum they reared themselves again and again, walls of white fury. The rain conspired with them, lashing the ground. The sightseers were all gone. The wind shrieked malice as it hurled itself against mankind. The waves roared. Lightning split the sky. The sea was black. The world was black. THE STORM REIGNED.

June Holmes,
Peterborough.

THE SNOWDROPS

The little churchyard was in a village some two or three miles from where we lived, a distance easily covered by bicycle. From the front it appeared very neat and trim; the railings and the wrought iron gate shone black as though newly painted and the yew trees that flanked the stone pathway were trimmed to perfection. Beyond the yews, however, the graveyard straggled into disorder. Here and there, a newly dug grave was heaped with fresh brown earth and adorned with wreathes of bright flowers, and there were one or two of the older graves which showed evidence of tender care over the years, but in the main the graves were overgrown and neglected.

We had gone there first a year before and had visited it often since. There were four of us altogether, although Wendy did not always come. It was Wendy, in fact, who had begun it all by telling us about the death of her little sister and the boy next door on the railway lines behind our streets. The children were only two years old at the time and each mother had made the tragic mistake of believing her child to be playing in the other child's garden. This sad little tale had so captured our imagination that we had set out to find their graves in Isleworth cemetry, a task that had proved difficult at first because they were so tiny and almost completely overgrown. It was only the dis-

364

covery of a small marble vase bearing the name of Robert Logan and the date of death that had enabled us to identify the graves at all.

Having discovered the graves, we came regularly to tidy them, bringing wild flowers or flowers from our gardens. We even extended our activities to include the tending of several other children's graves that we found there.

Beyond the boundaries of the graveyard there was a meadow and, to the left of this, a small area of woodland. Sometimes in the meadow there were two horses and we would come prepared with apples and sugar-lumps to feed them.

One day in February the four of us cycled to the churchyard after a few weeks' absence, due to Christmas and bad weather. It was a frosty morning and there was little we could do to the graves because the earth was frozen solid. We looked over the fence to see if the horses were there, but it must have been too cold for them to be out because there was no sign of them. But in the wood, sheltered by the trees and bushes, grew drifts of snowdrops just asking to be picked.

We scrambled over the fence and began to gather the flowers, tripping over one another in our eagerness, when I suddenly came across a clump of daffodils in bud. At about the same time Wendy discovered crocuses. I looked at her and she looked at me. Somebody's garden! We beckoned the other two and began to withdraw. Too late! A woman coming out of the house with a basket of washing saw us, banged her basket down on the path and advanced upon us, shouting. We all took to our heels and fled, over the fence, across the churchyard and out at the gate. We leapt onto our bicycles and four front wheels wobbled into action, whilst the woman, who had now reached her front gate, continued to shout at us to return. Even in our haste and agitation we could not fail to notice the inscription on the gate: "The Vicarage" it proudly proclaimed. We had been picking the vicar's flowers!

Across the road an upstairs window opened and the head of an old lady appeared. She had evidently put her own interpretation on the little scene outside the churchyard.

"Robbing the graves! You should be ashamed! I knowed you were up to no good. I seed you here afore. I knowed you were up to no good!"

We had gathered speed now and made our escape at last, leaving the two angry voices fading away behind us. We were full of righteous indignation at the injustice of the accusations, and hot with embarrassment at having made such a mistake. We should have realised that snowdrops don't usually grow wild in such profusion. Isleworth was going to be effectively out of bounds to us for quite a while.

But those beautiful "wild" snowdrops brightened four rather drab kitchens long before the first shafts of spring sunshine began to filter in at the windows.

P. Kerslake,
Peverell, Plymouth.

THE FATHER

The girl's hair shone like a golden halo in the piercing light from John's car headlamps. "The young fool," he muttered angrily "Thumbing a lift after dark – she's asking for trouble." He stopped. He didn't make a habit of giving lifts, but who knows – he may be instrumental in saving her life. She would be safe with him.

John Laidler was an ordinary, mortgage paying, hard working Scot, with a semi-detached, a loving wife Helen and two children, one of each sex. In fact he was "Mr. Average". Fifty years old, he had worked as a draughtsman for the same Company for over thirty years.

Occasionally he had to travel to Birmingham in connection with his work and it was one Friday night, returning from one of these trips, that he saw the girl.

She slipped easily into the seat beside John. In answer to his question she said she didn't know exactly how far she would be going as she was meeting her father. He started to give her some advice about accepting lifts from strangers, but stopped abruptly as he realised she was quietly sobbing. He started to say he was sorry but she interrupted him and her voice was soft but clear.

"If only people knew," she kept saying "They would lead very different lives. How selfish I've been, opting out, never considering anyone else's feelings, never thinking of my parents' sufferings, not being able to say 'I'm sorry'."

John cut in on her ramblings "You can say 'sorry' now to your father." "Oh no," she almost laughed, "you don't understand."

They had reached the Scottish border. Suddenly there was a blinding flash and when John could see again, the girl had vanished, but he could hear a plaintive cry "Father, Father, Father".

John couldn't remember how he arrived home, but there he was, being welcomed by Helen and the children. Thankfully he relaxed in his armchair. He hadn't had time to read the paper that morning. The headlines stood out starkly, "Girl killed near Scottish Border". There was a picture of the girl. He knew she had met her "Father".

Hilda Kneebone,
Dalton-in-Furness, Cumbria.

366

THE HAGGI HUNT

The year was 1978 and the Tourist Board in Scotland were gleefully rubbing their hands together as tourists from all over the globe poured in their thousands into Scotland. The Government had decided to lift the ban on tourists taking part in the annual Haggi Shoot, and had announced that the Haggi was fair game to anyone with a licence to carry a gun during the months of January and February.

The travel agencies and the hotels had never known a winter season or indeed a summer season like it, as people swarmed in from abroad. The Scottish landowners were also delighted as they arranged for shooting parties to hunt the Haggi on their land for exorbitant fees. There were a few Scots glum at the fact that their sole right to hunt the Haggis or, as they are collectively known the Haggi, had been taken from them and a small section of the community had formed a Haggi Protection Society, fearful that the increased numbers hunting that funny little creature could lead to its extinction.

The first hunting party had arrived at the estate of MacTavish of Glenachie and their guide was to be young Ewan MacTavish, youngest son of the present Laird. As he looked at his father's clients he could not suppress a smile. Indeed they were a comical lot, dressed in plus fours and deerstalkers with rifles of every size and description. Solemnly wiping the grin from his handsome young face, he informed them that they could leave their guns with his father in the house until they returned from the hunt. The party looked at the young lad in amazement – how could one hunt the Haggis without a gun?

Sighing, Ewan wished with all his might that the Tourist Board had seen fit to produce pictures of the Haggis to let people see just how tiny it really was. Through the years an aura of mystery had built up over the appearance of the little beastie, indeed some people even doubted its existence, preferring the cynics' opinion that it was made from oatmeal, liver etc., and served under false pretensions as being Scotland's National Game. He started to explain to the awed group that the Haggi, contrary to popular opinion, was not a large ferocious animal but indeed a tiny red and brown spotted beast similar to a cross squirrel hamster. He went on to explain that they lived in clumps of vegetation where their colouring provided excellent camouflage from predators who were mainly man as their fellow animals did not care for their spicy flesh. To kill the Haggis, you needed a bow and arrow and a lot of luck.

Later that day, armed with their medieval weapons the party gaily set out with high expectations of returning that evening with braces of Haggi. On and on they trekked mile after mile until they reached the foot of Ben Fruachan (mountain of tears) and approaching a clump of vegetation Ewan signalled to his party to form a semi circle and flinging back his auburn-topped head let out a weird cry "Whee aha, Whee aha". To the astonishment of his party, suddenly from out of the undergrowth appeared literally hundreds of Haggi, their inquisitive noses twitching. So taken aback by their sudden appearance, the party forgot their purpose in being here until they were recalled by Ewan's arrow sailing through the air to land plum centre in a little Haggis. The rest of the timid species scattered and ran in terror as arrows flayed the sky. At last all was quiet again and Ewan discovered much to his secret delight only a few haggi had been killed. Putting them into a large canvas sack the party continued hunting and as Ewan listened to the excited babble of many tongues, he wondered if the true size of the Haggi would ever be known to the world as a whole, for he had the strangest feeling that the Haggis would grow in size when these gallant huntsmen told of their fierce struggle with the Haggi.

Perhaps he could be forgiven for his cynical thoughts, after all Haggi hunting has been a national sport in Scotland for centuries and to all who know the size of the beastie it is considered poor sport, but to a foreigner to our shores who until this year had only heard of the Haggi and who even in his inner heart disbelieved its true existance today's hunt had taken on the qualities of hunting for a prehistoric monster.

Jillian Anne Millar Lees,
Kirkcaldy, Fife.

REMINISCENCE, 1939

The day we had been expecting and dreading had come – the day chosen by "the powers that be" for our school children to be evacuated from our London Suburb to a place of safety – we knew not where – we did not know when. I was on my knees washing the kitchen floor when quite suddenly I turned to look out of the window which was level with my head. A long queue of children, orderly and rather quiet, were traipsing down the lane towards the station. Each child had a small box slung over his or her shoulder, which contained a gas mask – a now familiar sight. Clutched tightly in their hands were oddly shaped parcels or bags. Worried teachers were hurrying the children along, a few mothers, who perhaps lived near the school and guessed what was happening, stumbled beside the children, many silently weeping. I knew that my two sons were not with this group, as they attended a school in another district, and would leave from a different station. My heart ached so terribly as I watched, I tried to pray, but could only whisper "Oh God – oh please God – ."

At last it was over – the "Pied Piper" had vanished taking our children away. I bowed my head and finished washing the floor – with my tears.

Doris Martha Logsdail,
Hastings, Sussex.

Gordon Robb eased his dugout canoe past the rocks slithering into the sea at Toke headland and aimed for the No. 2 River estuary. The pale yellow flicker of the sun peeping over Good Luck Hill on his right told him dawn was breaking. He would just be in time to catch the turn of the tide – the best time for line fishing for barracouta off No. 2 River beach.

Strong, firm strokes of his curved paddle edged his craft into the flotsam scattered along the tideline. Tin cans, bits of wood, half eaten apples and the occasional surprising article of clothing bobbed inexorably towards the shore.

It was where this floating refuse tip met the debris carried from the hill villages in the poachers' pockets of No. 2 River that the fish gathered on the incoming tide to feed. Sometimes Gordon felt embarrassed by the predictability of the live bait wriggling along his line. A dull repast compared to the bits of sandal and paper hankies that seemed to appeal to the diners of the deep. But he always caught enough to eat with some spare to sell. That was fine.

A far cry from the accountant's job he had left in Edinburgh, however, many years before. He couldn't quite remember now – and certainly didn't care.

Only a few minutes had passed but already the sun was burning through the early morning haze. Another cloudless West African day as it would be every day until June. And then the rain when No. 2 River washed down some really appetising treats from the hills.

Gordon cast the first line of the day amongst the "nonsense" as his Creole friends called it. Where the marker plopped into the water he noticed a scrap of floating newspaper. Responding to the echo of a habit Gordon reached over to retrieve it. If it was printed, it demanded to be read. That was the kind of conditioning he had once decided to leave behind.

Just the corner of a page. No indication of which newspaper it was. Nor the date. It was in English – and the headline was definite enough. "TWELVE DIE IN GLASGOW RIOTS."

Below, the story ran, "Twelve people, three of them teenage girls, died as rival demonstrations clashed in Glasgow yesterday. George Square was a battleground as a fifteen thousand strong rally of supporters of the Scottish 'Government in exile' was broken up by a counter rally organised by the Patriotic Front. The Patriotic Front supports the recent intervention by the army to restore Scotland to the United Kingdom. A police spokesman estimated casualties at over three hundred, including forty-eight of his own men. Casualty wards were swamped as scores of tear gas victims . . ."

Frustrated by the story ending in mid sentence Gordon turned the fragment over. The other side informed him of some of that day's market prices.

Gordon's mind started to drift back to his homeland and its agonies, hatreds, problems, violence, indulgence when a sharp tug on the line in his left hand brought him back to reality. The marker had disappeared below the surface. Definitely a snapper. Without thinking, just concentrating, he dropped the scrap of paper over the side to free his right hand for landing his breakfast. The tide having by now turned, the morsel of newspaper floated back out to sea. Gordon didn't think of it again.

H. McGrittie,
Edinburgh.

AS ONE DOOR CLOSES

The little country bus jogged along. Hazel sat by a sun-warmed window, luxuriously day-dreaming. She saw in her mind's eye the house, shabby but homely. A mysterious voice seemed to whisper "There was once a man who built a house and . . ." The bus shuddered to a halt. Hazel realised she'd reached her destination, a pretty little village, her childhood home and dear to her heart. One hundred or so miles she had travelled for a last look at her old home . . . to say farewell . . . to collect a box of papers and odds and ends. There'd been little time on her last visit to look through these fragments from the past.

An hour later, she sat on an upturned box by a blazing fire, the inevitable and much-needed cup of tea by her side. Gradually, her hot drink cooled as she delved, fascinated, into some of the history woven by previous occupants, her family. Here was a letter written by her great-grandmother, from another world it seemed – "I am not very happy at aa-ll. Jeannie has lost two wee bairns afore. But God has blessed her wi' another on the way, I hope for her, pore thing, that all will go well. Marriage makes a great difference in a family."

Another letter read "Dear Mother, I hope you keep well. I am fine just now. I will send on some more money soon . . ." That was Uncle David whom she'd never met. He had emigrated while still in his teens to America. Why, she had often thought, had he left home, when, as eldest son in the family of eight, with his mother a widow, he'd be needed most? The answer was here. He was happy to be able to send help to his mother and younger ones at home.

A Sweetie

Hazel sipped her cooling tea thoughtfully, then picked up an old yellowed account book. Here were Granny Grant's neat entries of the profit and loss in her wee shop, where she was at her best. "A sweetie for the bairn" she'd often say, taking several out of a big glass jar. Tho' it nibbled into her profit at the end of the day, she was a happy person, leaving behind her a wealth of cherished memories in the wee closeknit community.

Aunt Helen was the youngest of the Grant family. Hazel remembered her blue eyes and curling auburn hair and wondered why she'd never married. A faded postcard from the battle-fields of France, World War I, could well be the answer. "Dearest Helen, I think of you every minute and long to be with you again. Pray it will be soon. Yours as ever, Bill." Perhaps he lay in Flanders like so many others.

A sepia-coloured photograph showed Mother and Father Grant, serene and proud of their brood who surrounded them. The wee loons in kilts looking sullen and displeased, the lassies frilled to their chins, not too happy-looking either.

Now a different era. In World War 2 fashions had changed but faces were as fresh, young and innocent, as off to war they marched, some, alas, never to return. Those who did, to pick up the threads again, were disoriented for a time. The world was so rapidly changing.

Stood Fast

A sigh escaped as Hazel recognised herself in these thoughts. Now her generation occupied the wee hoose. This was their time.

The home that had already seen and heard so much still stood fast, a haven almost unchanging as the family came and went, married and brought new life to the old rooms. Carry-cots and "nibs chariots" in every corner, nappies to dry festooning the fireside.

There was little time for the past in these days, of thinking back to the wee shop with its tinkling till, the tall sweetie jars and the goodwill spread by "a sweetie for the bairn". There was still plenty of coming and going. Friends from the south often stopped by for a wee chat to stay several hours if not several nights.

Life moved on ever faster, gathering momentum till the "ever-young" grew older and the "bairns" became teenagers.

That was the sad time. The imperceptible but inevitable ageing of the grand-parents, those gallant veterans of two world wars; of trying to "keep their peckers up" while one's own spirits plunged to zero, thinking of a time, not too far distant, when only memories would remain.

One did one's best to try to ease those latter uneasy years, but how little it was one realises!

Life goes on and, happily, there are good things still along its way. The hoosie looked as always, windows eyeing the world, sometimes wearily in wind and rain but full of bright hope when bathed in golden sunshine.

A Link

Hazel added more wood to the fire. Not so many visits to the north now – no-one in these rooms to envelope us all with the warmth of their love.

It was then the tears flowed. Tears that remained unshed in the last few years of crises now spilled over, bringing strange sweet relief as if they had waited a long long time. In public the stiff upper lip was fine and necessary, but in private, defences down – there is a time to weep. Granny Grant would understand.

The little room was filling with dusk and the electricity had been turned off. "I should be scared," Hazel thought to herself. "It's funny, I don't feel alone – I'm part of the vast family of the world, striving for better things, often to slip and stumble but picking ourselves up and on again – searching for the truth of life. Even these scraps of paper have explained a lot to me."

Long ago, she mused, about five generations, a man built a house – this one – or any one, for his family with his love.

It was filled with dreams, some to be fulfilled, others to fade away. But this home has been lived in to the full.

Whatever they left behind of themselves – of faith, hope and charity, of gaity and courage in adversity, Hazel found herself breathing a little prayer that these great qualities would never be lost – more than ever were they needed.

Making sure the fire was completely out, she produced her torch and made her way to the front door. There was a phone call she had to make at the corner callbox. Excitement overcame her sad feelings for the auld hoose, she turned the key in the lock for the last time, and with a light step, went out into the darkness.

Happiness

Nervously, Hazel dialled a number. After an endless second, her son's voice came low-pitched to her ear.

"Mum, or should I call you 'Gran' – Yes it's true – you have a grandson and all's well. Kay and I – well, you know – we're absolutely delighted. How soon can you come down here? The new Grandad is as excited as a schoolboy." A pause, then he went on "Mum, it's daft, but I hope the house knows – say goodbye from us."

If her step was light before, she simply flew back to the house. The moon had risen, a shining disc. Hazel, stood for a full minute before the old front door, a minute of prayer and thankfulness and bright with hope for the future, as the moonlight winked back at her from a shining window.

C. F. MacKinnon,
Perth.

IN THE PARK

Going for a stroll in the park. It was a warm sunny afternoon. Some day in the week or Sunday. Mark often went for a walk in the park. Not with friends, no, to the park he went on his own. He didn't like to be distracted. And his friends like to chat, throw the ball, keep running. Sometimes they teased him because he liked to take his time and watch.

"Look at Mark! He's frozen to the ground. Can't move his legs, found a leopard in a tree!" This amused him. He didn't care what they thought of him in the park. Outside the park he would compete with them, chase the ball and throw it back. He would join in their stories about home, fantastic descriptions, last night's movie on TV. But in the park all was different. He didn't want intrusions.

He walked briskly along. It occurred to him that he had already passed three times two old ladies on a bench. He looked at them. They seemed engaged in serious conversation, but suddenly the one in the red coat diverted her gaze into Mark's direction. "Those aren't the days like they used to be," she said. Whatever could that mean? Mark puzzled. Grown-ups talk a lot of the past. What good is it when there's so much to look forward to?

He noticed that he had stopped in his tracks and was looking intently at the two ladies. They too regarded him. It was obvious, they were talking about him. Saying something he did not understand. He decided to leave the park.

On his way out he saw a narrow path winding around a stream into a part he had never walked before. Why had he never seen it? He had known this park as long as he could remember. Curiosity led him on. It was shady there. Tall trees obscured the sky as though they wanted to wipe out the sun. Nobody around except for a dog, who in passing sniffed at his trousers and dashed off. Thick bushes bordered each side and Mark wondered about snakes.

Something red caught his eye. A small woollen glove half down in mud. Thrown away or lost? He wanted to pick it up but then afraid that the mud would soil his hands or knowing that the object was useless he discarded the thought. He saw a bench by the water. He scrambled down to it. On sitting down he noticed an inscription: "In loving memory of my wife Emily who loved these trees, this bench, this walk."

It was certainly her husband who had it inscribed, he thought. She must have been an old lady. No date. But he could tell. Perhaps they were pensioners, taking this walk every day on the way home from shopping or in the evening when the sun began to set. She must have known the country. Was brought up there. Then they had moved to the town and she had found this park. Mark looked around. He could see the old lady arm in arm with her husband. They would rest just here, opening a sandwich freshly bought from the delicatessen. A cup of home-brewed tea from a flask. They watch the squirrels hastening up and down the trees.

"The sparrows are very persistent today, aren't they, dear?"

"Yes. Look, this one's really cheeky. The way he snatches all the crumbs for himself."

"Can I have my apple, dear?"

"Yes. Here you are. I just finish this and then we must be getting along."

The place was quiet. But the voices were distinct. A stream of wind circled through the thick foliage of the trees, then wiped the surface of the grass.

He sat listening. Further off some kids played "hide and seek". He watched for a while then turned his head. There was so much mystery here in colours and shapes – it bewildered him. He saw figures and faces in treetops, discovered strange forms in roots and branches and drew them with his fingers. He hurled a stone in the water. If he could live here, be the keeper of this park, take care of it. He'd love it. He must tell his father. He could arrange it. It was good to be here. He could understand the old lady. For the first time in his life he felt the identity of a grown-up. For the first time he felt he was ready for them.

Something told him that it was time to go home. He got up, pocketed a leaf from the ground and made his way towards the gates. All the way home he kept whistling to himself.

I've just finished work. I often come here to this park. I can relax here. I have a favourite bench up there by the band-stand. I read the paper or I just sit and think. The weather's been good recently. I was able to come every day. Every day this week except yesterday when I went to the dentist. There's so much you can look at here and it does you good. So much green. Green's good for your eyes, they say. I wonder why. I heard the other day at a lecture somewhere that the colour green doesn't exist. He said it was a combination of blue and yellow that produces green. Green's not a natural colour. But how is it that everything in nature is green. If this is not natural, what makes grass green, leaves green? There must be somebody one can ask. But what if everybody knows except me? Perhaps they've all been told at some time or other except me? I could ask Jim at work tomorrow. He's a mechanic, he ought to know. Because this is really important. Green grass – how? I've never heard anybody mention it. Never read it anywhere. Suppose they all know? Everybody was told at school and I missed it. What then? It's too late to ask now.

I've often come here but I've never thought about this before. Strange really. I like parks. As a young boy I used to have a favourite one. I remember I went there every day, twice in summer. I knew a lot about parks in those days. But this never occurred to me. Perhaps nobody worries about it. People come here, some of them regularly till the end of their lives. Some love it here, some find it relaxing, others come for the exercise, but there are some who are really in-fatuated with the place. They even have their names inscribed on benches when they die. Just look at this one: "For my dearest wife who found so much peace and enjoyment here." Do I want to know, I ask myself? No. I already know. Know what it does to me. And as for others, they have to find out themselves. No good telling them. They won't believe it. And look! Inscriptions on every bench all over the place. All the same, the same lettering, the same words, identical. At first I used to read them. Used to stop at each bench and read what it said. The more I read the better I felt. I felt peaceful inside. But now I walk past them.

Mark had met Sylvia at evening class. They were both interested in literature. A few weeks after the first evening they started meeting outside class. They liked walking. Especially at weekends. When it was fine they went to parks and walked for hours. They discussed things.

Mark: "One Sunday we went to a museum. It was really a sort of castle converted into exhibition halls. There was a large park surrounding it. We'd come out and started talking about the exhibits. We walked around the building – very leisurely. There was a gravelled path with benches on either side. As we approached the back of the building we noticed that there was hardly anybody sitting there. The sun was round the other side and people like to sit in the sun. The empty benches looked as if saluting wedding guests walking down the aisle on their way out of church. Walking towards the glaring sun. Sylvia stopped and bent down to read something. She motioned me closer.

'Look, Mark! Isn't this a lovely way of remembering somebody dear. It means so much, don't you think?!'

I read it. And I remembered. The first time as a little boy. How I used to believe it. Don't I believe it now? Here with Sylvia. I think it's true, I can feel it. The same invigorating sensation surging through me. The freshness.

I turned to Sylvia and said, 'Yes, a wonderful idea. There's so much expressed in these words. It makes me happy.'

Sylvia smiled and took my arm. I couldn't tell then whether I felt like that because of her presence, whether it was the happiness of being in love, or whether it was a moment of childlike love brought back to me from when I was young. I couldn't tell then and I find it difficult now."

Sylvia took Mark's arm and they slowly walked past the benches.

Christine McNeill,
London.

375

AS YOU SOW – SO SHALL YOU REAP!

During the last war years, a young airman resolved to attend and assist at a premier meeting of a new "Padre" who was to initiate some religious Doctrine to the present non-religious camp.

The outcome was a close friendship between "Padre" and airman, the latter becoming a great aid at services and after becoming confirmed after instruction from the Padre he used to serve at confirmation, and often read the lesson at the Sunday evening service.

Eventually a gradual change – the airman noticed that he had acquired such an inherent spirit of happiness that he simply had to give some to others somehow! Also he noted that a certain grudging respect was being given to him by the majority of men on the campus.

Fellow airmen came to him with problems which he would resolve, or else he would give comfort to them verbally – but he never discussed religion.

One evening the airman entered a room in the canteen, where, to his surprise, a big party was going on between Sergeants and Corporals and one person was in the act of taking off his shirt whilst standing on a table singing a bawdy song – complete silence – everybody stood as if frozen! Quickly and for the first time noticing the real effect of his personality the airman quietly went to the bar, ordered a pint and sat at a vacant table looking as if nothing had happened! Soon everything went on to full swing.

One day the airman felt ill – very ill – went "sick" and was rushed to Hospital on a stretcher. A private room, Doctors, Nurses, a long syringe in the backbone, a curled up needle, another long syringe, result – a shake of the head then complete oblivion for 5 or 6 weeks!

It was evening when the airman stirred, opened his eyes and saw beside his bed, outlined in mystic light, bareheaded in a cowled robe the form of Jesus himself! The young airman was not afraid but looked in quiet wonder for some unknown time before he fell asleep or became unconscious – he is not sure.

Another three weeks and the young airman was up and about, slowly with sticks at first, then to another ward with occupants and then home to England and holiday, for I am told this happened in Scotland.

The Padre said it could not have been so! I feel it makes a good parable for HER MAJESTY'S JUBILEE – Don't you?

Edwin John Mitchell,
Nuneaton, Warwickshire.

The river gurgled round the stone on which a dipper bobbed while on the other bank an oak tree leaned over the water, a sole survivor of the forest which had been destroyed by fire. Young birch trees, however, had gradually taken their place.

The girl lay back contently in the early evening sunshine, thinking of the other life in Edinburgh which seemed so far away, with its crowded streets, people hurrying to and fro and no-one knowing anybody. After a day teaching, she returned each night to a cold, empty flat.

The girl got up, stepped over the fence at her back and began walking along the boundary of a field which was used by Scouts for camping. Willows hung over a pool in which minnows darted. A little later the water divided, rushing over and round some stepping stones in one direction and in the other, flowing quietly and smoothly towards a sluice gate for the lade that once fed the mill.

Over the stone bridge the ground steepened towards the boundary fence. The girl pushed the wicket gate and stepped out on to a grassy track, as she had done so many times in the past. One on the left was a copse, behind which the burn twisted and then pointed north between two fields.

At a crossroads the track joined a recently surfaced road. On the right the road led past farm cottages, several houses and the village school before it joined the main road. (Near this junction the village of Aldie began.) Ahead houses were strung along the road like beads in a necklace, these scattered houses being known as the Back Aldie.

To the south stretched fields, bisected by the main road. Beyond was the moss, a large area coloured brown, where they say a horse and cart once sank. When the mist blew over the waving grasses on a cold day, it was not difficult to believe such stories.

There was a railway line when the girl went to secondary school but the station had been closed for some years, the track having been removed and the station house sold. The community had been left to rely on the rural bus services but gradually these were being curtailed.

Further south fields and farms stretched into the distance, merging nto a long, low ridge of hills. The names of the farming families changed little with farms being passed from father to son, generation after generation. Neither the weather nor the seasons changed. Every year the fields were ploughed and planted and the crops harvested as winter passed to spring and spring to summer.

The girl approached a tumbledown cottage used as an outhouse, behind which was a small field with haystacks, bounded on the north by a row of beech trees.

A sheep farmer stood at the door. He chatted to the girl first about the weather as all farmers do and then about people they knew.

"Old Harry died last week. Passed away in his sleep."

He then went on to mention some of the dead man's qualities.

"There's no many of the old ones left, Mary. A lot of new folk have come in from the towns. There's new folk in Ashfield. Brown's the name. The man's an architect – partner, they say, in a firm in Edinburgh. It's a long way to travel but he's no the only one these days. His wife's a bonny lass, terribly polite but pleasant. She doesn't mind daein' things for the place, no like some o' them that just sit on their backsides when they get home. She has a job in a lawyer's office."

The conversation continued for about another ten minutes and then they went their separate ways.

As she approached Ashfield, an old house with a bell from a ship above the porch, she remembered the story that it was haunted by an old lady, who sat knitting in the study. The girl had occasionally been in the house since she had played with the children who lived there when she was about ten or eleven, but she had never seen the ghost.

The field opposite belonged to her mother, a widow. Once rows of strawberries had been planted there. Now it was let to John Anderson, the sheep farmer to whom she had spoken. Three long rows of redcurrant bushes ran parallel to the house and in between were rows of blackcurrant bushes and gooseberry bushes.

The road ran between the two fields which belonged to the market garden. Part of the field on the left was let out to the same farmer but a wide strip had been fenced off to grow raspberries, gooseberries and vegetables.

Mary walked on and then turned. The evening sun was setting behind Avalon, casting a glow over the green hillside. On a low ridge, cattle walked slowly along a path, while in a neighbouring field sheep grazed peacefully, white specks among the gorse and broom.

As she neared the house, a solitary blackbird dipped on the telephone wires above the roadside. Suddenly its deep-throated song floated over the velvet air. The world seemed a beautiful place. She would stay here.

Janet C. O'Brien,
Edinburgh.

TREASURE OF WHITE HEATHER ISLAND

Off the Scottish western sea-board there lived on White Heather Island Iona and Rory Craig. Their father was a fisherman who had his own boat, the "JAMIE". The children often went on fishing trips with their dad and would bring home a catch of codling, haddocks or if lucky a lobster from the creel. On returning from sea Mrs. Craig would have ready a delicious tea of oatcakes, butter from the churn, wild bramble jelly, eggs from the brown hens. Best of all, mother would fry some of the newly caught fish. However one sunny day Iona and Rory instead of going with the boat decided to explore the beach and nearby caves. As they strolled along the shore they picked up many coloured pebbles and popped them into a strong bag. During the long winter evenings with parents and friends they would polish the pebbles. A fine collection of semi-precious stones they acquired by their skill.

On reaching the caves Iona and Rory entered the gloomy taverns. Seagulls swooped noisily around, strange sounds seemed to come from all corners. Iona was looking all around her when she accidentally stumbled over a box made of strongwood and encrusted with shells and ancient sea-weed. Iona on picking up the box tried to force it open but with no success. Rory made an effort as well, but was out of luck. With disgust Rory threw the box away, but in doing so, the box bounced off a large rock whereupon the box burst open, and out fell a little brass-bound box complete with lock and key. Iona who was nearest to the box lifted it up. On turning the key into the lock the lid sprung open and lying on a piece of faded crimson velvet were two miniature brooches each surrounded with tiny brilliant diamonds. On closer examination Iona and Rory could distinguish on one brooch the features of a finely dressed lady and on the other a portrayal of a handsome gentleman with a plaid flung across his shoulder. Iona and Rory excited by their find raced quickly home. Parents and friends were called upon to scrutinise the find, most were of the opinion the little portraits were of Flora MacDonald and Bonnie Prince Charlie. Perhaps Flora MacDonald knowing she would perhaps never meet with Bonnie Prince Charlie again had thrown the box containing their portraits into the sea as they were being rowed over to the mainland from the Isle of Skye where she had met the Prince at her parents' home on the island. The box had been buffeted about the Hebridean seas for many, many years and perhaps had lain as long in the caves of White Heather Island until Iona fell over the box. Iona and Rory handed over their treasure to the authorities who rewarded the brother and sister for their honesty and also for finding the historical portraits. The little miniature brooches with the famous characters painted on each now lie in an Edinburgh Museum, famous for many Scottish antiquities, but the caption below the brooches proudly states the treasure was found by Iona and Rory Craig of White Heather Island.

Catherine Ramsay,
Edinburgh, Midlothian.

Now in my Pension years, I recall the most memorable event in my life!

It was a great step for me to take from my country home in Lostock Hall, Lancashire, to work in the City of London where I took a Typist's post in the Civil Service in February, 1937. I had been booked into a Hostel, run by Southport people, in Clapham South, where we paid 21s. 0d. per week for bed, breakfast, evening dinner and full board at weekends, with 1d. charge for use of the electric iron in the basement laundry room and 2d. for a bath! The hostel was close to Streatham where we could shop and go to a Theatre to see good plays occasionally.

The highlight of my stay in London, however, was the great occasion of the Coronation Procession of their Majesties King George VI and Queen Elizabeth on 12th May, 1937. Being holiday on that special day, and as the underground stations were remaining open all through the previous night, we set out from the Hostel at 2.30 a.m. equipped with food, fruit, sweets, flasks, newspapers, etc., travelling from Clapham South underground station on the Northern Line, changing to the Bakerloo Line at Charing Cross for Trafalgar Square station as we'd decided that Pall Mall would be a likely place to find room. Emerging from the underground we heard a lot of noise most of which was shouting pedlars selling all kinds of souvenirs, including small mirrors on sticks to act as periscopes. When we finally arrived at Pall Mall, we noticed pedlars had displayed their wares on sandwich boards, others were rushing around with a variety of things on trays slung over their shoulders. It was like an open market and people were chatting happily, despite the early morning chill. Some were already sleeping on rugs, others just smoking or having snacks. There was so much going on around us that the time passed quickly enough, though the dawn revealed a very dull sky and we hoped the sun would come out later on.

About 9.00 a.m. or earlier, people came along to fill the reserved seats in the stands whom we enjoyed watching. They were dressed very smart for the occasion. Union Jacks were numerous and the large banners bore large crown symbols and were silk-fringed at the base which was pointed. Forces personnel, soldiers, sailors, royal air force officers lined the routes and along ours, two officers were distributing food from a big box to fortify them for the long wait. They were very good-humoured, chatting to the people and answering continuous questions.

Later, we could hear the heavy gun salutes from the Tower which apparently signified the actual moment of Coronation, and parts of the Abbey ceremony were broadcast outside to the millions of people awaiting the return procession to Buckingham Palace. Young men had even climbed trees to get an overall view. We could also hear the bands which were stationed along all routes playing in between the broadcasts. On the procession's approach, the officers sprang to attention on the command of their C.O. and, you may guess, great excitement prevailed, with cameras, binoculars and periscopes appearing in hundreds amongst the crowds.

Different contingents headed the procession, both mounted and unmounted from all Defence Forces of the Empire; the King's Own Regiment riding their beautifully groomed white horses in red and gold uniforms and fur busbies were particularly resplendent. It is not possible to detail all detachments, Royal Air Force, Navy, Infantry, Army, Yeomen, and Royal Marines playing their respective bands. All were so colourful and smart for the occasion, the band playing being very enjoyable and impressive.

Next came the carriage procession of Prime Ministers, the first conveying Sultans with Troopers of Lancers as escorts, also the Prime Ministers of Northern Ireland, Southern Rhodesia, Burma, South Africa, New Zealand, Australia and Canada, all with their own escorts, the Canadian Mounted Police especially smart. The United Kingdom Prime Minister, the Rt. Hon. Stanley Baldwin, who received special applause, was escorted by the Metropolitan Mounted Police.

Great interest grew when a State Landau was sighted with escort preceding the Glass Coach seating Her Majesty Queen Mary and their Royal Highnesses Princess Elizabeth and Princess Margaret whose happy faces we could see through the windows and, oh, what beautiful jewels in Queen Mary's crown and how sweet the little Princesses looked in theirs.

The Escort with Standard followed and again one cannot in words do justice in describing this, nor the various King's troops, the Colonial and Dominion Officers, and the Yeomen of the Guard, general favourites known as "Beefeaters" in their red and black uniforms with white ruffs, black hats with tassels around, red stockings and buckled shoes. Also the massed bands of the Household Cavalry so rousing and enjoyable, preceding the Royal Household carriages, the Commissioner of Police and others.

When their newly-crowned Majesties in the State Coach came into view, there was a tremendous acclamation from the people. Men doffed and waved their hats amidst ceaseless cheering and clapping with thousands of Union Jacks fluttering like grass in the wind; the King wearing the Imperial Crown, the Queen also radiant waving a white-gloved hand and both smiling happily as they acknowledged the people's homage. It was a very moving moment!

The coach was followed by the Officer Commanding and Sovereign's escort, Life Guards and Horse Guards making a splash of rich colour in their red and navy tunics with gleaming helmets plumed in white and red respectively, their horses trotting proudly along. Then the Earl Marshal preceded the Standard, he being largely responsible for the Abbey arrangements and those of the procession.

Their R.H.s the Duke & Duchess of Gloucester and the Duke & Duchess of Kent in their carriage came last with more of the Guard escorts, all magnificent and impressive.

The procession was ending and unfortunately it started to rain and, although we got very wet, due to the underground entrances being greatly congested and our inability to get to the trains for a time, we eventually arrived at the Hostel, tired but extremely happy to have witnessed such a marvellous event which would always remain a most memorable occasion.

Elizabeth Smith,
Preston.

KILRAVOCK CASTLE

Kilravock Castle lies on the north bank of the River Nairn and it has been the home of Col. and his Lady wife. The two ancient estates of Kilravock Castle, the ancient family seat of the Rose or De Roos, also included Holme Rose (today home of Lord Croy, former M.P. for Moray and Nairn).

There is some doubt as to whether this family derives from the old renowned family of Norman Celtic origins. They bear a boar's head between bonjets on their coat of arms. This thirteenth century Castle itself is a very interesting and impressive building of great extent on sharply rising ground above Nairn meadows. The old square keep of 1460 rises to the east, simple and lofty, with five storeys above. To this was attached in the seventeenth century the large and commodious five storey gabled house with stair turrets and dormer windows.

Many prominent people came to this lovely ancient castle including Mary, Queen of Scots in 1562. Here too came Prince Charles Edward Stuart, who slept in the Castle the night before Culloden, the last battle in Scotland. His enemy, Cumberland, slept in Nairn. Here too came Sir Walter Scott, who wrote his book, The Thane of Cawdor, and then we are leaving out the most illustrious visitor of all – Robbie Burns himself, the Scottish National poet.

The Rose family came here in 1541. There is seventeenth and eighteenth century work behind the Georgian facade. Nearby are several famous places: Caedor, home of the Earl and Countess of Cawdor, Moy Hall belonging to MacIntosh of MacIntosh, and of course the battlefields of Culloden.

It was to Kilravock that a young girl named Jean aged seventeen came to work as a kitchen maid. Previously she had been working in a seasonal job at Darnaway Castle, home of the Earl and Countess of Moray. As Jean came up the castle drive of Kilravock she gazed in wonder at this ancient five storey high castle with its towers and battlements. On entering, she found that the staff were elderly and their forbears had served in this castle for generations and they spoke the Highland tongue.

The Col. and Lady Rose had a baby son and on a famous occasion, King George and Queen Mary were to call at the castle for the Baby Heir to be presented to them. The great day dawned and the Col. waited with his Lady wife on the steps of the castle, resplendent in Highland dress. A step lower down stood the Nanny with the baby dressed in his robes. At one side of the castle courtyard were lined all the guests from the surrounding castles; at the other side, stood the servants, and all the estate workers. On each side of the castle drive were soldiers from nearby Fort George and the Pipe Band awaited the Royal Party to escort them into the castle courtyard. It was indeed a very impressive scene.

Queen Mary wore a grey costume with a white frilled blouse, and a blue toque hat with grey veiling. King George was in a navy suit. The year was 1922.

When the Royal party left, the soldiers came into the servants' hall as they were hungry. One young soldier gripped Jean's hand and said, "Hey, lass, same again, I am hungry." "Coming up, Sir!" replied Jean. So it was that Jean and the soldier boy from Glasgow met.

The soldier boy came up to the castle often until he came to tell Jean that the regiment was drafted to India. They said their farewell on the castle drive.

"Promise me, Jean, you will write to me every week," he said.

"I promise," replied Jean.

"Promise me you will wait here at the castle until I return. Then I shall come and claim you as my bride," he said.

"I promise."

So two young lovers parted there on the castle drive.

A year later Jean got an official letter from his C.O. saying with regret that soldier boy had died of fever, and had been buried out in India. Jean just took the official letter to my Lady, and gave a month's notice.

Jean had been in the castle for four years and everybody waved goodbye to her as she went down the castle drive; she turned once to look back at the castle and then she reached the road that was to take her to another castle down south.

Baby Heir was killed at El Alamein in 1942 aged twenty, Jean still receives word from Miss Elizabeth Rose, 25th Laird of Kilravock Castle. The castle is now run by the Christian Aid Society to raise funds to help poor and hungry people, not only at home, but all over the world.

Jean Stewart,
Elgin, Morayshire.

Sometime during the night the wind had dropped. Now the frost held the feathery whiteness of the snow in a great stillness just where the wind had driven it.

Telegraph poles, wires, fences, trees were silhouetted, with a dark contrasting clarity, against their partial covering of storm-driven snow. Above his head, last autumn's unfallen beech nuts each lifted a snow-puffed candle to the pale grey sky. The trees up the hill beyond the river were more finely silver-traced, trunks, branches, and twigs intricately laced, further and further into the distance.

His were the first prints in the crisp snow: so it was he who found the dead bird, still and limp on the undisturbed snow.

He took it in his hands, the soft smoothness of the feathers warming him. But for its drooping head it could have been alive. Its neck was broken. It had probably struck an overhead wire. He thought it was a kestrel or a sparrowhawk: someone would know. He had seen them overhead, hovering and gliding – but never close, like this.

He studied it carefully, opening the strong hooked beak with his fingers, feeling the scaly yellow feet and the sharpness of the talons. It had vivid yellow-circled eyes.

He pulled the wing feathers, and the wings unfolded like old fashioned ladies' fans. He stroked the downy feathers, banded in chestnut and brown and grey and brown. He decided to pull one or two and wear them in his curler's bonnet.

He gave a deft tug.

At that moment he saw a dazzling yellow streak of lightning in the sky, followed almost immediately by a dull rumble of thunder like snow falling off a roof.

Startled, he dropped the bird. The wind was rising again, and millions of feathery flakes were already falling gently, settling on the dead feathers, covering the bird.

He stood watching, for a long time, not noticing the snow on his clothes.

Some small bird or mouse would maybe live another day in this magic, cruel world of snow, while the once powerful bird lay where it had fallen.

Only when the feathery snow-flakes had completely covered it did he go on his way.

Ursula Stoaling,
Keith, Banffshire.

A DAY TO REMEMBER

"Follow my instructions exactly, Mrs. Morrison, and everything will turn out fine, there will be no trickery." On hearing these words, Jean Morrison felt a panic stir deep within her and knew that she must fight it, at all costs she must remain calm, or her meeting with this man could end in failure. It was barely ten minutes since he had made himself known to her, even so she sensed he would allow no mistakes on her part.

Six months ago, when, after much thought, she had taken the first step which she hoped would change her life, she had given no thought to this day, but now she realised her efforts were to be put to the test.

"When you're ready Mrs. Morrison," the man's cold voice broke into Jean's thoughts. She took another look at the grim unsmiling face and his steely eyes sent a shiver through her. It was a lovely warm April day, but Jean suddenly felt very cold. Breathing deeply to steady her nerves, and with the man at her side, she set off.

There was to be no idle talk on this journey, no trivial remarks about the weather, her companion chose to speak only when he wanted her to change direction. This happened so often that Jean began to wonder if they were going round in a circle. Only once did the man lose his composure, that was when Jean stopped suddenly and she sensed rather than saw him stiffen, he gave a slight gasp, then, seeing nothing was amiss, he brusquely told her to keep moving.

"Stop in front of that red building." Jean obeyed. "Now Mrs. Morrison, the time has come when you must answer some questions regarding the code." Jean's heart missed a beat, her mouth was so dry she felt she would be unable to utter a word. She had been memorising the code signs for months, nevertheless, she found herself praying silently, "Dear God, please dear God, let me say the right things to this man."

She could not bring herself to look at him as she answered his queries. There was a long silence. Finally Jean turned her head. She was amazed! He had gone! The man who had filled her with so much dread had vanished, and by her side was a kindly looking man whose grey eyes were warm and friendly, he smiled and then started to speak.

"I am pleased to tell you Mrs. Morrison that you have passed your driving test, congratulations." The examiner held out his hand. Jean relaxed her grip on the steering wheel and wept.

Margaret Tills,
Dunfermline, Fife.

A family of swans lived happily in and around the boating lake, at a certain well known holiday camp in Wales. They had the place to themselves during Winter and the baby swans played hide and seek in the reeds and bushes around it. Sometimes Father Swan had to chase away intruder snakes – but he was sure in his mind that their holiday camp home was a nice place for little swans to be.

In the early Spring, the only human beings around were the camp gardeners, who were getting the gardens ready for the new season's campers. The gardeners were very kind to the swan family, feeding them scraps of food from their lunch tins; so they became good friends.

When the Summer came, things changed. The lake became filled with little squeaky rowing boats, filled with laughing squeaky children, and some of the naughty ones even lashed out at the baby swans as they passed close by and that was more than Father Swan could stand.

And so, one morning when Mother Swan and her hungry little ones clucked noisily in for breakfast, they found that Father Swan had disappeared and when at dinner time he still hadn't shown up, Mother Swan was quite worried. She thought of all the nasty things that could have happened to him. The baby swans had none of such fears and just carried on with their game of hide and seek and left all the worrying to Mother.

Suddenly, just as Mother Swan had begun to fear the worst, there was a loud, joyous, "Honk, Honk", and gazing down at them from the bank flapping his huge wings, excitedly, was Father. "Bring the babies over here," he honked.

Mother Swans never question the intentions of Father Swans. They just do as they are told; so she hastened her offspring to the side of the bank near to father exclaiming as she did so "Where on earth have you been?" Father Swan stuck a proud beak high into the air and trying to look mysterious, honked "I've been exploring" and flapped his wings again. "Whatever for?" replied Mother Swan, "We've been worried to death about you."

Father Swan stuck his chest out until it looked as if it might burst "We are going to move house!" he honked. "Good Gracious," said Mother Swan.

The baby swans got very excited and let off lots of squeaky joyful sounds and then Father Swan proclaimed his really big news. "I have found a new lake!" he said, with a great booming honk, "and it is right in the middle of a wood and there isn't a boy, girl, or rowing boat to be seen." "Hurrah, hurrah!" honked the little swans. "We want to see it, we want to see it!"

Then Father Swan assumed great authority "Now Mother," he said, "We'll start at once; It's a long way and we'll have to go through the car park and up on the main road. You go in front Mother and the little ones behind you. I will guard the rear."

Mother Swan gathered her children behind her, honked out a warning for them to keep close behind her and then set off for the car park at a fast pace. What an adventure it was for the little swans; they passed rows of shining new cars in the car park; headed straight up the main road almost running to keep up with the parent swans and what a sight they were with Father Swan swaying from side to side, protecting them from the back. And all the way, little boys and girls wondered where they were going.

It was a long long way and the baby swans soon began to tire. They began to wish that Father Swan hadn't found a new lake and they felt like crying. Mother Swan had always taught them to be good triers, however, and so they struggled on.

Then, all at once as if by magic, they found themselves looking down into a deep valley and the cool blue waters of Father's new lake. And it was – right in the middle of a wood and there wasn't a boy or a girl or a rowing boat, anywhere to be seen. The little swans forgot their tiredness at once. "Hurrah!" they honked, "Let's hurry and be first in," and they waddled down to the water as fast as they could go but just as they reached it there was a loud splash! Oh dear, there was Father Swan looking majestic like a king, proudly swimming on the blue blue water. "Doesn't Daddy look fine!" the baby swans honked. "Come on in!" said Father Swan.

So they all splashed down into the water and they all liked it so much that they vowed never to return down the long road that led through the car park to a children's boating lake at a certain holiday camp in Wales.

And so . . . if ever you, dear children, go for a holiday at Mr. Billy Butlin's holiday camp at Pwllheli in Wales, don't expect to find Mr. and Mrs. Swan and family, among the rowing boats on the lake.

Because . . . you just won't!

John Tinkler,
Scunthorpe.

KLONDIKE DAYS IN EDMONTON

1890 was the start of the goldrush era – everyone was caught with the gold fever.

Edmonton became the stopping place for thousands of men passing through on the way to the gold infested Yukon. Naturally Edmonton began to grow and prosper. In 1962, the Edmonton Exhibition Association came up with a Klondike theme as a tribute to the history of the past.

As the last two weeks of July draw nearer, you can sense the excitement in every street-corner. Pseudo fronts are put up in front of buildings to represent log style cabins. Western style doors are put on the entrances to bars. People begin to plan their wardrobes to correspond with 1890's style – western outfits for the cowboy inclined and top hat and tails and long dresses for the more stable type. Activities are planned including something for everyone. The whole city seems to take a backward step in time.

Well the time is here. First is the gigantic sourdough breakfast which goes on each morning for the full two weeks. Now what more could you ask for – juice, flapjacks, sausages and coffee; as much as you like, all free of charge.

Then "Operation Arrest" goes into effect. Police cars are stationed on the outskirts of the city. The first car or truck to pass them coming into Edmonton is stopped. The people are arrested. First, they are escorted all over Edmonton; take part in some of the day's activities and later taken out for a meal in one of Edmonton's many night clubs. In all, 14 cars are stopped – one each day and all the people inside each car get the same treatment.

The Exhibition grounds open. Here once again are activities for young and old alike ranging from midway rides, fashion shows to man the daredevil and horseracing. Gamble, Las Vagas style in the Silver Slipper Saloon – or pan for gold in the Chilfoot Mine, or take a walk through Klondike Village and visit an old time general store, barbershop or post office. Even take in stage shows with popular entertainers, like Roger Miller or Bobby Vinton.

Spend a relaxing day sailing down the river on a homemade raft or go shopping in one of Edmonton's shopping centres to Klondike music and entertainment.

Stroll about the streets, listening to the bands or join in the fun of a garden party.

Now here is the best part – the parade. Sometimes you can stand for up to two hours to see it all as it can be up to two miles long. It can include 100 to 200 floats – of all descriptions and sizes, 100 bands from all over the world and about 50 clubs and associations.

Babysitting facilities are found all over the city. Here parents of young children can pay a small charge and have their child or children looked after by experienced people while they go out and enjoy themselves.

Night-time at the Exhibition grounds finds you watching the fireworks and listening to hear if your number gets drawn which would entitle you to a colour T.V., or a steer, or a camper, or a car. On the last day, a ticket gets drawn to see who wins a complete furnished house which is taken to the place of your choice and put down, with foundation included in expenses.

Meanwhile in downtown Edmonton, you can join in the laughter and gaiety of the night clubs. Have a bash at a can-can dance or join in a sing-along or even have a real live shoot-out.

All in all come the end of the two weeks, you are glad to return to the 1970's. It was fun, but exhausting.

Mary Waddell,
Greenock.

388

THE NIGHT OF THE GHOST

It was a cold, wet, windy night. I lay tossing and tumbling in my bed, trying desperately to forget what Clare had said and go to sleep. At the time she had said it, I just laughed, but now, being night, I was frightened, very frightened. Of course, I was never one to believe in ghosts, but what she had said and the way she had said it . . .

I got up, switched on my torch and shone it on the small ornate clock by my bedside, hoping against hope that it would be past midnight, but it was not, it was only 11.30 p.m. Slowly I walked across to the window and opened the curtains. The big empty house stood there in the gloom, silent and derelict. It frowned down on all who passed, remembering, it seemed, the time it had rung with laughter, from the parties and dances there. The big desolate garden had been let fall to rack and ruin. The trees which grew round the house, stood silently in a veil of mist.

I could have cried for that house, I loved it, I don't know why. But not tonight, no, tonight was different. An owl hooted and made me jump. A bat screeched and flew out of a window of the big house.

I shuddered, remembering again Clare's warning, "It's tonight," she had said, "You'd better be careful."

I laughed and asked her what on earth she was talking about. By this time she had gone deathly pale and was staring disbelievingly at me.

"You, you're laughing," she stuttered. "How can you? You must be out of your mind," she went on.

I stopped laughing and looked amazedly at her, frowning slightly. "Don't you know what happens tonight?" she questioned.

"No, I'm sorry, I really don't know," I returned, half laughing again. "This is the night," she began, with a strange mysteriousness in her voice, that made my heart beat faster. "This is the night that the ghost walks," she concluded. "Ghost! Ghost!?" I repeated scornfully, "I don't believe in ghosts."

I shuddered again as the vivid recollection of Clare shrugging and saying, "Please yourself, the house is opposite yours, not mines and I can't say I'm sorry." Then she walked away, leaving me standing staring after her. I jolted myself back to reality and shone my torch on the clock again. It said 11.45. I knew I had to go over to that house. I quickly pulled on my dressing gown and slipped quietly out of the house, taking care not to wake my parents.

Once outside, I found the rain pouring down in great torrents, but I hardly noticed the weather. My mind was completely occupied with what was to happen. I arrived at last, at the big oak door and, mustering up all my strength and courage, I pushed it with all my might. It creaked slowly open, revealing the dark and dingy interior and as I advanced, I grew more and more afraid.

At last I saw a staircase, which I ascended. At the top it was a little lighter. A crash resounded! I stood stock still, not daring even to breathe! Then, in front of me, was a ghostly apparition of a woman, clad in white robes and laughing hysterically. I screamed! She came floating towards me. I stood there, unable to move, unable to think. Then she stopped, just as suddenly as she started and began to sing. Her voice rang out in earpiercing splendour. The song grew louder and louder, then, with a scream of hatred, she disappeared. For the next few minutes, I stood there, staring at the place where she had been. Then I turned and ran out of the old house, never to return.

Linda Margaret Walker,
Forfar, Angus.

C. JOHN TAYLOR SELECTION

UPON BEING SIXTY

"Almost as a kind of protest about the popular cliche 'Life Begins at 40!', and just after my 60th birthday, I wrote the following poem . . . Each stanza is true . . . hope you enjoy reading it!"

Sixty's
Such a glorious age!
Over-turned,
So many a page!!
Grandchildren;
Almost, form a queue,
All loving souls, to visit you!!!

From
The home;
All children gone!
Sons,
And daughters, every one!!
Save Duncan;
Sturdy, youngest son,
moreover;
His,
Boisterous, teenage days are over!!!

Mother's
Gone,
To Heaven above!
Joining those,
Whose endless love,
From
Celestial places far; yet near!!
Guides
Their loved ones; still down here!!!

Father's
Journeying on,
At almost ninety!
Surviving
World War One; for
"Blighty"!
Served he,
Again, in World War Two,
   unscratched
With
Churchill leading;
His kind, proved Hitler,
"over-matched"!!!

392

Sixty's
Such a glorious age!
You feel
So young; yet look a sage!!
A prophet;
Composer; genius, or
    simpleton;
When
The heart is young
Life has only just begun!!!

Music's
Godly food!
So Shakespeare said,
Man:
Truly filled,
Should be well-read!!
Experience teaches;
Better than academics do!!
Age,
Improves us;
Matured wine "out-tastes"
    the new!!!

Young love,
is "swell"!
Or so, some tell!
Barred,
No holds;
Convention, can get to H – – l!!
My love,
Through years and years;
Has grown most sweet;
My love,
'Tis morning, noon and night,
My life complete!!!

Sixty's
Such a glorious age!
Unruffled;
No envious words; jealousy;
    rage;
Serenity unaffected,
Earlier ambitions are impostors
    revealed;
Creating tensions hardly ever
    healed!!

Sixty's
Angels near, beside us,
    everywhere!
Sounds of music,
Friendly voices; daffodils
    growing there!!
With love, by the shore, seen
long ago,
Sharing our cares; as the
Master taught us, so.

Sixty's
Such a glorious age!
Unfolding
Days, always amaze!!
Whatever's been,
Is coming yet;
Heav'ns own course, before
    us set!!!

WINSTON CHURCHILL

These sceptred Isles, beleaguered as of yore,
Three hundred thousand men on Dunkirk's murky shore.
Flower, of the Nation's manhood
Held, in Hitler's grasp
Perplexed, bewildered, bleeding sore,
Faced by far, a grimmer task,
Than Harry's band, on Crispin's Day,
Nelson's, in Trafalgar Bay,
Glory, seemed so far away,
Fear, or falter not, nor sway
We'll live to fight another way,
Immortal Churchill, called on all, to pray!

We shall defend our land, so dear,
No space permit invaders here!
Surrounding seas with ring of steel,
Closing ranks, exterminating those who deal
In evil Propaganda's squeal,
Overhead, disturbing September's skies
of blue,
Pock-marked, noisy, "Battles to-the-death" ensue
Immortalised for me, and you,
By Churchill's words about "The Few".

Sands of Africa, with blood made red,
Forever ours, where sons lay dead,
Years of torment, failure,
Disappointing loss, and pain,
Mocking Rommel scores again
Mussolini's charger's ready
Cairo trembling, weak, unsteady,
Friend, foe, expecting agony
Churchill quietly sends Montgomery
Men of the "Eighth" reject defeat,
Achieving victory, absolute, complete!

Onwards still, tho' rough the way
From El-Alamein to V.E. Day
Feats of arms by land, by air, by sea,
Heroes join the glorious company
Of those, from ages past, who died that we,
Surviving free, shall not forget their chivalry,
We honour those, as well as he,
Who led us to the victory,
Winston Spencer Leonard Churchill's name,
Emblazoned ever in our Halls of Fame.

A DUMB FRIEND WHO BECAME BLIND

Tiny Cairn
Bold, as burnished brass,
Adorned in youth
By mask, of Rembrandt black.

Visible scarcely
'Midst the early morning grass
Your piercing bark
Echoing: puts rest, to rack!!!

A virgin still,
At three years old,
'Cross harbour,
To mate; by boat, he's sped!

Awaiting "lady",
All fussy, bold;
Discovering "over-keenness"
Oft' thwarts th' marriage bed!!

Thrice,
The sailing "groom"
is brought to "bride",
And thrice, "Mac" fails to act!

Perseverance
Eventually, is satisfied;
As consummation
Indubitably becomes a fact!!

The taste
O' love across the bay
Dormant
Passions; ever-growing, did arise!

Bold "Mac"
Would swim the sea, each day,
For what?
Needs no surmise!!!

Good things,
Unfortunately must end,
Away,
His love, in time, they send.

Swear I, oftimes,
Turns he, with sightless gaze,
To Easdale's Isle and dreams

Of sweetness
Without guile,
Reliving, once again,
A little while
The springtime of his days.

A thousand welcomes
"Mac" has given
To folks "just met", or dear,
With wagging tail, excited dance,
And bark; to make it clear!

For taste o' tablet,
Sweet as honey,
Has meanings;
Never touched by money.

Thrilled to greet you
Letting you know
Without a word;
Saying "hello"!

A Highland welcome's
Awaiting here
So filled with love,
With true good cheer,
That Heav'n itself,
Seems very near.

Ancient now,
is "Mac-E-Boy",
No sight
Left in his eyes.

Still barking daily,
Oft' with joy,
Greets he,
Each new sunrise.

Splendid,
In spirit; upright, unbent,
Self-pity
Knows he not!

Almost it seems
"Mac-E-Boy's" been sent
To show us mortals
How to grin
and bear our lot!!

ISLANDS OF BEAUTY

A New Poem in English and Gaelic

ISLANDS OF BEAUTY	EILEANAN BOIDHEACH
Islands, Of beauty and mystery!! How; With only words to use, Can I Express what you mean to me?	Eileanan, Lan maise agus diomhaireachd! Ciamair Ann am briathan A chuireas mi an ceill 'Ur tuigse dhomh?
Islands, Of magic and history? With My love I first saw thee; Time, Seems inadequate to measure eternity!!	Eileanan, Lan druidheachd agus eachdraidh! Comhla ri 'm ghaol Chunnaic mi sibh an toiseach. Tha tide new-fhreagarrach Gu tomhais siorruidheachd!!
Islands, Of birds; wind and sea!! Are, There musical instruments Capturing, your infinite symphony?	Eileanan, Lan eun; gaoth agus mara! A bheil innealan-ciuil A' glacadh 'ur co-sheirm neo- mheasraichte?
Islands, Of clouds; mountains fair! Paint I; for a million years, Your beauty's inviolate; beyond compare!!	Eileanan, Sgothach, le beanntan aillidh! Deal bhadh mi; Fad deich ceud mile bliadhna, Do sgeimh neo-thruaillte; gun choimeas!
Islands, Of people, ever young! Cherishing ancestry, Ages countless Cannot tell, whither you were sprung!!	Eileanan, Tir nan Og! Ag arach sinnsearachd. Cha chuir Linntean do-aireamh an ceill Co as a thainig sibh!!
Islands, Where sparkling waters flow! Playing Melodies; dancing downwards; Seawards; On to where . . . we'll never know!!	Eileanan, Le uisgeachan loinnreach A' ruith gu ceilearach! Damhsa sios D'on chuan; 'S air adhart . . . a' gabhail cursa!
Islands, Which spread your lights, Equally, For the great and small; tho' Millions, Never here, will never miss, their rights!!	Eileanan, A' sgaoileadh 'ur soillearachd Gu reidh, D'on bheag's mor; ged tha Miltean, Chan annan seo, Nach ionndrainn gu brath an coir!
Islands, Whose sunsets, touch the heart! Heav'ns, Made manifest, for all to sense, To know, With God; we're each, and all, a part!!	Eileanan, 'N am laidhe grein', a'buintuinn criahe! Neamhan, Air an taisbeanadh, gum beachdaich gach duine. Bhiodh fiofrach, Maille ri Dia, Gur cuibhroinn sinn, gach aon, gu leir!!
Islands, Unique, so dear, to Thee! Always; Now, and forever be; Nearer, with God, to me, In dreams, as in reality!!	Eileanan, Annasach, cho priseil Dhuit a Dhe! Daonnan, An nis, agus gu siorraidh, Bidh na's fhaisg dhomh, cuide ri Dia, 'Nam bhruadar, mar 'na m' fhirinn!!

Gaelic translation by Catriona MacLeod Taylor of the Isle of Lewis.

Verse 1.
Islands where dancing waters flow
Playing melodies dancing down-
wards
Seawards to where we'll never
know
Islands of beauty Isles of the Sea.

Chorus 1.
Islands of beauty Isles of the Sea
Whispering softly come home to
me
Islands of beauty boats sailing by
Breezes enchant me passing
clouds sigh.

Chorus 2.
Islands of beauty magic to see
Wave crests make music love's
harmony
Islands of beauty pearls of the
west
Sunsets paint glory bringing
sweet rest.

Verse 2.
Islands of birds wind and sea
Islands unique so dear to thee
Fairer than dreams you'll ever be
Whispering softly come home to
me.

Chorus 3.
Islands of beauty stars shining
bright
Heavens own stillness my hearts
delight
Islands of beauty where ere may I
roam
Always you're waiting calling me
home.

Chorus 4.
Islands of beauty in my memory
Mother is singing softly to me
Islands of beauty Isles of the Sea
I hear you calling come home to
me.

Author of "Night Must Fall" and other works, famous screen and stage star. For years travelled the world's leading theatres presenting a Charles Dickens one man entertainment, comprising characterisations, with readings, from the great Victorian novelist's most illustrious stories.

EMLYN

Master of macabre tales,
Genius from the hills of Wales,
Across the world in Dickens' guise,
As "Sidney Carton's" moving ditties
Uplift with "Tale of Two Cities"
Or "Fagin", twisted one who lies,
For him the "Artful Dodger" tries
To pick a pocket for a prize
Hypnotising watchful eyes,
Victims, with complete surprise,
Find they just can't realise
What's gone forever, and is missed,
Fills up the tale of "Oliver Twist".

Williams now with voice of "Scrooge",
Treats us to a grand deluge
Of whimpering, whining, pathetic chatter
Christmases appearing on his platter.
Past; where meanness chills the marrow,
Here's "Tiny Tim", so lean and narrow.
The future; shown is filled with tears
Where goodness all but disappears.
Mercifully, we are back somehow
To present times, the here and now.
Loud Christmas carols fill the air
His wealth with all old "Scrooge" will share
This story's filled with thrills, ghosts, joy,
To touch the heart of girl and boy.

Welshman Williams' versatility,
Demonstrating his ability,
Wistfully convincing in each part
"Micawber's" ever so beguiling
"Up will something turn," says he, smiling,
Changing mood, 'tis quite an art,
As characters immortal start
Bewildering, before our eyes, they dart
Enchantment's brief, but pure, delight,
A thrill in store, and this each night,
As Dickens, resurrected, comes in sight,
Hidden Emlyn, ensuring all is right.

GREATLY BE-LOVED*

FROM HEAVEN,
I HAVE TALK-ED, WITH YOU!
MY VOICE,
NEITHER NEEDS,
NOR USES, SOUND!
CREATED I,
ETERNITY . . . MAN-KIND TOO!!
THE SEAS; HEAV'NS;
EVERY-THING
ABOVE . . . AND
BE-NEATH THE GROUND!!!

MAG-I-CAL
MUSIC'S A PART OF ME!
OUR CHILDREN'S
EVER-Y SMILE!
EACH MOTHER'S
LOV-ING HEART;
SERENITY!!
AND GOOD-NESS
MAKING
ALL LIV-ING
WORTH THE WHILE!!!

TRUE LOVERS
PACTS: UN-SELFISH ACTS
MARTYRS: GIVING THEIR ALL DID SHOW
JOURNEYING HEAV'N-WARDS,
CALL-ING "LET GO"!
LEAVE GREED, AMBITION, PRIDE AND SELF;
ALL EARTHLY THINGS BEHIND.
TRUTH; GRACE;
PERFECT PEACE;
EVERLASTING JOY!
YOU WILL; THEN; SURELY FIND!!!

* *"I have Talked with you from Heaven."* Holy Bible, Exodus, Chapter
20, Verse 22.

RICHARD BURTON

"*After receiving an unusual invitation to view Richard Burton's T.V. film in which the Welsh film-star portrayed Winston Churchill, Britain's War-time Prime Minister, C. John Taylor was moved to write the following poem.*"

RICHARD BURTON

Film star
Burton's blue eyes frolic,
Insanely
When he's alcoholic,
Unrehearsed,
Uncoerced,
Double-double vision,
He proclaims,
With practised precision,
Matching signs,
With sounds, on television!
Mentally
Befogged and sore,
Becoming,
Almost just a bore,
Expensively
Partaking of the cure!
Affirming,
He will take no more!!
The studio
Audience calls encore!!!

A spouse,
Who Cleopatra played,
Big bosoms,
Bejewelled, all arrayed!
In goats' milk
Bathing, undismayed!!
Technicians,
Cameras at the ready,
Find it tough,
Emotions to keep steady,

Actors,
Young and old, feel "heady"!!
"Mark Antony
Will you stand here?"
Director's voice
Calls, sharp and clear
Breathing hard,
When she comes near,
Thrice painted eyes!
With lips to match!!
Her brain
Is pounding, "What a catch!!"
Burton caught,
Costum'd, cannot detach!!!
Touching flesh,
Forgetting what has been,
Whisp'ring,
"Blast that infernal machine,
On stage,
Or off, you'll be my queen!!"

Across
The world, and in a whirl,
Masquerading,
As lovers, boy and girl,
Fame,
Plays tricks for, as you hurl
Stories,
Intimate, for love or money,
Americanising
"Dear" for "honey"!
Tantalisingly,
From climes more sunny,
Than Wigan,
With th' pier of George Formby fame,
Or Glasgow,
Dripping wet with rain!
Welsh Wales
Just won't be the same
For fans,
On wages poor and low!
Inflation's
Cruel, fast, then slow!!
Where
Does all the money go?

Remorselessly
From screen, sound, box of B.B.C.

Imagining "empty lives"
"Short-changed" on warmth, love, glee,
Flaunting egg-sized
Diamonds foolishly, to many, and to me!!
Eventually achieving
Less than nought for thee!!!
Discounting possibly
Pseudo-sympathy,
"Lizzie
Do you agree?"
"Does your former mate
Of Celtic ancestry?"

Real people,
In all walks of life, today,
Find love,
Babes, tears, then laughter on the way,
A simple scene,
Not strained but true,
Effortlessly here,
Made clear, for you!!
"Box-bogglers",
Thwarted when the power,
Unceremoniously
Obliterates "Movie-Hour",
Impatience show,
So off to bed!!
Or make
A pot o' tea instead,
Out goes the cat! . . .
The doggie too!!
Relieved,
Returning 'fore the brew,
'Tis cool enough,
For you, to drink,
"The Radio Times",
I'll check, you think!
"What's this?",
Tomorrow night at eight, with Burton,
An epic film,
Technicoloured, I'll see for certain!
Time,
Has no meaning when th' day is ending,
Resting birds,
And trees, with racing moon are blending,
Irritations,
Surreptitiously, mending,
Some simple thing!

A church-bell's ring?
Outside,
The peace, descending!!

Welsh
Ages past, are built in there,
Begetting
Voice, beyond compare,
By practice,
Polished, as a jewel rare!
Shakespearean
Pathos, rings the rafters!
Osborne's wit,
Wins shallow laughters!
Burton,
Now as Becket, falls!
From Agincourt,
He loudly calls!!
"It's hellish
Working to these empty stalls!!!"
Forgetting,
"Silent as the grave," a set can be,
Small price,
To pay, for actors filming, with the I.T.V.!!!

"Come then
Let us to the task!
In
Just one word, 'tis victory!!
However
Long, or hard the road may be,"
Honoured
Welshman called to
Speak,
With lisping mimicry, great Churchill's charge,
Abandoning humility,
Courting publicity! Releasing your barrage!
Denigrating
One, who freedom's flickering light,
Nurtured;
Who alone, could lead the fight!
To victory!!
Over might, bad faith, insanity, shame,
By calling
Winston; coward! you harmed your Burton fame!!!

Distance lends
Enchantment; under the sun there's nothing new!

405

Cliches,
Both applicable, to your "Taming of the Shrew!"
The version, earlier,
Starred Mary Pickford, with Douglas Fairbanks Senior,
Despite no sound,
So many found, 'twas to yours, indeed superior!!!
In "Anne
of the Thousand Days", you rise,
Hidden,
'Neath Henry the Eight's disguise,
Emerging, authentic!
Forceful! compelling! 'twas sad to say goodbye!!
Dear Charles Laughton's role,
You effectively stole, a fact we can't deny!!

Ev'ry trial,
'Tis truly said,
Makes
Us stronger grow!!
Preaching's,
Easier than practice is,
'Tis now,
'twas ever so!!!
Burton, Richard,
By repute millionaire, remember this,
Worldly riches,
Haven't yet, or ever will, guarantee bliss!
Gifts,
Divinely given, developed, grow and spread!!
Your life,
Insignificantly begun, by work, has foged ahead,
World-wide you're known:
Your films are shown;
Your image,
Has
For many;
Eased life's strain!!
Grateful souls
Wish you
"All the best", and again,
True happiness find,
Peace of mind,
Heaven's abode!

"For the least of them do it,
If you would
Ease my load!!"

THE CHILDREN'S SHOW

In a charity fund raising effort, a CHILDREN'S ART EXHIBITION was arranged for the children of Scotland. Selected entries were displayed, visitors using a ballot paper (provided for the purpose) voted for the pictures of their choice. Ten prize winning pictures were later featured, from Glasgow, on a coloured television programme. The Exhibition raised almost One Thousand Pounds for charities. C. John Taylor, after visiting the Exhibition, wrote his poem entitled, "OUR CHILDREN'S SHOW".

THE CHILDREN'S SHOW

On Seil Island here's a Show
To uplift the heart!
Children, from every-where we know,
Proudly, exhibit their art!!

Colours, shapes, symbols!
People, Sea-scapes, Flowers,
Wizards, Warriors, Birds, Bulls,
Pleasures awaiting: for hours and hours!!

One exhibitor; Walter of Fife!
Using pencil; with gifts, from above,
Portrays Mohammed Ali; like life!!
"The Greatest"; Wise-cracking; "Mouthing" self-love!!!
Astonishingly; one "tot" aged only two!
Just a bonny boy; yet paints he a tree!!
Another older boy, in water-colour, for you!
Pictures Jesus; healing; as in reality!!!

Clydesdales; sturdy, fully-harnessed, plough here!
"Wendy" from Cumbria, drew these!!
Spitfires; attacking Germans, quite near,
Re-created; by Craig Peacock, realistically; with ease!!!

Gordon Russell; paints birds beside Kilbride!
Sheep; endlessly grazing, by a mill-side, at Kent!!
Hazel Ann's jockey, from Fort William, can really ride!
Marvel at Miss Currie's "Glasgow Close"; so old; so bent!!!

Come then to Seil Isle; to see the Show,
Tell all your friends; everyone you know.
This lovely Highland Spot's beyond compare,
Rolling Skies, Mountains fair, Children's pictures, everywhere!!

In the distance,
Crisp, and clear,
Asking
Each morning to appear,
Tho' drowsy night,
Still lingers on,
Moon, and dreams,
Have not yet gone!
Roving sheep; disturbed,
Make plaintive bleat,
Sounds of early birds,
Squealing seagulls meet;
Unmistakably now,
His chest and neck puffed out, raised,
The "Cock-a-doodle's" call
To mates; and us, our God be praised,
Each time, the sound is heard,
My mind goes backwards; to the long ago
The High Priest's lackeys
Whipping Christ;
Peter saying No!!
Denied He; the Master sent
To show the heavenly way of love;
Whose everlasting grace
Lives here: as in, the realms above!!!

CHARLES CHAPLIN—
NEW KNIGHT – OLD CLOWN

Master of mirth,
We, on this earth
Acknowledge the dearth
Of men, of your worth,
Four score years and more, we surmise
Passed away, before the "Arise,
Sir Charles" was, by Majesty spoken.
'Tis we suspect just a token
To you, with your fame
Your inimitable cane
And enduring acclaim
Charles Chaplin's the name
No jesters retain
Our respect and affection
Or approached your perfection
Tramp, dictator, comic, King and
Now a Knight!
Mankind's genius of laughter
And sheer delight!!

Written on 2nd January, 1975 – on hearing Chaplin at long last had been Knighted.

THE GOOD SHEPHERD

Children of Seil Haven!
Not so very, long ago;
Red Indian, costumes making:
For the village, Christmas, show!

Fierce "braves": war-painted: gory!
Accompanying "squaws"; so fair:
Re-enacting, an old, story!
Mind-chilling; well-documented; rare!!!

"Signed-treaty", after treaty,
White-men failed to keep!
Slaughtered he; our buffalo!
Forced us: to mountain steep!!

Pray God; of our Fathers!
Send us, at last; a Chief!
Resilient: resolute: a warrior!
To ease our burden: lift our grief!!

Skies slowly moving; grey and dull!
One unsuspecting morn.
Where "Big-Chief Sitting-Bull",
Reconnoitred Little Big Horn!!

Riding down below; in the early light!
Famed for prowess, gallantry!
Far travelled: seeking a fight!
Came the U.S., Fifth Cavalry!!!

Massed braves; well armed; hiding!
Operating a plan!
"Pray let the fools, keep riding"!!
Said the Red Men: man to man!!!

Silent rings of rising smoke,
Spelt out, the trap: well baited!
Unsuspecting sons of white folk,
Rode on: where death, awaited!!

Encircled in that valley!
Exposed on every side!
No time to think, manoeuvre: tarry!!
Sustained by soldiers' pride!!!

Fast falling to increasing blows!
Every man, that they could muster!
Defending "Old Glory"; and God knows,
Their long-haired General Custer!!!

Dying beside Sergeants: Bugle Boys!
Majors, Medicos: Old Campaigners!
Horses terrified: shattering infernal noise!
Drowning the Padre's last "God Save Us".

After the deeply moving sorrow
Inevitably, had passed away!
Politicians; extolled a new morrow!
Ignoring realities: proclaiming a new day!!

Hunting grounds: happy for a thousand years!
Vacated, now: by the Great Spirit's Red Men.
Warriors frustrated; alcohol saturated: such tears.
Regretting never will their Fathers' like be seen again!!

*The above poem is about an oil picture painted from life by the Poet/
Artist, C. John Taylor. In the picture, in costumes they made themselves,
are the children of Seil Isle who, in the village hall, in a play movingly
recounted in mime and dance the story of the survival struggle of the
North American Indians. A struggle certainly contributed to by the
white man's continually enlarging encroachment upon the Indians'
homelands and which culminated in the famous historic "Battle of Little
Big Horn". Fighting under their great strategic warrior Big Chief
Sitting Bull, the final victory against the armed forces of the Government
of the United States of America was achieved by the native tribesmen.*

THE PRINCE OF WALES!

This Royal Prince!
Placed by Destiny
Apart from men, tho' worthy;
Of less noble birth!
Whose ancestors indutiably
Provide him, and us; with
Famous and familiar examples,
Of Royal Lives, affecting
For good or ill, countless
Millions of people, who lived;
Worked, loved and who, inevitably
Departed, from this ageless earth.

May he emulate the finest
Of his breed! revealing thus,
Within his one person, miraculously,
A combination of their virtues!!
Bodeceia's resistance!
Edward the First's prowness!
Richard the Lion-Hearted's idealism!
Robert the Bruce's resilience!
Henry the Fifth's oratory!
Elizabeth the First's father's glamour!
And her obstinacy!
The attractiveness of Prince Charles Edward Stewart!
The determination of George the Second!
The longevity of Victoria!
The diplomacy of Edward the Seventh!
The goodness of George the Fifth!
With his second-sons mastery over debility!
Forgetting not, the devotion of Queen Elizabeth
Two and Prince Philip, Duke of Edinburgh!

May his life be blessed! God inspire
Him to true leadership, making his life, and
Ours stimulating; fruitful: worthy: peaceful!

Let his light so shine, that all men will say:
"Truly, this is a Prince amongst the people".

ROBERT BURNS
"1759–1796 – SCOTLAND'S NATIONAL POET"

Robert Burns. Born on 25th January, 1759 near Ayr. Financially un-
successful as a farmer. Seven years an Exciseman. Enjoyed fame,
thro' his poetry and songs for ten years, prior to his death, at Dumfries,
on the 21st day of July, 1796,

Poem written on Burns' birthday, 25th January at Durban, South Africa

Burns' "spouse"
Tolerant, wise, resigned
Or "second-sighted",
Watching o'er him,
As with alcohol
His gifts are blighted.

Learning nought from sensuous excesses,
"My love is like a red, red rose"
He presses,
Moving as a bee,
From one to t'other,
into her soul,
He sends a shudder.

'Tis "Bonny Mary of Argyll"
Or yonder "Lass o' Ballochmyle"
Society dames
Of so-called style,
Red-heads from
The "Royal Mile".

Virgins deflowered, bide a while
Young ones, eager, without guile,
Entranced, bewitched, by "Rabbie's" "wild"
Glad with him to "rest" a while
'Mangst the hay, against the stile.
Awaiting spouses, without smile,
Bearing up, and great with child!

Years, you'd think, would wisdom bring,
To him, who made the whole world sing,
Songs of love, and "Auld Lang Syne",
Lifting souls, of every clime,
Not just for now,
But for all time!

Poems too, to touch the heart,
Of just plain folk, and those who're "smart",
Amassing, wealth 'ere they depart,
To havens, where
No shadows fall,
True love's unmeasured there
For all.

Immortal "Rabbie" joined them early,
Passing on, aged seven and thirty,
From realms above
With gift of hindsight,
Sees he himself,
In clearer light?

Pondering still,
Was it all right?
Tasting muchly,
Mock delight.
Or questions he,
"Now who returns
To come, to earth,
With Rabbie Burns?"

Reincarnation's mystery,
Unwrapped perhaps 'twill never be,
Abodes apart, where Rabbie's now, and known,
May well, to him reveal, marvels of harmonious tone,
Symphonies of song, an everlasting throng,
Where characters belong, fascinating, undiscovered yet,
    beyond our ken,
Larger than life, outside human strife, revealing again
How here, to live, to grow, to love, to know, to be,
Guided to eternity.

Come what may, he'll know today,
Below we say,
True genius only partly used, abused,
Knowing not the farthest sea, of creativity,
Shortened prematurely,
Captivated, by wine, by women, by song, in turns,
Unique, irrepressible, immortal, ROBERT BURNS.

POETS AND POETS LAUREATE

Following are listed a selection of famous Poets and Poets Laureate. Their works in various forms are published widely and can be read with interest and growing satisfaction as the reader's life unfolding, acquires added dimension and experience. Sir John Betjeman (b. 1906) is now Poet Laureate (1972).

Arnold Matthew
(1822–1888)
Auden, W. H.
(1907–1973)
Belloc, Hilaire
(1870–1953)
Blake, William
(1757–1828)
Bridges, Robert
Poet Laureate 1913
(1844–1930)
Browning, Robert
(1812–1889)
Browning, Elizabeth
Barrett (1806–1861)
Burns, Robert
(1759–1796)
Byron, Lord
(1788–1824)
Campion, Thomas
(1567–1619)
Chesterton, G. K.
(1874–1936)
Clare, John
(1793–1864)
Coleridge, Samuel Taylor
(1772–1834)
Collins, William
(1721–1759)
Cowley, Abraham
(1618–1667)
Cowper, William
(1731–1800)
Crabbe, George
(1754–1832)
Davies, W. H.
(1870–1940)
De la Mare, Walter
(1873–1956)
Drayton, Michael
(1563–1631)
Dryden, John
Poet Laureate 1670
(1631–1700)
Eliot, T. S.
(1888–1965)

Fitzgerald, Edward
(1809–1883)
Gay, John
(1685–1732)
Goldsmith, Oliver
(1728–1774)
Graves, Robert
(b. 1895)
Gray, Thomas
(1716–1771)
Hardy, Thomas
(1840–1928)
Herbert, George
(1593–1633)
Hood, Thomas
(1799–1845)
Hopkins, Gerard Manley
(1844–1889)
Housman, A. E.
(1859–1936)
Hunt, Leigh
(1784–1859)
Johnson, Dr. Samuel
(1709–1784)
Jonson, Ben
Poet Laureate 1619
(1573–1637)
Keats, John
(1795–1821)
Kipling, Rudyard
(1865–1936)
Lamb, Charles
(1775–1834)
Langland, William
(1330–1400)
Lawrence, D. H.
(1885–1930)
Lear, Edward
(1812–1888)
Lovelace, Richard
(1618–1658)
Marlowe, Christopher
(1564–1593)
Masefield, John
Poet Laureate 1930
(1878–1967)

Moore, Thomas
(1779–1852)
Peacock, Thomas Love
(1785–1866)
Pope, Alexander
(1688–1744)
Raleigh, Sir Walter
(1552–1618)
Rossetti, Christina
(1830–1894)
Rossetti, Dante Gabriel
(1828–1882)
Scott, Sir Walter
(1771–1832)
Shakespeare, William
(1564–1616)
Shelley, Percy Bysshe
(1792–1822)
Sidney, Sir Philip
(1554–1586)
Southey, Robert
Poet Laureate 1813
(1774–1843)
Stevenson, Robert Louis
(1850–1894)
Suckling, Sir John
(1609–1642)
Tennyson, Alfred, Lord
Poet Laureate 1850
(1809–1892)
Thomas, Dylan
(1914–1953)
Thompson, Francis
(1859–1907)
Thomson, James
(1700–1748)
Vaughan, Henry
(1622–1695)
Wilde, Oscar
(1856–1900)
Wordsworth, William
Poet Laureate 1843
(1770–1850)
Yeats, William Butler
(1865–1939)

The Compiler of PRIZE-WINNING POETRY C. John Taylor. The Poet/Artist with his Oil Portrait of H.R.H. The Prince of Wales.

Annually, during the months of May to October there is an Exhibition of his work which is open to visitors. Located upon Seil Isle, opposite picturesque Easdale with the beautiful mountains of Mull and Iona's Sacred Isle in the distance, The Exhibition Gallery, Studios and Poet/Artist's home, are truly nestled in a highland haven!

The nearest town to Seil Isle is Oban. By ancient reputation, long known as the "Queen of the Western Isles". Oban is a fascinating town; justifiably proud of its record of extending genuine 'Highland' hospitality to visitors old and new, Oban is unique, quaint, well furnished with Shops, Restaurants, Hotels, Theatres, a Cinema, and a modern Swimming Pool. From Oban's piers delightful sailing is daily enjoyed by visitors, especially the 'old folks' and the children.

From Oban Special Excursion Buses leave every day, Sundays included, to C. John Taylor's Seil Isle Artists Exhibition. Motorists enjoy the sixteen road miles from Oban to the Exhibition (The A.A. Route is B.844). The journey passes historic Loch Feochan, from which for centuries, Scotland's Kings were taken in sailing vessels to their final burial grounds; onwards beyond remote Loch Seil, over the famous bridge which crosses the Atlantic Ocean and so onto Seil Isle: then follows three miles of panoramic views, until finally nestling beside the ocean, at the head of a centuries old slate built Highland Village, lies the Highland Artist's Exhibition. Inside original works of Art abound, to delight the eye: to stimulate the imagination. Hereunder is a list of the places through which a motorist from the South would travel.

From GLASGOW *Via* Balloch Luss Tarbet Arrochar Inveraray Taynuilt Oban.

From EDINBURGH *Via* Stirling Callander Lochearnhead Crianlarich Dalmally Taynuilt Oban.

Leave Oban via Soroba Road, passing the High School and on through Kilmore, beside Loch Feochan. Turn right at main road sign marked "Easdale" (A.A. Route B.844), travel four miles to road bridge which connects Mainland to Seil Isle. Three miles onwards to Easdale and The Highland Arts Exhibition.